2005

EXCAVATING EGYPT

GREAT DISCOVERIES FROM THE PETRIE MUSEUM OF EGYPTIAN ARCHÆOLOGY

UNIVERSITY COLLEGE
LONDON

BETSY TEASLEY TROPE

STEPHEN QUIRKE

PETER LACOVARA

ATLANTA

MICHAEL C. CARLOS MUSEUM

EMORY UNIVERSITY

2005

Photography by Mary Hinkley except for
Michael McKelvey: cat. nos. 20, 36, 40, 41,
49, 55, 66–8, 70, 95, 96, 110, 118, 121, 134,
136, 153(A, C, D), 160; and Renée Stein: cat no. 77.

Drawings cat. nos. 49, 80, 115 by Nina West;
cat. no. 43 by William Schenk.

Designed by Times 3, Atlanta.

Printed in the United States of America
by Pro Graphics.

This exhibition is made possible
in part by grants from the
Massey Charitable Trust and the
Georgia Council for the Arts.

THE PAST IS VANISHING BEFORE OUR MODERN [EYES,
IT] CHANGES YEARLY AND DAILY.
THERE IS EVER LESS AND LESS TO PRESERVE AND EVERYTHING POSSIBLE
MUST BE GARNERED BEFORE IT HAS ENTIRELY VANISHED.
THE PRESENT HAS ITS MOST SERIOUS DUTY TO HISTORY
IN SAVING THE PAST FOR THE BENEFIT OF THE FUTURE.

SIR WILLIAM MATTHEW FLINDERS PETRIE

CONTENTS

FOREWORD

Excavating Egypt: Great Discoveries from the Petrie Museum of Egyptian Archaeology, University College London features the extraordinary archaeological achievements of Sir William Flinders Petrie. At a time when excavation often seemed little more than a treasure hunt, he saw the need to develop scientific methods and techniques for the practice of archaeology. He insisted on the value of everything found, whether eye-catching or not, and he built up a large collection of excavated objects of all types intended specifically to train young scholars and familiarize them with the material remains of ancient Egypt. In 1913, his collection was bought for University College London by public subscription to form the Petrie Museum.

The development of the Egyptian collection in the Michael C. Carlos Museum has followed a different path, beginning with the generosity of an Atlanta business man, John Manget, who in 1920 provided funds to purchase antiquities in Egypt and continuing with the extraordinary 1999 purchase of the collection from the Niagara Falls Museum. The aim, however, has been the same: to provide a study and teaching collection for the University and surrounding community and to educate students and visitors about ancient Egypt through its material remains.

It is, therefore, extremely appropriate and exciting, given the similar aims of the two institutions, to bring this exhibit drawn from the Petrie Museum to the Carlos Museum to further the education of the Emory and Atlanta communities. Petrie himself was by all accounts an inspired teacher, as Margaret Murray observed: "He could and did give lectures that held his audience breathless for the boldness and convincingness of his theories and explanations. And more than once at the close of a lecture the audience clapped vigorously, a rare thing for a college audience to do after listening to a routine lecture." His inspiration lives on in the collection he created, and we are the beneficiaries of his conviction that such a collection was a necessary part of learning about ancient Egypt.

GAY ROBINS
Samuel Candler Dobbs Professor of Art History
Emory University

ACKNOWLEDGMENTS

The possibility of organizing an exhibition devoted to the life and accomplishments of W. M. Flinders Petrie, the "father" of Egyptology, as told through the antiquities he unearthed and the research he conducted, was exciting to say the least. As discussions turned into action plans, the magnitude of this endeavor became palpable, escalating the excitement and sharpening the expectations for the final product.

Exhibitions demand the concerted efforts of many, and in this case, required cross-Atlantic coordination. A significant undertaking indeed, but when such a collaboration is successfully accomplished, the results are far greater than the sum of its parts. We have many people to thank for making this exhibition a reality. Our gratitude goes first and foremost to Dr. Peter Lacovara, Senior Curator of Ancient Art at the Carlos Museum, and Dr. Stephen Quirke, Curator of the Petrie Museum. Without their combined vision and dedication to the legacy of Flinders Petrie—the preservation and teaching of the history of ancient Egypt, as well as the more recent past—this project would never have come to fruition.

This exhibition highlights not only the unparalleled collection of the Petrie Museum, but also the extraordinary staff of that institution, who tackled this effort with unflagging good humor, despite tight deadlines and cramped quarters. Museum Manager Sally MacDonald provided levelheaded support and counsel throughout, deftly negotiating the complexities of museum and university policy. Our thanks go to Tracey Golding, Judy Joseph, and most especially to Hugh Kilmister for their skillful management of all manner of details, including the photography and packing of the objects in London. The thorough examination of the objects by conservator Felicity Woor was invaluable. At University College London, we are also particularly grateful for the enthusiastic support of Peter Ucko and Nick Merriman.

On this side of the Atlantic, the complex logistics of an international exhibit, including the transfer of the objects from London to Atlanta and then on to succeeding venues, have been coordinated with painstaking attention and good humor by Registrar Todd Lamkin. Assistant Registrar, Stacey Gannon, has provided invaluable support, supervising additional photography in Atlanta, overseeing the unpacking of the objects, and organizing materials for other venues. Amanda Leenerts, graduate student and intern, supplied inestimable assistance in a variety of areas, from registering objects to proofreading catalog text. We are also grateful to volunteer Sylvia Teasley and student intern Dana Haugaard.

Heartfelt appreciation extends to Betsy Teasley Trope, Associate Curator of Ancient Art for her research and writing skills, patience, and terrific sense of humor not to mention her relentless pursuit of perfection. Renée Stein, head of the Carlos Museum's Parsons Conservation Laboratory, masterfully supervised the transport and conservation of the objects within challenging time constraints. She was ably assisted by volunteers Joan Sammons-Hodges and Eleanor Ridley, and student interns Emily Nomura, Erin Falbaum, and Sara Bellis. The beautiful installation, as it opened at the Carlos Museum, is a testament to the high energy and flawless taste of Nancy Roberts, Coordinator of Exhibition Design, who overcame demanding circumstances with her usual calm and patient demeanor. Her staff, Tony Howell, Winston King, and Bruce Raper, worked tirelessly and with characteristic excellence. Elizabeth Hornor, Director of Education, and Julie Green, Manager of School Programs, created an array of exciting programs and interpretive materials to complement the exhibition, with the capable assistance of Nina West.

The financial and budgetary complexities of an international traveling exhibition have been dexterously handled by Manager of Personnel and Budget, Darlene Hayes and her assistant, Pam Clark. Mark Burell, Manager of the Museum Bookshop, and assistant Cecilia Pike facilitated publication of the catalog while capably meeting the Egyptian and archaeological demands of the public. Bernard Potts, Manager of Operations, and his dedicated staff provided cheerful support throughout the project. In the office of the director, Joyce Daniels assisted in countless ways, always with the voice of reason and good humor.

Director of Development and External Affairs, Lucie André, and Development Specialist Jessica Fuller worked tirelessly to bring the exhibition and catalog to completion. Gail Habif, Coordinator of Public Services, and Leigh Burns, Manager of Visitor Services, ensured the success of the many events and activities supplementing the exhibition. Publicity and media affairs have been deftly orchestrated by Allison Germaneso Dixon, Coordinator of Marketing and Public Relations. We must also extend our gratitude to Associate Director Catherine Howett Smith, whose management skills and sage advice contributed immeasurably to the realization of this project.

We are grateful to the Georgia Council for the Arts, which continues its tradition of support for the Museum and enables us to share our work with a broad audience. We also thank the Massey Charitable Trust which invested early and generously in the exhibition and catalog.

Many other colleagues provided input and advice, for which we are grateful, including Jasper Gaunt at the Michael C. Carlos Museum; John Tait and Margaret Serpico at University College London; Joyce Haynes and Yvonne Markowitz at the Museum of Fine Arts, Boston; Diana Craig-Patch at The Metropolitan Museum; and Lorelei Corcoran at the University of Memphis. We must also thank William Size of the Department of Environmental Studies at Emory University for his meticulous analysis of many objects in the exhibit.

We are indebted to catalog authors, Tom Hardwick and Sabrina Gomez-Deluchi, for their contributions of time and scholarship, while working under an extremely compressed timeframe. The attentive and patient proofreading of Elizabeth Hornor, while juggling numerous other projects, has been invaluable. Mary Hinkley and Michael McKelvey provided the wonderful photographs for the catalog. The line drawings for both the catalog and the exhibition were expertly drafted by William Schenk and Nina West. We must extend special thanks to Robert Evans of Times 3 for producing an exquisite catalog—it is always a delight to work with him and to benefit from his superb sense of design.

This collaborative exhibition between the Michael C. Carlos Museum at Emory University and the Petrie Museum of Egyptian Archaeology, University College London highlights the unique contributions of university museums to the realm of public scholarship. Our collections are at the service of scholarship, and through the myriad educational opportunities exhibitions offer, can inspire all who experience them to think farther and deeper than before.

BONNIE SPEED
Director
Michael C. Carlos Museum at Emory University

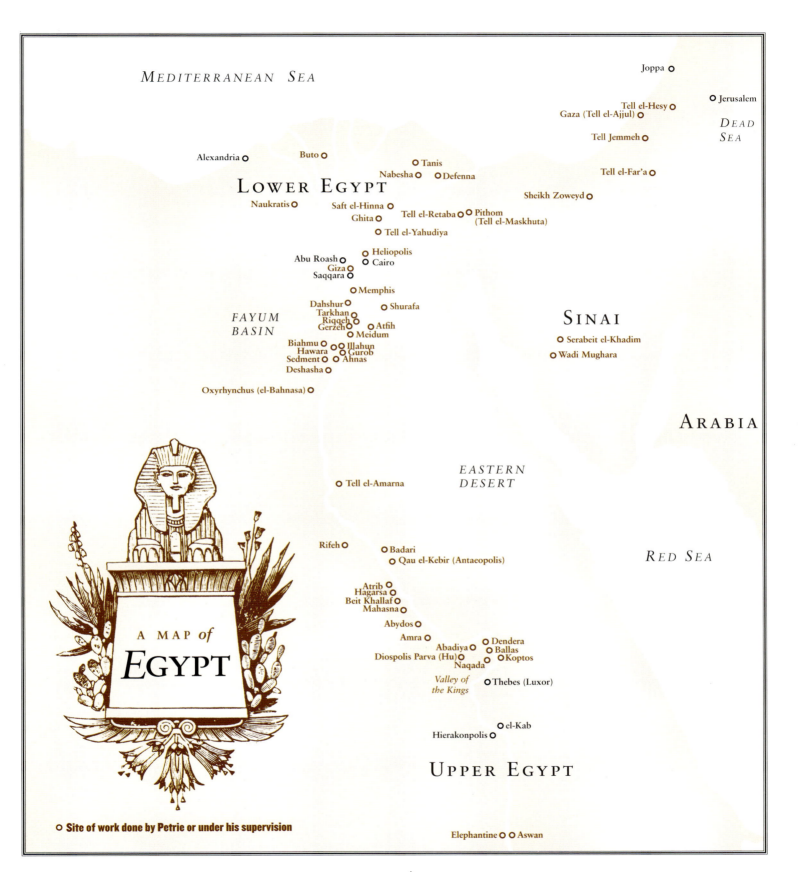

MEDITERRANEAN SEA

Joppa ○

○ Jerusalem

Tell el-Hesy ○

Gaza (Tell el-Ajjul) ○

DEAD SEA

Tell Jemmeh ○

Alexandria ○   Buto ○

LOWER EGYPT

Tanis ○
Nabesha ○   ○ Defenna

Tell el-Far'a ○

Naukratis ○
Saft el-Hinna ○
Ghita ○
Tell el-Retaba ○ ○ Pithom
(Tell el-Maskhuta)

Sheikh Zoweyd ○

Tell el-Yahudiya ○

Heliopolis ○
Abu Roash ○   ○ Cairo
Giza ○
Saqqara ○

Memphis ○

Dahshur ○   ○ Shurafa
Tarkhan ○
Riqqeh ○
Gerzeh ○   ○ Atfih
Meidum ○

SINAI

○ Serabeit el-Khadim

FAYUM BASIN

Biahmu ○ ○ Illahun
Hawara ○ ○ Gurob
Sedment ○ ○ Ahnas
Deshasha ○

○ Wadi Mughara

Oxyrhynchus (el-Bahnasa) ○

ARABIA

EASTERN DESERT

Tell el-Amarna ○

Rifeh ○

○ Badari
○ Qau el-Kebir (Antaeopolis)

RED SEA

Atrib ○
Hagarsa ○
Beit Khallaf ○
Mahasna ○

Abydos ○

Amra ○
Abadiya ○   ○ Dendera
Diospolis Parva (Hu) ○   ○ Ballas
Naqada ○   ○ Koptos

Valley of the Kings   ○ Thebes (Luxor)

○ el-Kab
Hierakonpolis ○

UPPER EGYPT

A MAP of EGYPT

○ Site of work done by Petrie or under his supervision

Elephantine ○ ○ Aswan

CHRONOLOGY OF ANCIENT EGYPT

PREDYNASTIC PERIOD (Upper Egypt)

Badarian	4800–4200 BC
Naqada I (Amratian)	4200–3700 BC
Naqada II (Gerzean)	3700–3250 BC
Naqada III (Late Gerzean–Dynasty 0)	3250–3100 BC

DYNASTY "0" (ca. 3100–3000 BC)

An uncertain number of rulers, including Scorpion and Horus King Narmer

ARCHAIC PERIOD (ca. 3000–2686 BC)

DYNASTY 1	3000–2890 BC

Seven rulers, including Horus Kings Aha, Djer, Djet, Den; and Neith Queen Meryet (or Queen Merneith)

DYNASTY 2	2890–2686 BC

Nine rulers, including Hotepsekhemwy, Nynetjer, Seth Peribsen, and Horus-and-Seth Khasekhemwy

OLD KINGDOM (2686–2125 BC)

DYNASTY 3	2686–2613 BC
Djoser Netjerikhet	2667–2648 BC
DYNASTY 4	2613–2494 BC
Sneferu	2613–2589 BC
Khufu (Cheops)	2589–2566 BC
Radjedef	2566–2558 BC
Khafre (Chephren)	2558–2532 BC
Menkaure (Mycerinus)	2532–2503 BC
Shepseskaf	2503–2498 BC
DYNASTY 5	2494–2345 BC
Userkaf	2494–2487 BC
Sahure	2487–2475 BC
Neferirkare Kakai	2475–2455 BC
Shepseskare	2455–2448 BC
Raneferef	2448–2445 BC
Niuserre	2445–2421 BC
Menkauhor	2421–2414 BC
Djedkare Isesi	2414–2375 BC
Unas	2375–2345 BC

DYNASTY 6	2345–2181 BC
Teti	2345–2323 BC
Meryre Pepy I	2321–2287 BC
Merenre Nemtyemzaf	2287–2278 BC
Neferkare Pepy II	2278–2184 BC

A few later rulers, possibly including a queen, Nitiqret

DYNASTIES 7/8	2181–2160 BC

An indeterminate number of ephemeral monarchs

FIRST INTERMEDIATE PERIOD (2160–2055 BC)

DYNASTIES 9/10 (HERAKLEOPOLITAN)	2160–2125 BC

Eighteen rulers, including Akhtoy (Achtoes) I, Nubkare, and Merykare

EARLY DYNASTY 11 (THEBAN)	2125–2055 BC
Sehertawy Intef I	2125–2112 BC
Wahankh Intef II	2112–2063 BC
Nakhtnebtepnefer Intef III	2063–2055 BC

MIDDLE KINGDOM (2055–1650 BC)

LATE DYNASTY 11	2055–1985 BC
Nebhepetre Montuhotep II	2055–2004 BC
Sankhkare Montuhotep III	2004–1992 BC
Nebtawyre Montuhotep IV	1992–1985 BC
DYNASTY 12	1985–1773 BC
Sehetepibre Amenemhet I	1985–1956 BC
Kheperkare Senusret I	1956–1911 BC
Nubkaure Amenemhet II	1911–1877 BC
Khakheperre Senusret II	1877–1870 BC
Khakaure Senusret III	1870–1831 BC
Nimaatre Amenemhet III	1831–1786 BC
Maakherure Amenemhet IV	1786–1777 BC
Sobeknefru Sobekkare (Regnant Queen)	1777–1773 BC
DYNASTY 13	1773–AFTER 1650 BC

A large number of kings, most of them ephemeral, governing from Itjtawy

SECOND INTERMEDIATE PERIOD (1650–1550 BC)

DYNASTY 14

Minor rulers in the eastern Delta, probably based at Tell el-Daba; predecessors of Hyksos Dynasty 15

DYNASTY 15 (HYKSOS)   1650–1550 BC

Six rulers, including Apophis

DYNASTY 16 (CONTEMPORANEOUS WITH DYNASTY 15)

DYNASTY 17 (THEBAN)   1580–1550 BC

About fifteen rulers, ending with:

Seqenenre Tao	ca. 1560 BC
Wadjkheperre Kamose	1555–1550 BC

NEW KINGDOM (1550–1069 BC)

DYNASTY 18   1550–1292 BC

Nebpehtyre Ahmose	1550–1525 BC
Djeserkare Amenhotep I	1525–1504 BC
Aakheperkare Thutmose I	1504–1492 BC
Aakheperenre Thutmose I	1492–1479 BC
Maatkare Hatshepsut	1473–1458 BC
Menkheperre Thutmose III	1479–1425 BC
Aakheperure Amenhotep II	1427–1400 BC
Menkheperure Thutmose IV	1400–1390 BC
Nebmaatre Amenhotep III	1390–152 BC
Neferkheperure Amenhotep IV (Akhenaten)	1352–1336 BC
Ankhkheperure Smenkhkare	1337–1334 BC
Nebkheperure Tutankhamen	1333–1323 BC
Kheperkheperure Ay	1323–1319 BC
Djeserkheperure-setepenre Horemheb	1319–1292 BC

DYNASTY 19 (RAMESSIDE)   1292–1185 BC

Menpehtyre Ramesses I	1292–1290 BC
Menmaatre Seti I	1290–1279 BC
Usermaatre-setepenre Ramesses II	1279–1213 BC
Baenre Merneptah	1213–1203 BC
Menmire Amenmesse	1203–1200 BC
Userkheperure Seti II	1200–1194 BC
Akhenre-setepenre Siptah	1194–1188 BC
Satre-merenamen Tausret (Regnant Queen)	1188–1186 BC

DYNASTY 20 (RAMESSIDE)   1186–1069 BC

Userkhaure-setepenre Sethnakht	1186–1184 BC
Usermaatre-meryamun Ramesses III	1184–1153 BC
Heqamaatre-setepenamun Ramesses IV	1153–1147 BC
Usermaatre-sekheperenre Ramesses V	1147–1143 BC
Nebmaatre-meryamun Ramesses VI	1143–1136 BC
Usermaatre-setepenre-meryamun Ramesses VII	1136–1129 BC
Usermaatre-akhenamun Ramesses VIII	1129–1126 BC
Neferkare-setepenre Ramesses IX	1126–1108 BC
Khepermaatre-setepenptah Ramesses X	1108–1099 BC
Menmaatre-setepenptah Ramesses XI	1099–1069 BC

THIRD INTERMEDIATE PERIOD (1069–664 BC)

DYNASTY 21 (TANITE)   1069–945 BC

Hedjkheperre-setepenre Nesbanebdjed (Smendes)	1069–1043 BC
Neferkare Amenemnisu	1043–1039 BC
Aakheperre-setepenre Pasebakhenniut I (Psusennes)	1039–991 BC
Usermaatre-setepenamun Amenemope	993–984 BC
Aakheperre-setepenre Osorkon	984–978 BC
Netjerkheperre-setepenamun Siamun	978–959 BC
Titkheprure-setepenre Pasebakhenniut II (Psusennes)	959–945 BC

DYNASTY 22 (BUBASTITE)   945–715 BC

About ten rulers, including:

Hedjkheperre-setepenre Shoshenq I	945–924 BC
Usermaatre Osorkon II	873–844 BC

DYNASTY 23   818–715 BC

Rival rulers at Thebes and in various northern principalities

DYNASTY 24 (SAITE)   727–715 BC

Shepsesre Tefnakht	727–720 BC
Wahkare Bakenrenef (Bocchoris)	720–715 BC

DYNASTY 25 (IN EGYPT)	747–656 BC		**DYNASTY 31 (SECOND PERSIAN PERIOD)**	343–332 BC
Menkheperre Piye	747–716 BC		Artaxerxes III	343–338 BC
Neferkare Shabaka	716–702 BC		Arses	338–336 BC
Djedkaure Shebitku	702–690 BC		Darius III	335–332 BC
Khunefertemre Taharqa	690–664 BC			
Bakare Tantamani	664–656 BC		**GRAECO-ROMAN PERIOD (332 BC–AD 642)**	
DYNASTY 25 (CONTINUING IN NUBIA)	653–CA. 300 BC		**MACEDONIAN DYNASTY**	332–305 BC
Senkamenisken	643–623 BC		Alexander III, "the Great"	332–323 BC
Anlamani	623–593 BC		Philip III Arrhidaeus	323–305 BC
Aspelta	593–568 BC		Alexander IV	323–305 BC
			PTOLEMAIC DYNASTY	305–30 BC
LATE PERIOD (664–332 BC)			Ptolemy I Soter	305–285 BC
DYNASTY 26 (SAITE)	664–525 BC		Ptolemy II Philadelphos	285–246 BC
Wahibre Psamtek I (Psammetichus)	664–610 BC		Ptolemy III Euergetes I	246–221 BC
Wehemibre Nekau II (Necho)	610–595 BC		Ptolemy IV Philopator	221–205 BC
Neferibre Psamtek II			Ptolemy V Epiphanes	205–180 BC
(Psammetichus)	595–589 BC		Ptolemy VI Philometor	180–145 BC
Wahibre Haaibre (Apries)	589–570 BC		Ptolemy VII Neos Philopator	145 BC
Ahmose Khnemibre (Amasis)	570–526 BC		Ptolemy VIII Euergetes II (Physkon)	170–116 BC
Ankhkaenre Psamtek III			Ptolemy IX Soter II (Lathyros)	116–107,
(Psammmetichus)	526–525 BC			88–80 BC
DYNASTY 27 (FIRST PERSIAN PERIOD)	525–404 BC		Ptolemy X Alexander I	107–88 BC
Cambyses	525–522 BC		Ptolemy XI Alexander II	80 BC
Darius I	521–486 BC		Ptolemy XII Neos Dionysos (Auletes)	80–51 BC
Xerxes I	486–466 BC		Cleopatra VII Philopator	51–30 BC
Artaxerxes I	465–424 BC		Ptolemy XIII	51–47 BC
Darius II	424–405 BC		Ptolemy XIV	47–44 BC
DYNASTY 28	404–399 BC		Ptolemy XV Caesarion	44–30 BC
Amyrtaeus	404–399 BC		**ROMAN, LATER BYZANTINE, EMPIRE**	30 BC–AD 642
DYNASTY 29 (MENDES)	399–380 BC		Augustus	30 BC–AD 14
Baenre-merynetjeru Nefaarud I			Tiberius	AD 14–37
(Nepherites)	399–393 BC		Claudius	AD 41–54
Maatibre Hakoris (Achoris)	393–381 BC		Nero	AD 54–68
Nefaarud II (Nepherites)	381 BC		Trajan	AD 98–117
DYNASTY 30 (SEBENNYTOS)	381–343 BC		Hadrian	AD 117–138
Kheperkare Nakhtnebef I				
(Nectanebo)	381–362 BC		**COPTIC PERIOD (LATE SECOND CENTURY AD–AD 642)**	
Irmaatenre Djedhor (Teos)	365–362 BC			
Senedjemibre-setepeninhur			**ARAB CONQUEST (AD 642)**	
Nakhthorheb II (Nectanebo)				
(last native king)	362–343 BC			

WILLIAM MATTHEW FLINDERS PETRIE

WILLIAM MATTHEW FLINDERS PETRIE has been called the "Father of Egyptian Archaeology" and the "Father of Scientific Archaeology." Such high praise is well deserved, as Petrie bridged the gap not only between the nineteenth and twentieth centuries, but also between archaeology as a search for "treasure" to a real science. Many of the methods still used today in excavation and analysis of objects were devised originally by Petrie. Having written more than a thousand articles and innumerable books, his scholarly legacy is unrivalled by anyone before or since. In addition, as a teacher as well as a field archaeologist, Petrie trained or influenced just about everyone working in Middle Eastern archaeology for over a century.

Petrie was born in the town of Charlton, England in 1853, and from the circumstances of his birth, seemed destined for his future career. His maternal grandfather, Captain Matthew Flinders, was a famous explorer who circumnavigated Australia and surveyed many of the islands in the region. His mother, Ann Flinders, and father, William Petrie, an inventor and amateur surveyor, were both interested in ancient mythology and the history of the Bible. They met attending a meeting of the Mutual Information Society, a discussion group that included Piazzi Smyth, who was to write "Our Inheritance in the Great Pyramid," which postulated that the monument encoded the mystical knowledge of the ancients in its measurements.

As a rather sickly only child, the young William Matthew Flinders spent much of his time reading and became intrigued with a local curiosity shop that sold ancient coins. He began to haunt the Coins and Medals department of the British Museum and to collect for them, quickly learning how to spot forgeries. His father also taught him how to use an old quadrant found in a junk shop. Petrie's interest in the past and surveying grew, and he accompanied his father on expeditions to map standing stones, the most important being Stonehenge. The plan he made of that great ruin was by far the most accurate that had ever been produced and it, along with numerous others, was presented to the map room of the British Museum. This lead to an interest in ancient systems of measuring; working through the collections in London, Petrie produced what is still an important work on ancient measures, "Inductive Metrology, or the Recovery of Ancient Measurements from the Monuments," published in 1877.

Petrie, father and son, soon devised a plan to go to Egypt and measure the Great Pyramid to test Smyth's theory. With enough money saved, the young Petrie sailed for Alexandria in 1880, anticipating that his father would join him in Egypt. From Smyth, Petrie had an introduction to Dr. James Grant, who had founded a sanitarium outside of Cairo and begun collecting antiquities. Grant and his family took the young adventurer

Petrie outside the tomb in which he lived at Giza, 1880.

under their wing and helped him get established. After meeting with Auguste Mariette, a French scholar appointed as the head of Egypt's Antiquities Service, Petrie, ever frugal, moved into an abandoned tomb at the Giza necropolis, setting up a hammock as a bed. In the heat, he would often work only in his underwear, claiming that, "if pink, they kept the tourist at bay, as the creature seemed to him too queer for inspection."

Petrie was painstaking in his surveying triangulation, back-checking each measurement he made, so as to ensure the accuracy of his plans. Though intent on his work, Petrie was not unaware of the ravages going on around him. He wrote: "it is sickening to see the rate at which everything is being destroyed, and the little regard paid to its preservation." Before leaving for Egypt, Samuel Birch, Keeper of Antiquities at the British Museum, had asked Petrie to make a collection of small objects, pottery, beads, and the like, hoping to get some idea of the date of these various classes of material. Prior to this, such material was little regarded, since museums and collectors were only interested in sculpture and inscribed monuments. Petrie, already aware of the importance of small finds from his coin collecting days, did an exemplary job of gathering and analyzing these neglected artifacts. In particular, he was intrigued with tools and their marks found in and around the pyramids, clues to how they were made. By the summer of 1881, it was too hot to continue working, and Petrie returned to England to write up his survey notes and present his finds to the British Museum.

He prepared for a return to Egypt, building his own camera and tripod. By the time of Petrie's arrival, Gaston Maspero had succeeded Mariette as head of the Egyptian Antiquities Service and was trying to systematize archaeological work in Egypt. He made Petrie a temporary employee of the Egyptian Museum to facilitate his work at the pyramids. During this season, Petrie also made a trip up the Nile with the Reverend Archibald Sayce, an Assyriologist with an abiding interest in ancient Egypt. Returning to Giza, Petrie finished his survey of the pyramids, concluding that Smyth's theories were wildly wrong, and headed back to England.

In the meantime, developments were taking place in London that would have a profound effect on Petrie's future career. In 1873, an intrepid English novelist and journalist, Amelia Edwards, had made a trip similar to Sayce's, and had recounted her journey in a volume entitled *A Thousand Miles Up the Nile*, which became a best seller. Edwards, like Petrie, was moved by the ruination of the ancient monuments and wrote:

> I am told that the wall paintings which we had the happiness of admiring in all their beauty and freshness, are already much injured. Such is the fate of every Egyptian monument, great or small. The tourist carves over it with names and dates...the 'Collector' buys and carries off everything of value he can. The work of destruction, meanwhile goes on apace. There is no one to prevent it, there is no one to discourage it. Everyday more inscriptions are mutilated—more tombs are rifled, more paintings and sculptures are defaced.

Miss Edwards was able to prevail upon Reginald Poole, Keeper of Coins at the British Museum, and Sir Erasmus Wilson, a wealthy surgeon and Egyptophile who had helped bring the obelisk now on the Thames embankment to England, to found a "Society for the Promotion of Excavation in the Delta of the Nile." The society was particularly interested in the ancient cities of the Delta, which they hoped could shed light on the Biblical accounts of the Israelites' sojourn in the land of the pharaohs. The Committee decided to engage as its first excavator the Swiss Biblical scholar and philologist, Édouard Naville. Naville had no previous experience as an excavator and was largely interested in inscribed monuments. Nevertheless, there was great enthusiasm for his first season of work in Egypt and enough money poured into the fund to send out a second expedition. Sayce, a member of the Committee, recommended Petrie to head that.

While Naville was dismissive of anything that was not carved in stone, Petrie carefully collected everything he found and his ever-watchful eye led to many important discoveries. Exploring in the Delta, he discovered the remains of the Hellenic colony of Naukratis, and noted "Oh what a feast of pottery! The whole ground thick with early Greek pottery, and it seemed almost a sacrilege to walk over the heaps with fine black lustrous ware crunching under one's boots. It seems as if I was wandering in the smashings of Museum vase-rooms."

At San el-Hagar (Tanis), he discovered a house that had been burned, which could be dated by coins to AD 174. Never before had such an intact group been carefully excavated and recorded; all at once, the material culture of Roman Period Egypt was defined. Elsewhere on the site, with painstaking care, he was able to recover a trove of papyri that had been burned, but were still partially legible.

The following season, enough money was raised to send a young Oxford student, Francis Llewellyn Griffith, out as Petrie's assistant. Working at Tell Nabesha (Tell Far'un), they discovered the remains of a temple site, which Petrie was able to date by identifying a foundation deposit of King Amasis, located by digging in the wet sand with his toes. He also conducted work that season at Tell Defenna (Daphnae), where he discovered the remains of a large fortress of Amasis.

The flurry of work drained the resources of the Committee, by then known as the Egypt Exploration Fund, and the death of Sir Wilson removed their principal benefactor. Unable to finance multiple expeditions, the directors of the fund were forced to choose between Naville and Petrie, deciding on the more established Naville. Miss Edwards, who had been excluded from the deliberations, was outraged, writing: "not to send out Mr. Petrie would be very unjust; he has worked harder than Naville ever worked, and has brought home richer results." Indeed, the two men could not have been more different. Naville spent extravagantly while Petrie lived the most spartan existence, to put as much into the work as possible. Petrie was an engaged and innovative thinker, while Naville was an aloof traditionalist.

Determined to return to work in Egypt, Petrie was commissioned by Francis Galton, who was engaged in research on genetics, to photograph and record different racial types found in Egypt. This was the unfortunate beginning of the eugenics movement, whose proponents attempted to validate their ideas of racial superiority by projecting them back into the past. Like other Egyptologists of his day, Petrie was badly misled by these ideas.

Petrie embarked for Egypt in November of 1886, accompanying Francis Griffith on a study trip down the Nile. While there, Petrie learned of an anonymous benefactor who would fund a season for him the following year. Petrie returned to Egypt in 1887 to prospect for a new site. Eugène Grébaut had succeeded Maspero and gave Petrie permission to excavate in the area of the Fayum. At the site of Hawara, almost at once he came upon a major discovery: under the body of a woman, he found a roll of papyrus inscribed in Greek with the text of the *Iliad*, which was later presented to the Bodleian Library in Oxford. His most significant discovery, however, was the vast cemetery of mummies wrapped with

A display of finds from Hawara at University College.

encaustic panel portraits over their faces in place of the traditional mummy mask. It was startling to see such lifelike renditions of the ancient residents of the Nile Valley. As per his contract, Petrie divided his finds with the Egyptian Museum in Cairo, Grébaut keeping some of the best portraits, but giving the bulk of the discoveries to Petrie. Petrie's finds were brought back to London and displayed, appropriately enough, in the Egyptian Hall at Piccadilly. The exhibition was a sensation, particularly among the Orientalist painters, notably Sir Lawrence Alma Tadema, Edward Poynter, and Holman Hunt, who welcomed Petrie into their circle.

Petrie had little trouble in raising money for a return to the Fayum. He opened the pyramid there and in the muck of the flooded burial chamber located the name of Amenemhet III, the builder of the monument. Another feat of excavation came in the flooded tomb of Horwedja of the Twenty-sixth Dynasty. Petrie noted:

one swings down a rope ladder for 25 feet, then squeezes through the top of a doorway nearly choked [with debris], and at once slides down the slope inside into the water. The whole of the walls are pitch black, owing to some deposit or growth when the water has filled the chambers. So it is very dark and the candle only just shows you where you collide with floating coffins or some skulls that go bobbing around. One wades in carefully, the ground being strewn with slippery sodden wood, bones and mud.

He continued to look at the monuments of the area, moving on to the pyramid at Illahun, which he was able to ascribe to Senusret II on the basis of inscribed blocks found in the ruins of the mortuary temple of the pyramid. A more enticing and more rewarding discovery lay to the north. Here, mounds of debris appeared to be residential in character, and at this place he called "Kahun," distinguishing it from the pyramid, he found a regularly built housing complex for the workers who constructed and later maintained the tomb of Senusret II.

Petrie excavated and mapped the town in a systematic fashion, recovering toys, papyri, utensils, furniture, and most importantly, masses of pottery to add to the corpus of dynastic vessels he had been assembling. Although scoffed at by Naville, Petrie had realized early on that the myriad potsherds that littered every ancient site in Egypt were the most important clues one could find to unravel the secrets of history and by painstakingly recording the context in which the material was found, one could eventually build up a corpus spanning all of Egyptian history. Particularly interesting, too, were the imported wares Petrie found here and at the neighboring site of Gurob. Unfortunately, he left the work at Gurob to an assistant named W. O. Hughes-Hughes, who was far less meticulous than Petrie and eventually left, notes and all, not to be heard from again.

Petrie had been approached by the Palestine Exploration Fund to do some investigation on their behalf, and in 1890, left for Jerusalem. He chose the site of Tell el-Hesy, where he excavated and recorded the first stratigraphic section in archaeology, cutting into the *tell*, or town mound, which revealed the levels of occupation like layers in a cake. He also began to compile a corpus of Palestinian pottery.

Petrie returned to the Fayum the following fall and began excavating the pyramid of Meidum, which he correctly surmised formed the transition from the Step Pyramid to the true pyramid. He also conducted work at the great *mastaba* tomb of Nefermaat (see cat. no. 11) that had been excavated by Mariette years before and had fallen into a bad state of ruin. Many of the inlaid reliefs and paintings were later salvaged in the 1909–10 season at Meidum.

The following year Petrie decided on a site that he had visited with Griffith on his study trip: the ruins at Tell el-Amarna. Soon after his visit, a woman digging in the mud had unearthed cuneiform tablets that proved to be the diplomatic correspondence of the "heretic" pharaoh, Akhenaten, with vassal states in the Levant. This piqued Petrie's interest, given his research on interconnections, and he was happy to have a place to work far from the intrigues of Cairo.

Petrie was able to trace the walls of a number of massive buildings that proved to be the palaces and temples of the pharaoh and his wife, Nefertiti. Although the walls of the structures were largely razed, the pavements of these palaces were remarkably intact and decorated with beautiful mural paintings, which Petrie carefully recorded. He took on as an assistant a young Englishman named Howard Carter, who had been funded by Lord Amherst, a wealthy collector. Petrie thought him affable enough, but dismissed the man who was later to find the tomb of Tutankhamen as "no use to me to work him up as an excavator." Although Carter was entranced by the sculptures in the strange style of the Amarna period, Petrie was delighted to find the palace workshops, strewn with the remains of glassworking and faience manufacture, along with foreign pottery.

While Petrie was working away in Egypt and Palestine, Amelia Edwards had busied herself expanding the work of the Egypt Exploration Fund, and had made an exhaustive lecture tour of America to raise support for its work. She was a great admirer and supporter of Petrie, who in turn, collected many beautiful pieces of sculpture and antiquities for her collection. However, the pace proved to be too much for her, and she succumbed to a series of illnesses, finally passing away on April 15, 1891. In the terms of her will, Miss Edwards set up funding for a Professorship in Egyptian Archaeology at University College, London, the only institution of higher learning that would admit female students. She did everything but name Petrie in the particulars of the bequest, which came along with her library and her collection of antiquities. Petrie undertook to set up the Museum and the teaching program before returning to Egypt in 1892.

There was again a change in the Antiquities Service with the appointment of Jacques de Morgan as director, a far more accomplished scholar than his predecessor. Petrie asked to work at the site of Quft (ancient Koptos), to which de Morgan readily agreed. Here, he found a series of temples superimposed on one another, dedicated to the cult of the ancient fertility god, Min. Petrie's most important discovery from the site was three very early and primitive sculptured torsos of the god. De Morgan generously granted two of the three figures to Petrie in the division of finds, which he presented to the British Museum. However, Wallis Budge, now the Keeper of Egyptian Antiquities, dismissed them as "unhistoric," so Petrie offered them to the Ashmolean Museum instead. They would later be joined by some of his most important discoveries of material dating to the beginnings of Egyptian civilization.

The workmen trained at Quft became specialized in archaeological excavation and, known as *Quftis*, many other archaeologists used them because of the skills imparted to them by Petrie. Petrie was careful to reward any important finds with a handsome *baksheesh* and employed many of these men for decades, bringing them all over Egypt to dig with him.

The following season, he explored the sites of Naqada and Ballas on the opposite side of the Nile from Quft. At Naqada was a temple to the god Seth, but from there north spread a vast series of cemeteries that proved quite a puzzle. They were filled with pottery the likes of which had rarely been seen before, and bodies placed in crouched positions that were not mummified. Adding to the mystery was the fact that in the over two thousand graves he opened that season, there was not a scrap of inscription anywhere to be found. Petrie, blinded by the migration theories popular at the time, theorized that this was a "new race" that had moved into the Nile Valley after the collapse of the Old Kingdom.

Moving southward in the following season of 1895–6, Petrie worked in western Thebes, digging around the mortuary temples of the pharaohs buried in the Valley of the Kings. He found many beautifully carved blocks fallen away and reused. His most celebrated find that year was an enormous stela of Amenhotep III. When the monument was lifted, the back revealed a lengthy inscription listing peoples conquered by Merneptah, the king who had reused it. One name seemed to puzzle the epigraphers, "Isiriar," which Petrie at once recognized as Israel. He mused, "won't the Reverends be pleased!" and the discovery made headlines around the world.

The adulation Petrie was receiving finally brought the Egypt Exploration Fund to their senses. When they implored him to come back again to work for them, Petrie agreed, but insisted on more autonomy than he had before. He worked that season for the EEF at the Old Kingdom site of Deshasha, and also made a number of important purchases, including an ebony cosmetic tray in the form of a Nubian serving girl.

Upon his return to London, Petrie set up the usual exhibit of the finds granted to him by the antiquities service before they were dispersed amongst the supporters of the work. One female visitor to the exhibition caught his eye, and on making her acquaintance, he learned that she was working at University College, drawing Classical antiquities for the painter Henry Holiday. Her name was Hilda Urlin and Holiday, a member of her parents' circle of friends, had used her as a model before noting her skill as a draftsman. Petrie seems to have pursued her with the same vigor he did anything that interested him, at first putting her off, but finally winning her over before they were married on November 26, 1896. They set off on their honeymoon to, of course, Egypt. Hilda fit naturally into the expedition lifestyle; she loved Egypt and ran the camp with cheerful efficiency, as well as undertaking most of the drawing and recording of the finds.

Hilda Petrie

Stopping in Cairo, they had a chance to look over de Morgan's latest finds, and Petrie, who rarely admitted a mistake, was forced to acknowledge that his "new race" theory was wrong and that the strange pottery and unmarked graves he had found at Naqada and Ballas actually belonged to Egypt's Predynastic or Prehistoric phase. Without written records, however, everyone was at a loss to date this new material more precisely. This is where Petrie showed his true genius; in the thousands of pots he had found, he noticed that some were imported from Palestine, while others seemed to be Egyptian imitations. Not all the local copies were the same, however, leading Petrie to theorize that the changes might correspond to stylistic developments over time. He ordered the graves and their contents using little strips of paper with the vessels running from the wide, imported examples to narrow cylinders. The end of the sequence could be tied to a historical date, since some were inscribed with royal names of the first two dynasties. He called this process "sequence dating," now called seriation, which remains an important tool for archaeologists and art historians today.

That same year, J. E. Quibell, who had been trained by Petrie, was working at the site of Hierakonpolis and discovered some of the most important records of the earliest history of Dynastic Egypt. Less well trained was a French archaeologist named Amélineau, who was working concurrently at another important early site: Abydos. There, he had found the graves of the kings of the First and Second Dynasties, but had ravaged them looking for beautiful objects. In 1899, Maspero, who was once again head of the Antiquities Service, was appalled at what Amélineau had done and granted a concession to Petrie to salvage what he could. Petrie did a masterful job of reconstructing the history of the site and putting the tombs in historical sequence. He continued working at Abydos and the surrounding area for several seasons.

Unfortunately, the Fund's resources were again low due to attrition in the American branch and scandal in the Boston office, prompting first the Boston Museum, then University Museum in Philadelphia and later The Metropolitan Museum in New York to cut back on their contributions in order to finance their own expeditions. Once again, instead of choosing Petrie, the Fund opted for Naville, who was working on the temples at Deir el-Bahri.

Petrie then founded his own mission, the British School of Archaeology in Egypt. Like the Egyptian Research Account he had established after his first break with the Fund, the British School would continue the same rapid publication for which he had become famous. His first campaign was also one of his roughest, exploring the wilderness of the Sinai and carefully recording the temple at Serabeit el-Khadim. In this lonely outpost of Egypt, he found some of the earliest examples of alphabetic script that he termed "Proto-Sinaitic." Following that expedition, he returned to work in the Delta, at Tell el-Yahudiya and Tell er-Retaba.

In the following seasons, he worked at Giza, the nearby cemetery site of Rifeh, Meidum, and Memphis. He also excavated the early necropolis at Tarkhan that had unusually well preserved organic remains. In 1912–3, Petrie returned to the Fayum and the pyramid of Lahun. Around the perimeter lay a series of tomb shafts that had been plundered in antiquity. In one of the shafts, Petrie discovered a sealed niche containing a wealth of gold jewelry with inlays and beads of semi-precious stones that had belonged to the Princess Sathathoriunet. Maspero was munificent in letting Petrie retain most of the treasure, which was later purchased by The Metropolitan Museum in New York.

Hilda Petrie, possibly at Dendera, 1897–8.

Forced to take a break from excavation during the First World War, Petrie used the funds from the sale of the Treasure of Lahun to catch up on his publications. It also gave him time to spend with his children, John and Ann. Once the war was over, Petrie returned to the Fayum to work again at Lahun, Kahun, and Gurob. In 1921, he moved to the rich cemetery at Sedment and returned to Abydos, where he made many great finds, as well as at Qau in the 1923 season. Despite this success, Petrie increasingly experienced difficulties with the bureaucracy in Cairo now that his old friend Maspero was gone, souring him on future work in Egypt. Furthermore, with the discovery in November, 1922, of the tomb of Tutankhamen, by his former assistant, Howard Carter, Petrie may have felt the center of Egyptological attention shift from him. In addition, his American rival, George Andrew Reisner, was also lauded for many of the same qualities as Petrie.

Still, he was honored with a knighthood in 1923 and a grand celebration at University College in celebration of his 70th birthday. But by now, Sir Flinders as he was usually called, longed for a change, and with Hilda at his side, decided to work in Palestine. While he continued his same rough and ready existence, time had taken its toll and he became less and less able to work. He died after a long illness in Jerusalem, on July 28, 1942. Hilda lived on until 1956 and attended a grand centennial party celebrating Sir Petrie's birth. She became a great archaeologist in her own right and Petrie dedicated his autobiography "to my wife on whose toil most of my work has depended." Today, Petrie's legacy remains not only in his numberless publications, but also in the great department he founded and the museum he so carefully tended.

CHRONOLOGY OF FLINDERS PETRIE'S WORK

1853	Born, Charlton, England
1880	Travels to Egypt to survey pyramids at Giza
1881–3	Continues work at Giza
1882	*Abu Roash*
1884–6	Excavates on behalf of Egypt Exploration Fund (EEF), under direction of Édouard Naville
1884	*Tanis*
1885	*Naukratis*
1886	*Nabesha, Defenna (Daphnae)*
1887	*Aswan, Western Thebes, Dahshur*
1888	*Biahmu, Arsinoë*
1888–9	*Hawara*
1889–90	*Kahun, Gurob*
1890	*Illahun, Tell el-Hesy*
1890–1	*Meidum*
1891–2	*Amarna*
1893	First Edwards Professor of Egyptology, University College London
1893–4	*Koptos*
1894	Founds Egyptian Research Account (later British School of Archaeology in Egypt)
1894–5	*Ballas, Naqada*
1895–6	*Western Thebes, Ramesseum*
1896	*Oxyrhynchus (Bahnasa)*
1897	*Deshasha*
1897–8	*Dendera*
1898–9	*Abadiya, Hu (Diospolis Parva)*
1899–1904	*Abydos*

1900–1	*Mahasna, Beit Khallaf, Amra*
1903–4	*Ahnas, Sedment, Gurob*
1904	*Buto (Tell el-Fara'in)*
1904–5	*Wadi Mughara, Serabeit el-Khadim*
1905	*Tell el-Maskhuta*
1905–6	*Tell el-Yahudiya*
1906	*Tell el-Retaba, Saft el-Hinna, Ghita*
1906–7	*Giza, Rifeh, Bala'iza, Shaganba*
1907	*Atrib, Hagarsa, Deir el-Abyad*
1908–13	*Memphis*
1908–9	*Qurna*
1909–10	*Meidum*
1910–11	*Hawara, Mazghuna, Gerzeh*
1911	*Shurafa, Atfih*
1911–12	*Tarkhan, Kafr Ammar*
1912	*Heliopolis*
1912–13	*Tarkhan, Riqqeh*
1913–14	*Illahun, Harageh*
1919–20	*Illahun, Kahun, Gurob*
1920–1	*Gurob, Sedment*
1921–2	*Abydos*
1922	*Oxyrhynchus (Bahnasa)*
1923–4	*Qau el-Kebir, Badari (Hemamiya)*
1926–7	*Tell Jemmeh*
1928–30	*Tell Far'a*
1930–4	*Gaza (Tell el-Ajjul)*
1935–7	*Sheikh Zoweyd*
1937–8	*Gaza (Tell el-Ajjul)*
1938	*Transjordan Survey*
1942	Died, Jerusalem

THE PETRIE MUSEUM—
PAST, PRESENT, AND FUTURE

WILLIAM MATTHEW FLINDERS PETRIE (1853–1942) is justly celebrated in the name of the Museum, for he towers over the landscape of early archaeological endeavor in the Nile Valley. However the visitor should be alerted to a host of other celebrated archaeologists who contributed to the formation of the extraordinary university collection of 80,000 Egyptian and Sudanese antiquities. Indeed, many of the most beautiful and most alluring exhibits were acquired by others at sites that Petrie never visited, or decades after he died. Several of these highlights were collected by the inspiring traveler, writer and fundraiser Amelia Edwards (including cat. nos. 17 and 139). Her energetic agitation lies behind the creation of what is still the main channel for British funding for excavation in Egypt, the Egyptian Exploration Society. The Society started life as the Egypt Exploration Fund in 1882, when Petrie was just embarking on his Egyptological career.

Amelia Edwards

Petrie himself had first traveled to Egypt in 1880 at the age of 27, to survey the Great Pyramid. For the next five decades he was at the forefront of the development of archaeology in the country, before turning in the 1920s to the archaeology of Palestine. In general he worked at a much higher number of sites, and with much greater speed, than an archaeologist would today, not least because he saw his life as a mission of rescue archaeology— to retrieve as much information as possible from sites that were shrinking dramatically in size as Egypt modernized and the population expanded.

During the Petrie decades there was no government grant to fund excavation—money was needed to pay for travel, accommodation, food, packing costs, labor costs, photography, drawing, and publication. Excavators had to seek funds, or work for societies that raised money for archaeological work in Egypt. Petrie obtained his funding from Amelia's Egypt Exploration Fund (EEF) until 1886, and again from 1896 to 1905. Partly in recognition of this funding problem, partly in the framework of colonialism, the Egyptian Antiquities Service allowed out of Egypt a certain proportion of finds, excepting any required for the great national treasury of antiquities, the Egyptian Museum in Cairo. Foreign excavators then distributed finds among their sponsors, provided that they remained in the public domain. This distribution system extended around the globe and fulfilled an implicit, if not explicit, educational mission to reveal the glorious history of ancient Egypt to all nations. Petrie himself sought to maximize the potential benefit of this web both by his lectures across the British Isles and by his contacts with sponsors overseas. In one of his pioneering initiatives he encouraged the roots of Egyptian archaeology in Japan, sending finds to the Kyoto University collection. In this way, Petrie finds are now

*Petrie in the museum
at University College,
after 1921.*

located in at least one hundred and twenty museums around the world, from New Zealand
and Australia, to South Africa, to Europe, Canada and, from the beginning, the United
States.

In the 1880s, most EEF finds were assigned to the British Museum, but a portion went
to Petrie and, for a teaching collection, to Amelia Edwards herself. From 1887–1892, he
relied on his own resources and the sponsorship of two wealthy enthusiasts—Jesse Haworth

and Martyn Kennard. Those years saw him at a series of magnificent sites: the first pyramid at Meidum, then the earliest dateable monument in the world; the Middle Kingdom town at Lahun, still the largest of its age to have been discovered in Egypt (below pp. 59–66); the New Kingdom palace of the royal women at Gurob (below pp. 79–84); the Middle Kingdom pyramid site at Hawara with its temple, the fabled Labyrinth of Greek historians, and its vast cemeteries of later ages, where Petrie found the astonishing panel portraits of the early Roman Period (below pp. 98–101); and, above all, the late Eighteenth Dynasty city at Amarna, founded by King Akhenaten in the first known gesture of dedication to one god—the "cradle of monotheism" (below pp. 67–78). A part-funder of his own excavations in these abundant years, Petrie retained about one third of all finds allowed out of Egypt by the Antiquities Service, the others going mainly to Manchester, through Haworth, and to the Ashmolean Museum, Oxford, through Kennard. So already by 1892, with his harvest from Amarna and the Fayum sites (Lahun, Gurob, Hawara), Petrie had amassed a collection of international stature, full of material not represented anywhere else, and providing an anchor by which archaeologists could date previously undatable material. On receiving one of the excavation reports, Adolf Erman, the great philologist and curator at Berlin, wrote to Petrie: "it is truly a joy now to be an Egyptologist."

It was at Amarna that Petrie heard news of the death of Amelia Edwards, in 1892. The following January, by the terms of her bequest, Petrie became the first Edwards Professor of Egyptian Archaeology and Philology at University College London. Along with funds to support the Chair, Edwards had left her collection and library. With this more permanent institutional base, Petrie was able to establish his own fund to support excavation in Egypt, the Egyptian Research Account (ERA). As with his work for the EEF, he was permitted by successive French directors of the Egyptian Antiquities Service to reward public museums sponsoring excavation by distributing to them a share of the finds allowed out of Egypt. After the annual process of distribution to the dozens of supportive museums worldwide, Petrie would retain both typical and enigmatic pieces for his own teaching collection at the university. As the active hub of this worldwide network of antiquities, the collection was beginning to take on its unique inquisitive character and unexpected scale.

In 1905, Petrie decided not to work for the EEF any more, and from that year the ERA supported a new institution founded by Petrie, the British School of Archaeology in Egypt. For the next three decades, the School played a prominent part in Egyptian archaeology, supporting excavations by not only Petrie himself, but also contemporaries and successors such as Reginald Engelbach and Guy Brunton. Although British troops were to remain in the country until after the Second World War, in 1922 Egypt became an independent kingdom with its own parliament. In the same year, Howard Carter discovered the tomb of King Tutankhamen in the Valley of the Kings. The Egyptian government opposed any suggestion of a division of this miraculous find, and Petrie became concerned that the political debate would put an end to the distribution of finds and so to his sponsorship. From the mid-1920s, he moved his activities to Palestine. There he continued to excavate, at sites along the Wadi Gaza where he expected to find evidence for relations between Egypt and the Bible lands. Excavating still into his eighties, he stopped his fieldwork only when growing violence in the area meant that he could no longer guarantee the security of his workforce.

After the death of Flinders Petrie in Jerusalem in 1942, his widow Hilda sought to keep the School alive, but postwar conditions in London made this difficult, and the BSAE formally came to an end in 1954, its assets vested in the UCL Department of Egyptology. The Department continued to excavate in Egypt, but now, for the Egypt Exploration Society and with government funding. Most people in the West are probably unaware, and might be surprised to learn, that there were still shares in the division of finds right down to the 1980s, including substantial gifts from excavations by Professors Emery and Smith at Buhen and Qasr Ibrim in Nubia, and at the Sacred Animal Necropolis of north Saqqara (below pp. 85–91). In addition, the postwar curator Reverend Anthony Arkell excavated in Sudan, identifying the Neolithic cultures of the Khartoum region, and one part of his finds was granted to University College. Other antiquities entered the university collection by bequest and gift. The Langtons, a British couple living in Cairo and friends of Professor Emery, bequeathed their gallery of cats from ancient Egypt, to be kept as a unit in testimony to the modern as well as ancient fascination for the feline. The College also received part of the bequests of Robert Mond and Guy Brunton, two of the leading figures in Egyptian archaeology in England in the 1920s and 1930s.

However, far the greatest postwar addition came when the Henry Wellcome Trust transferred to the museum its vast holdings in Egyptian and Sudanese antiquities. With an encyclopedic thirst for knowledge which Petrie would surely have recognized, the pharmaceutical pioneer Henry Wellcome had supported excavations by others, led excavations of his own at Gebel Moya in central Sudan, and sent his agents to the auctions of antiquities, with a particular eye for excavated material. In this way, Wellcome had acquired a prominent share in the finds from excavations by John Garstang at Meroe, capital of the independent Sudanese empire that withstood the power of Rome in the first centuries BC and AD (below pp. 102–111). The arrival of the thousands of Wellcome antiquities pushed the university museum beyond its capacity to make holdings accessible to research and lay visitors, and so, in the 1970s, the bulk of the unexcavated Wellcome items were transferred on to four public museums with a particular need at the time for Egyptian antiquities: University College Swansea, the Oriental Museum of the University of Durham, the Museum of the city of Birmingham, and the Liverpool Museum—all cities where Egyptian archaeology is also taught at university level. Most of the excavated material from the Wellcome Collection stayed at University College London. These include the finds from Meroe, now among the highlights of the Petrie Museum; together with the Arkell material, this provides an invaluable extension of its coverage into Sudan.

Despite the transfer of thousands of antiquities from the Wellcome collection and the more delicate organic materials to other national collections, the Petrie Museum has reached an equilibrium within its current home, the industrial stables where it was installed eventually, after return from wartime storage out of London. Its holdings amount to some 80,000 inventory numbers. Six thousand items are displayed on the shelves, and another two thousand in accessible, visible storage in the drawers of display-cases. The other 72,000 numbered items and groups are kept on site in cupboards around the displays: here, storage space, gallery space, teaching space, and study space are all one.

For the future, there are only two ways to deliver the collection to the great audience it deserves. The first is the touring exhibition, made possible in America by the initiative of the Michael C. Carlos Museum, Emory University, Atlanta. The second, crucial path forward is a new home, where the London visitor can find us. Here, we envisage every one of the 80,000 objects accessible, either on display shelves or in visible storage: no visitor should ever have to ask a curator with a key just to see an object that belongs either to no one or to all of us. We aim not just to open up the thousand and one stories within every one of those objects, but to ask questions, or better to ask our visitors to ask questions—we are, after all, a university museum, and if a university museum has a right to exist, arguably it is in the right of free and open debate. What rights do we have to look at these objects, not only the human remains, but all the items from those others we can never meet? Should they be outside the lands that produced them? How do we tell the stories, and in how many languages?

Sometimes technology can help, and we can capitalize on the breadth of subjects taught at University College London, across the arts and humanities. We have created sets of reconstructions of a range of sites in Virtual Reality, to explore not just how monuments and cities might have looked two, three, four, five thousand years ago, but how the all-too-persuasive medium of VR creates its own new reality, and how we can or cannot really learn from that. We are starting to ask questions about the specific ways in which an object helps or hinders learning—studying the magic of touch. Above all, we are asking ourselves who benefits from these collections, among all those captivated by ancient Egypt? We need to find ways of connecting with black African and Arab World audiences with their own strong, but different and often mutually exclusive views on ancient Egypt.

Traditionally, the subject of Egyptology has been separated from areas of time and space when and where Egyptian was not spoken. One way out of this isolation is to question the points of absolute rupture between one period and another, for example the transition from ancient Egyptian to Hellenized living, or from pagan to Christian, or majority Christian to majority Muslim. Under or over those seismic historical shifts, many aspects of life continued unchanged. The Petrie Museum contains material from all periods of Egyptian history, and offers unusual opportunities for that elusive "total history," still a noble goal because it reminds us that history is about humanity. Rehumanizing the past is the most important task for museums and universities today.

The present can rarely escape its own arrogance in relation to the past; it is too tempting to imagine that we are doing something for the first time, or better, than it has been done before. In Egypt, they say that nothing has been done for the first time. The ancient Egyptians modeled their *ma'at* or "sense of what is right," on the idea of an eternally repeating "first time," an originary power of Creation. At the Petrie Museum, we have a particular awareness of two pasts—the ancient, that attracts most visitors, and a more recent legacy from Amelia Edwards, Flinders Petrie, and the other indefatigably energetic pioneers of archaeology in Egypt, on their hard quest for knowledge of the ancient past. In the construction of a future, physical and practical, our hardest taskmaster and judge must be the spirit of Petrie, as the man who left such a remarkable collection to communicate to a twenty-first century.

CATALOG

CHRONOLOGY

Throughout his career, Petrie strove determinedly to recover history of the past. While he is renowned above all for his contribution to study of the prehistory of Egypt, he devoted as much care to the establishment of precise knowledge of king-lists and exact chronological data. Archaeology and prehistory stand, for him, not in opposition to the written record, but as part of the wider history that is the human story. His attention to historical sources led him to reconstruct out of the king-lists a chronology far longer than any Egyptologist would accept today; so many rulers are attested for the First and Second Intermediate Periods that Petrie assigned several centuries to both.[1] The shorter time span involved became clear only from advances in just the study of types of objects that Petrie pioneered: typologies of pottery, tools and weapons, funerary material, and amulets all serve to confirm the evidence of post-war analytical method, in particular Carbon-14 dating, that the Old Kingdom lies somewhere in the third rather than the sixth millennium BC. Reassessment of the king-lists themselves and of the other ancient written sources had already brought into play a short chronology, that still used in Egyptology. To be fair to Petrie, though, it is wise to keep a critical eye on the current consensus, and to test our standardized dates repeatedly against all the abundant available evidence.

In the third century BC, an Egyptian scholar called Manetho compiled a history of Egypt in Greek for the then ruler of the country, Ptolemy II, perhaps specifically for the new Library at Alexandria.[2] Manetho divided the previous rulers of Egypt into thirty, or in some versions thirty-one, groups called *dunastiai*, "power-units" (rather than "dynasties" in the sense of kings related by blood or marriage); the reasons for separating one group from another are not always entirely clear, but each group was related to a city in Egypt. The relation to the city is not stated; the group could have ruled there, been buried there, have originated there, but in each case it would be placed under the protection of the main deity of that city, according to the Egyptian conception of urban space and individual identity. Despite its very specific Egyptian-Greek home within early Ptolemaic Egypt, the king-list by Manetho is the most detailed to survive from antiquity, with years of reign for individual rulers and dynasties, and it is the only list to cover the entire period from the first kings to the arrival of Alexander the Great in 332 BC, marking the end of Pharaonic history. As a result, Egyptologists feel obliged to continue using it, writing still of an Eighteenth or Twenty-sixth Dynasty. Between 1818 and 1830, European Egyptologists came across three king-lists a thousand years more ancient: two hieroglyphic inscriptions in the temples to the cults of kings Seti I and his son Ramesses II at Abydos, and a hieratic manuscript from the village of draftsmen for the tomb of the king, at Deir el-Medina, also from the reign of Ramesses II.[3] The hieroglyphic king-lists at Abydos provide an edited sequence of

1 W. M. F. Petrie, *A History of Egypt Vol. IX. From the Earliest Kings to the XVIth Dynasty* (London, 1924).

2 G. Waddell, *Manetho*, Loeb Classical Library (London, 1940).

3 Donald Redford, *Pharaonic King-lists, Annals and Day-books. A Contribution to the Study of the Egyptian Sense of History* (Mississauga, 1986).

rulers, partly adapted to the space, perhaps also to the local traditions of those rulers accepted at Abydos during periods of disunity. The hieratic manuscript, the Turin Canon (so-called because now preserved at Turin) records year, month, and day totals for many reigns, and includes many kings omitted in the Abydos versions. However, it survives in extremely fragmentary condition, leaving many gaps in the sequences of rulers.

A full thousand years earlier again, lists of kings were inscribed on basalt slabs, perhaps for the temple of the reigning king. Only small portions of these most ancient lists survive. Petrie was able to acquire one fragment for his collection (cat. no. 1), and, given his keen interest in chronology, it is easy to imagine his delight at the prize. None of these lists makes allowances for contemporary reigns, and yet we know from other sources that Egypt sometimes fragmented into smaller units: at the most extreme, the great inscription of King Piy records his invasion of Egypt from Napata (in present-day Sudan) in the late eighth century BC, and the submission of a whole series of local rulers more than one of whom claims kingly status.[4] In a king-list, all these rulers would appear in linear sequence, not side by side, and a total of their reign-lengths would be misleading. King-lists also make no reference to the apparently recurrent practice of co-regency, where a king appoints his successor as junior king on the throne beside him, to avoid problems in succession.

For these reasons, king-lists do not quite fulfill their promise of bringing perfect order to the outline of political history. Instead, the historian must compile his or her own king-list out of the great mass of contemporary and posthumous references to each ruler. Here Petrie ranked second to none, acquiring for his own collection any available scrap of history, in the sense of a building block for the ultimate goal of an unbroken king-list. His *History of Egypt* aimed to deliver as complete a list of sources as he was able, and he could illustrate it at many points from his own collection.[5] From the perspective of modern history writing, this chronological record-collecting seems outdated, in thrall to a naive perception of history as a string of dates and events. Yet it would be unwise to judge Petrie too severely on this count. Something of Petrie, the calculating genius, is at work in his historical and chronological studies, a delight in the manipulation of numbers as well as a sense of the importance of all evidence in history and archaeology. Historical inscriptions amount to only one part of the evidence, but we do make full use of them. Sometimes they can bring a clarity and sharpness to an archaeological record: a foundation plaque with the name of a ruler can, when its context is clear, reveal which of two opposing forces constructed a temple or controlled a territory. More importantly, the chronological focus, almost an obsession to an outsider, reveals the guiding spirit of the age of its writer: if we ask, why did this sequence of major and minor rulers matter so much to Petrie, we can come closer to understanding the real advances he made, and to appreciate more fully his progress on dating by indirect means, such as sequence dating, at the point where the written record fell silent. At the level of the collection and its connoisseurship, it should be acknowledged that the quest for the name of the king, any king, brought to the Petrie Museum outstanding examples of art produced for kingship. Many of these "historical inscriptions" preserve unique evidence for the operation and profile of that kingship in its own time, in a society for which the record of a year of reign or of the name of the ruler signified a content far from the nineteenth century category of the historical, but close to it in its ideological power.

4 Robert Morkot, *The Black Pharaohs: Egypt's Nubian Rulers* (London, 2000).
5 First published in 1894 in the absence of a satisfactory textbook for his own teaching at UCL, the History ran to ten editions, including volumes by E. Bevan, J. Milne, and S. Lane-Poole for the Ptolemaic, Roman, and Islamic Periods.

1. Fragment of royal annals stone
Dynasty 5, 2494–2345 BC
Basalt
H. 7.5 cm; w. 8.1 cm; d. 8.7 cm
UC 15508

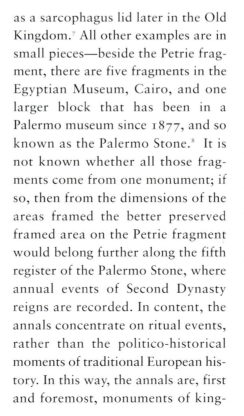

ON EACH smooth side of this fragment of stone may be seen hieroglyphic inscriptions arranged in vertical groups along horizontal registers, on the better-preserved side with clear framing lines. The upper largest area of inscription contains two registers, one with the events of a year, above another with linear measurements, generally interpreted as a record of the height of the Nile flood. A wide empty margin separates this framed area from the next framing line, below which may be seen the curving tip of the hieroglyph for "regnal year" and the sign for "to stand."

Inscribed basalt blocks of Fifth Dynasty date are the oldest Egyptian royal annals to survive. None have been found in context, and so their original location and architectural setting cannot be determined. They might have been set up in the temple of a deity, a temple to the cult of the king in whose reign they were carved, within his pyramid complex or, in the Fifth Dynasty, sun-temple. Petrie acquired this fragment at Memphis, but noted from inquiries that it might have come from Minya in Middle Egypt.[6] However, such monuments seem inappropriate to a regional town, and more at home in a national cult center, such as the temple of the god Ptah at Memphis, or the Fifth Dynasty monuments of kings at the nearby cemeteries from Saqqara to Abusir and Abu Gurob.

The largest annals block, 2.34 meters in length, survived by its reuse as a sarcophagus lid later in the Old Kingdom.[7] All other examples are in small pieces—beside the Petrie fragment, there are five fragments in the Egyptian Museum, Cairo, and one larger block that has been in a Palermo museum since 1877, and so known as the Palermo Stone.[8] It is not known whether all those fragments come from one monument; if so, then from the dimensions of the areas framed the better preserved framed area on the Petrie fragment would belong further along the fifth register of the Palermo Stone, where annual events of Second Dynasty reigns are recorded. In content, the annals concentrate on ritual events, rather than the politico-historical moments of traditional European history. In this way, the annals are, first and foremost, monuments of kingship. However, the inclusion of the linear measurements, apparently for the height of the Nile flood, bind that kingship to the dominant event in social and economic life in the Valley.

SQ

6 W. M. F. Petrie, "New Portions of the Annals," in *Ancient Egypt* (London, 1916) 114–20.
7 Michel Baud and Vassil Dobrev, "De Nouvelles Annales de l'Ancien Empire Égytien. Une 'Pierre de Palerme' pour la Ve Dynastie," *BIFAO* 95 (1995): 23–92.
8 Christine Ziegler, "Fragment of the Royal Annals," in *Egyptian Art in the Age of the Pyramids* (New York, 1999) 348–9, cat. no. 116.

2. Model razor inscribed for Djedkare Isesi

Dynasty 5, 2494–2345 BC
Banded chalcedony, pigment
L. 13.6 cm; w. 5.8 cm
UC 11771[9]

THE FORM of this artifact is most closely paralleled in the model razors found in Giza burials of the Fourth Dynasty, most notably the burial of equipment from the tomb of Hetepheres.[10] Even without its inscription, this razor stands out in its quality of production and its exceptional material, a gemlike vein of chalcedony as hard as any metal. Every line contributes to the refined restraint of the whole, in the geometric perfection so characteristic of the finest Egyptian art. The inscription is placed on the smaller rectangular face. The hieroglyphs are carefully incised, and record the name of the king in whose reign presumably the razor was sculpted: "the dual King Djedkare living forever." We can rarely identify the reasons for adding the name of a king to an object of practical use: it might be assumed that the name established either the property of the king himself, or, for objects given out at court, the favor shown to a subject of that king. In general, the name of the king acted as a powerful religious force, that could be deployed as a talisman for the protection and well-being of the individual. The constraints in such wider use of his name remain to be investigated. In this instance, the high quality of the artifact suggests production in the palace workshops, close to the heart of kingship.   SQ

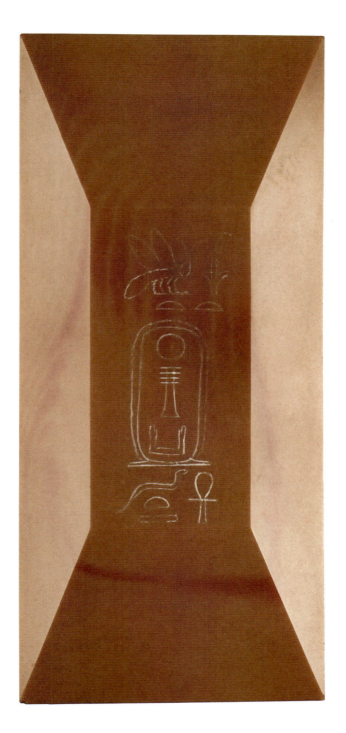

9 W. M. F. Petrie, *Objects of Daily Use* (London, 1927) 63, pl. 56, no. 9. Identified as a writing palette.
10 George Reisner, "The Tomb of Queen Hetep-heres," *BMFA* (Boston, 1927) vol. 25 supplement.

3. Cylinder vessel inscribed for Pepy I

Dynasty 6, reign of Pepy I,
2321–2287 BC
Calcite ("Egyptian alabaster"),
pigment
H. 14.2 cm; rim diam. 13.2 cm
UC 15791[11]

THIS CYLINDER VESSEL, with a wide flaring base and rim, is carved from a block of the translucent calcite sometimes called "Egyptian alabaster," quarried at Hatnub in the desert southeast of Amarna in Middle Egypt. Stone cylinder vessels such as this were used to contain scented oils, and played an important part both in the daily life of the elite and in temple rituals of deities and kings. The inscription on the side here records the names of King Pepy I within the cosmic frame of earth-line below, sky-hieroglyph above, and supporting pillar at each side in the form of the hieroglyph for a scepter with the phonetic value *was*, "power." The lower line of the inscription reads out symmetrically from the center "given life and power eternally." At center, a cartouche encloses the name taken by Pepy I on his accession to the throne, Meryre, "beloved of Re," facing left to his Horus name, another identity expressed after accession, Merytawy "beloved of the Two Lands," referring to Upper and Lower Egypt. The vertical line of hieroglyphs at the right side of the framed area reads "first time of the *sed*-festival." The *sed* is the most important festival of kingship, attested from the First Dynasty to the end of pharaonic history, and rendered in Greek inscriptions of the Ptolemaic Period as "thirty-year festival." Its rites were intended to rejuvenate the powers of the king, guaranteeing the unity and fertility of Egypt. Inscribed containers for the sacred oils for the festival for this and other Sixth Dynasty reigns have been found across a wide area; the very presence of the king's name as well as the prized contents would have made this a potent force for life.   SQ

11 W. M. F. Petrie, *Funeral Furniture and Stone Vases* (London, 1937) pl. 11, no. 93c.

4. Weight inscribed for Nebkaure Khety

Tell er-Retaba, Wadi Tumilat
Dynasties 9–10, ca. 2150 BC
Red jasper
L. 5.0 cm; w. 3.9 cm; d. 2.4 cm
UC 11782[12]

THIS WEIGHT is in the standard slab form, but, highly unusually, carved in red jasper, a prized semi-precious stone from the southeastern deserts. The inscription within the cartouche incised on the upper surface reads "[dual King] Khety Nebkaure living forever;" nine strokes are incised along one short end, identifying the block as the equivalent of nine "gold-measures" (see cat. nos. 87–8).

During the First Intermediate Period, when the country was divided in two, even the number of the northern kings remains uncertain, let alone their sequence. Manetho records a Ninth and a Tenth Dynasty of kings from Herakleopolis (Ihnasya), but too few monuments survive from the period either to explain this division, or to confirm it. Contemporary inscriptions refer to a group of northern kings as the House of Khety, the name of several. Against that background, every small, inscribed object acquires a particular historical value; this weight is the only known source from that reign.[13]   SQ

12 Petrie acquired the weight during his 1905–6 excavations of a series of sites between the eastern branch of the Nile Delta and the Bitter Lakes and Suez, mainly along the seasonally watered desert valley called the Wadi Tumilat. The site of the find, Tell er-Retaba, was the main town in the wadi until about 600 BC, when the population seems to have moved eastwards to Tell el-Maskhuta. W. M. F. Petrie, *Hyksos and Israelite Cities* (London, 1906) 32; pls. 32a, 33

13 King Nebkaure Khety does also figure, though, in a famous masterpiece of Middle Kingdom literature, the *Tale and Laments of Khuninpu* (widely known in Egyptology as the *Tale of the Eloquent Peasant*). In that literary composition, a "marshdweller" living in the Wadi Natrun, west of the Delta, is robbed on his way to market, and petitions the high steward in a series of increasingly desperate and angry speeches. After the first, the anonymous author of the Tale observes: "Now this marshdweller delivered this speech in the time of the dual King Nebkaure true of voice." It is intriguing that the Nebkaure weight comes from a landscape similar to the home of Khuninpu, though on the other side of the Nile Delta—the scrub and rocks of semi-desert valleys, too arid for agriculture, though watered enough for grazing herds and for small-scale settlements.

5. Scepter-head (?) dedicated by Senusret

Dynasty 12, 1985–1773 BC
Obsidian
H. 3.8 cm; w. 3.6 cm; d. 1.5 cm
UC 11264[14]

OBSIDIAN IS VOLCANIC GLASS, a hard and shiny material found only far from Egypt, one source being in Greece and another in Ethiopia. Its use always indicates elite status, here confirmed by the inscription, reading: "son of Re Senusret: he made as [...]." The phrase after the name of the king is part of the regular formula for a dedication to the cult of a king or deity: "he made as his monument for X." Three kings of the Twelfth Dynasty bore the birth-name Senusret, and in the absence of throne-name or archaeological context it is not possible to determine which is intended here; more monuments are known to have been dedicated by King Senusret I than the other two, but that remains uncertain grounds for identifying the ruler in this case.

No close parallels have been found for the form of the object. Its diameter and inner ring area seem rather impractical for a pot-stand; the drill-lines left rough on the interior suggest instead the space for a wooden shaft, with the obsidian ring as the head for a scepter. However, the ring would be flatter than surviving scepters, and it must be admitted that this beautifully produced artifact remains enigmatic; this indeed must have been part of its attraction to Petrie, inveterate problem-hunter, in addition to its value as evidence for chronology.   SQ

14 W. M. F. Petrie, *Scarabs and Cylinders with Names* (London, 1917) pl. 12, no. 12.2.33

6. Scarab amulet inscribed with the name of Thutmose III

Dynasty 18, reign of Thutmose III,
1479–1425 BC
Frit ("Egyptian blue")
L. 2.9 cm; w. 2.0 cm; d. 1.2 cm
UC 12034[15]

IN HIS QUEST for historical individuals, Petrie amassed one of the largest collections of scarab-shaped seal-amulets, as these are commonly inscribed with names and titles. This example is larger than the average scarab, and in a fine blue frit. The material is of similar ingredients to faience and glass, in different proportion; it was probably developed in ancient Iraq or Syria, but is now commonly known as "Egyptian blue."[16] Vast numbers of scarabs were inscribed with the name of King Thutmose III, the great conqueror who ruled in the fifteenth century BC; from the style of cutting, the motifs accompanying the name, and combinations with names of later kings, it is clear that "Thutmose III scarabs" continued to be produced for a thousand years after his death. Perhaps to distinguish him from the three other kings called Thutmose, perhaps on some symbolic reading of the name, these scarabs give not his birth-name Thutmose, but the name he added when he acceded to the throne, Menkheperre, incorporating both the sun-disk and the scarab itself (reading *kheper*). However, the size, style, and material of this example suggest that it was produced during the reign of the king rather than later.

The inscription on the underside reads "the perfect god Menkheperre, he who lays low Qadesh," referring to the Syrian city controlling the trade routes of the northern Levant. The scarab inscription may refer directly to a specific event, perhaps the battle of Megiddo, rather than to submission by the city to Egyptian armies during the repeated later campaigns of the king. Though a single phrase, the epithet reflects military history, and so may be considered the seed of the later more extended inscriptions in praise of kingship on the "commemorative scarabs" of his great-grandson, Amenhotep III (see cat. no. 7).   SQ

15 W. M. F. Petrie, *Scarabs and Cylinders with Names* (London, 1917) pl. 26, no. 18.6.14.
16 See Florence Friedman, ed., *Gifts of the Nile: Ancient Egyptian Faience* (RISD, 1998) 55; 256, cat. no. 181; 266.

7. Lion hunt scarab of Amenhotep III

Dynasty 18, reign of Amenhotep III,
1390-1352 BC
Steatite
L. 8.7 cm; w. 5.4 cm; d. 3.4 cm
UC 12256[17]

THIS LARGE STEATITE SCARAB, originally glazed, bears deeply sculpted and incised features of head, wing-cases, and legs, and is inscribed on the underside with eight lines of hieroglyphic inscription, giving the full five-fold titulary of King Amenhotep III, the name of his wife Tiye, and the record of a total of lions killed by the king "from regnal year 1 to regnal year 10: wild lions–102." For Amenhotep III, alone of all the kings of Egypt, several series of large scarab-shaped amulets were produced, most of glazed steatite and inscribed on the underside with hieroglyphic inscriptions in eight or more horizontal lines. Larry Berman has argued that all may have been issued in the eleventh year of that long reign.[18] Many imitations have been produced, making it difficult to give exact numbers without checking all items, now dispersed around the world.[19]

In Egyptology, these distinctive scarabs have been called "commemorative scarabs," and seen as tokens of royal propaganda sent out across Egypt and beyond, for examples have been found in Nubia, Sinai, and Palestine. However, this interpretation misses the crucial question of their place in kingship ritual, an aspect highlighted by Berman. Taken as a group, these "hunt and marriage scarabs" reveal a fundamental realignment at court after year 10 of Amenhotep III, perhaps specifically upon

the arrival of and marriage to Gilukhepa, a foreign princess from Mitanni, the western Asian great power nearest to Egypt. In the new constellation of forces at the palace, Queen Tiye may have been elevated at this moment to a new level of participation in the divinity of kingship, beyond any comparison with the Mitanni princess. A lake dug for Tiye presumably had cosmic and cultic significance, just as the slaughter of bulls and lions would emphasize the power of the king over the wild. In sum, these scarab series reflect a moment of religious as well as political change through the ritual of court, at the end of a first decade of rule. They express and project kingship in an unprecedented way, though within a millennium-old tradition of celebrating the

power of the name of the king at its most concentrated in kingship ritual (compare the *sed* kingship festival inscription on the calcite vessel of King Pepy I, cat. no. 3).   SQ

17 W. M. F. Petrie, *Scarabs and Cylinders with Names* (London, 1917) pl. 31, no. 18.9.2.

18 In Arielle Kozloff and Betsy Bryan, *Egypt's Dazzling Sun: Amenhotep III and his World* (Cleveland, 1992) 67–72.

19 The following summary offers a general account of this exceptional group of scarabs: Over one hundred record the number of lions killed by the king in his first ten years. Over fifty record the names of the king, his principal wife Tiye, her parents Yuya and Tuya, and the lands adjacent to his southern and northern borders. Just eleven record the digging of a great lake for Tiye near Akhmim in year 11. Perhaps five record the arrival at court of Gilukhepa, daughter of the king of Mitanni, the main rival to Egyptian power in Syria at the time, along with a retinue of 317 women. One or more record a hunt in year 2 in which the king killed 96 wild bulls (there are several modern copies with curious smooth-sided handle instead of scarab back).

8. Amulet with the name of Seti I

Probably from Memphis
Dynasty 19, reign of Seti 1,
1290–1279 BC
Faience
L. 7.9 cm; w. 5.0 cm; d. 2.8 cm
UC 12591[20]

THE GLAZED OVOID BLOCK is worn
away over the upper surface, obscur-
ing the original design, but the lightly
molded diagonal along the side and
the dip at one short end of the upper
surface make the identification as a
scarab amulet plausible. On the underside of the block the glaze is perfectly
preserved, with deep blue background
to fine blue-green hieroglyphic inscription and oval border. The hieroglyphs read: "the temple Light of King
Seti-beloved-of-Ptah, in the domain of
Ptah." "Seti-beloved-of-Ptah" is the
regular form for the name of Seti 1,
and the inscription would seem to
record the name of a temple to the cult
of that king in the city or region of
Memphis, where Ptah was the main
deity. The perfect execution of the
glazing is typical of the period before
and after the Amarna Period, when
polychrome faience is a prominent
feature of palace arts (see cat. nos.
152–3).   SQ

20 W. M. F. Petrie, *Scarabs and Cylinders
with Names* (London, 1917) pl. 39, no.
19.2.2.

9. Weight inscribed with the name of Taharqa

Dynasty 25, reign of Taharqa,
690–664 BC
Serpentinite
L. 5.1 cm; w. 3.2 cm; d. 1.9 cm
UC 16369[21]

THIS WEIGHT is sculpted from a veined, dark brown to black serpentinite, in the cuboid slab form typical of the Old Kingdom, but dated by its inscription to the Twenty-fifth Dynasty, a period when more ancient practices were being revived. The hieroglyphic inscription on the upper face reads "the son of Re Taharqa beloved of Osiris amid Sais." Taharqa was one of the kings from Sudan who controlled both the Napatan realm there and the Egyptian Nile Valley and Delta, making it one of the largest empires in African history.[22]

The rulers of Sais presented the principal opposition within Egypt to Napatan power, and therefore this inscription might be seen as evidence for a policy of pacification by Taharqa in the home-city of his main enemy. Although the term "amid Sais" indicates that Osiris was not principal deity of the place—the main cult at Sais was that of the goddess Neith—numerous references to a Saite cult of Osiris, god of the dead, demonstrate its importance. There were at least two great sanctuaries to Osiris;[23] the weight might have belonged to the temple inventory at either place, perhaps reflecting larger-scale monumental activity there by the Napatan king.

SQ

21 W. M. F. Petrie, *Ancient Weights and Measures* (London, 1926) 12; pl. 10, no. 2398.
22 Robert Morkot, *The Black Pharaohs: Egypt's Nubian Rulers* (London, 2000).
23 One temple was located in the city and another at the cemetery where, from about this very period, an image of Osiris was buried each year. See S. Woodhouse, "The Sun God, his Four Bas and the Four Winds in the Sacred District at Sais: the Fragment of an Obelisk (BM EA 1512)," in Stephen Quirke, ed., *The Temple in Ancient Egypt* (London, 1997) 132–51.

10. Foundation deposit plaque with the name of Psamtek I

Dynasty 26, reign of Psamtek I,
664–610 BC
Frit
L. 5.0 cm; w. 2.4 cm; d. 0.6 cm
UC 14840

THIS FINE-GRAINED, green frit, cartouche-shaped plaque, complete except
for the lower edge ends, is inscribed
on both faces, and it has no suspension hole; as a result, it has been identified as not an amulet, but a separate
integral object of a type placed in Late
Period and later foundation deposits.[24]
The two sides give the name of King
Wahibre Psamtek, so Psamtek I, Assyr-
ian-appointed governor of Sais and
then first king of the Twenty-sixth
Dynasty. The perfect proportions of
the design and the meticulous detail
in each hieroglyph are typical of late
eighth, and above all, seventh-sixth
century BC production, sometimes called the Saite Renaissance. SQ

24 As identified by Petrie in *Scarabs and
Cylinders with Names* (London, 1917) pl. 55,
no. 26.1.41.

SCULPTURE

11. Relief fragment from the tomb of Nefermaat

Meidum, *mastaba* 16
Dynasty 4, reign of Sneferu,
2613–2589 BC
Limestone, pigment
L. 12.3 cm; w. 9.05 cm
UC 30874

THE LARGE *MASTABA* TOMB[25] of Nefer-maat, located north of the pyramid of Meidum, was excavated by Petrie in the 1890–1 season and again in 1909–10, after the site had suffered the attacks of art-thieves.[26] Nefermaat was the eldest son of Sneferu and holder of the title "vizier," second in importance only to the pharaoh. Given his high status, one would expect an impressive tomb, but the *mastaba* of Nefermaat and his wife, Itet, was far more than that, standing out as one of the most singular experiments in Egyptian art.

A massive limestone chapel and false door were constructed at the northern end of the superstructure and decorated with offering scenes. Although the content of the scenes would later become standard in Old Kingdom tombs, here they are rendered in a unique way. Instead of the usual raised relief, the images were cut away below the surface of the wall in the technique of sunken relief, though in this instance, the interior surfaces were not carved and painted, but were left rough and filled with pigment up to the face of the stone. Perhaps mindful of the vandalism and weathering that had destroyed other tombs, Nefermaat recorded on his monument that "he made his *mastaba* in his unspoilable writing."[27] Unfortunately, this experiment did not succeed, since much

of the pigment later fell out of the carved areas, leaving Nefermaat's tomb, like Da Vinci's *Last Supper*, a magnificent failure.

Gaston Maspero, Director of the Egyptian Antiquities Service, fearing the fragile reliefs would deteriorate further, had Petrie remove them to the Cairo Museum where they may be seen in large part, today. Blocks and fragments from the smaller chapel of Nefermaat's wife, Itet, were distributed to museums in Europe and America. The items salvaged from the previous destruction of Itet's chapel included this fragment in the collection at University College. This small piece depicts the head of a man wearing a wreath of marsh plants around his head, and still retains traces of the original blue-green pigment. Other images of men from Nefermaat's tomb show them sporting such fillets. A preserved example of the illustration can be seen in a fragment of more traditional wall painting added at a later stage in the construction of the tomb.[28]   PL

25 The predominant form of Egyptian tomb from the Predynastic Period through the Middle Kingdom, so-called because its low, rectangular shape resembles a bench, or *mastaba*, in Arabic.
26 W. M. F. Petrie, *Medum* (London, 1892) 26–8, pl. 28; *Meydum and Memphis* (London, 1910) 4–5. This fragment is one of a group published without illustration in Petrie, *Objects of Daily Use* (London, 1927) 72, no. 282, where it is noted after nos. 282–6 "all the above pieces were found loose after the smashing of the sculptures."
27 Jürgen Osing, "Zu Spruch 534 der Pyramidentexte," in *Hommages à Jean Leclant BdE* 106/1 (1994) 282–3. See also Dorothea Arnold, in *Egyptian Art in the Age of the Pyramids* (New York, 1999) 199–201.
28 Arnold, *Egyptian Art in the Age of the Pyramids*, 202–4.

12. Head of a foreigner

Archaic Period, ca. 3000–2686 BC
Basalt
H. 17.0 cm; w. 14.9 cm; d. 7.9 cm
UC 14884

FROM THE VERY BEGINNINGS of Egyptian art, the image of the pharaoh vanquishing the traditional enemies of Egypt was a standard theme in sculpture. On statues, it would later take the form of coded images, with bows or lapwing birds representing subjugated peoples. In some early examples, however, three-dimensional images of conquered hostiles were employed. They often were incorporated into statue bases, where they were crushed symbolically under the feet of the pharaoh.

This head is rendered in the simple style of the Archaic Period, and is quite similar to a number of statue emplacements found within the Step Pyramid complex of Djoser.[29] The beard, round face, and high cheekbones are typical of Egyptian representations of Libyans, long a nemesis of the pharaonic Egyptians.[30] It has been suggested that this head could be part of a door socket,[31] although its upright position and three-dimensionality instead suggest a statue pedestal. A similar head with Nubian features purchased at the same time may come from the southern side of the same monument, in what would become the standard means of representing foreign peoples according to their geographical orientation.[32]   PL

29 Cecil Firth and James Quibell, *Excavations at Saqqara: The Site and Pyramid*, 2 vols. (Cairo, 1935) pl. 57.
30 Christine Ziegler, "Statue Base with Enemy Heads," in *Egyptian Art in the Age of the Pyramids* (New York, 1999) 174, cat. no. 6.
31 Anthea Page, *Egyptian Sculpture* (London, 1976) cat. no. 2.
32 Ibid., cat. no. 3. UC 14885.

17

13. Trial sculpture

Early Dynasty 4, ca. 2589–2532 BC
Limestone
H. 12.5 cm; w. 13.3 cm; d. 11.9 cm
UC 15989

THIS UNUSUAL LIMESTONE HEAD has a flush-cut base, back, and top, and clearly was intended as a trial piece rather than a finished work of sculpture, as indicated by the roughness of the bottom and the backs of the ears. While the piece has always been assigned to an early period, the suggestion that it is a depiction of "Narmer"[33] seems unlikely given the sophistication of its style in contrast to what little remains of First Dynasty stone sculpture.[34]

The rounded tabs of the crown in front of the ears suggest that the piece should be dated earlier than the reign of Menkaure (2532–2503 BC), when the strictly horizontal ear tab became standardized. The same broad features, widely spaced eyes, and blocky ears can be seen on an unprovenanced red granite head in Brooklyn which has been tentatively ascribed to Khufu.[35] The features of both of these images correspond to those of the tiny ivory statue Petrie found at Abydos, which is the only representation of the builder of the Great Pyramid that has yet been identified.[36]

Similar limestone studies have been found recently in excavations around the pyramid of Khafre,[37] suggesting that they were used to instruct artisans involved in the sculptural program of the temples.   PL

33 W. M. F. Petrie, *The Arts and Crafts of Ancient Egypt* (London, 1909) 31.
34 Hourig Sourouzian, "L'iconographie du roi dans la statuaire des trois premières dynasties," in *Kunst des alten Reiches* (Mainz, 1995) 133–54.
35 Christine Ziegler, "Colossal Head," in *Egyptian Art in the Age of the Pyramids* (New York, 1999) 194, cat. no. 21.
36 Mohamed Saleh and Hourig Sourouzian, *The Egyptian Museum Cairo: Official Catalog* (Mainz, 1987) no. 28.
37 Nicholas J. Conard and Mark Lehner, "The Excavation of Petrie's 'Workmen's Barracks' at Giza," *JARCE* 38 (2001): 46, 50; figs. 14, 15, 19.

14. Head of a king

Koptos
Dynasty 5, 2494–2345 BC
Limestone
H. 7.8; w. 7.6 cm; d. 9.2 cm
UC 14282

THIS SMALL HEAD excavated by Petrie at Koptos is one of the few Old Kingdom royal sculptures that survive from Upper Egypt.[38] It is likely that the head was originally part of a seated statue,[39] and is remarkably similar in style to a series of sculptures found in the mortuary temple of the unfinished pyramid of Neferefre at Abusir.[40] The head is comparable to a number of others that may also belong to the mid-Fifth Dynasty.[41]

The head, carved of a hard yellow limestone popular in that period, has suffered deterioration along the proper left side of the face due to weathering of an iron inclusion in the stone. The clumsy execution of the proper left ear and the striations on the left side of the wig imply reworking, either to repair damage or to effect an iconographic change. Catharine Roehrig has suggested that this piece originally may have had a falcon at the rear with its wings outstretched in a manner similar to the head of Neferefre, now in the Cairo Museum.[42] The remains of the prominent back pillar and the reworking of the head support this hypothesis. Such reworking of sculptures is hardly unknown;[43] the removal of the uraeus from the brow of the piece provides additional evidence of an effort to eradicate its royal attributes.   PL

38 W. M. F. Petrie, *Koptos* (London, 1896) 11. Catharine Roehrig, "Fragmentary Head of a King," in *Egyptian Art in the Age of the Pyramids* (New York, 1999) 316–7, cat. no. 101.
39 A base to a throne of similar proportion and material was found with it (UC 14283). Anthea Page, *Egyptian Sculpture* (London, 1976) 4–5; see also Margaret Murray, *Egyptian Sculpture* (London, 1930) 8–10.
40 Miroslav Verner, "Les Sculptures de Rêneferef decouvertes à Abousir," *BIFAO* 85 (1985): 267–80; Idem., *Forgotten Pharaohs, Lost Pyramids* (Prague, 1994) 143–50.
41 Roehrig, 316–7.

42 JE 98171. A. Bongioanni, et al., eds. *An Illustrated Guide to the Cairo Museum*, (Cairo, 2001) 54–5.
43 Peter Lacovara, "Menkaure," in Nancy Thomas, ed., *The American Discovery of Ancient Egypt* (Los Angeles, 1995) 126–7, cat. no. 39.

15. Figure of a man

Dynasty 5, 2494–2345 BC
Granite
H. 21.0 cm; w. 15.1 cm; d. 11.1 cm
UC 14313[44]

THIS SCULPTURE is preserved only from the waist up; under the navel is an indication of the belt of the kilt, but no other details of the costume remain. The man wears a shoulder-length, striated wig that is pulled behind the ears. The figure was depicted seated, as indicated by the bent position of both arms. While it originally may have been part of a sculpture portraying him cross-legged in the attitude of a scribe (see cat. no. 114), it is more likely that he was shown seated, on a block serving as a chair.

The torso and back pillar are carved in a single piece, inscribed with two columns of hieroglyphs. The incomplete inscription begins with an offering formula, invoking "Bastet, Mistress of Bubastis," suggesting that the provenance of the statue is Tell Basta (ancient Bubastis), in the eastern Delta. The name of the owner of the statue is missing, but it was not that of the man originally depicted. The inscription dates to a much later period, Dynasty 25 or 26 (747–525 BC), than the sculpture, which is typical of the Fifth Dynasty. In the column on the left, the name of the individual's mother is partially preserved, along with her title, "Mistress of the House."

While artisans during many periods of Egyptian history copied earlier styles, a practice known as archaism, there is usually a clue to their true date, which often has as much to do with technological advancements as with stylistic changes. Several factors suggest that this is not an archaizing statue, but rather an instance of reuse. Having only copper tools, the features on private granite statues of the Old Kingdom are frequently a bit summarily rendered. In addition, while red granite was used for a number of private sculptures in this era, it is far less common in later periods. The back supports of the Old Kingdom pieces were not inscribed, providing a "clean slate" for the addition of inscriptions such as this at a later date.[45] A great number of royal granite sculptures and architectural elements from the pyramid age were transported from the Memphite region to Bubastis and other Delta cities.   SG–D

44 Anthea Page, *Egyptian Sculpture* (London, 1976) cat. no. 7.
45 The mother's title, "Mistress of the House," is not regularly attested prior to the late Middle Kingdom, providing a *terminus ante quem* for the inscription and reuse of the statue.

16. Relief of a Nile god

Koptos, Temple of Min[46]
Dynasty 12, around the reigns of
Amenemhet I and Senusret I,
ca. 1985–1911 BC
Limestone
H. 39.2 cm; w. 48.8 cm; d. 7.9 cm
UC 14320

THIS PARTICULAR BLOCK depicts the head and shoulders of a figure carrying a tray of vessels.[47] The pose and pendulous breast identify it as a "fecundity figure," a personification of the bounty of nature, in particular of the Nile flood.[48] No coloration is preserved, but fecundity figures are often painted blue or green, recalling the color of the waters and growing vegetation. The figure carries a reed mat with conical loaf which can be read as the hieroglyph *hetep*—"offering." The two vessels carried are also the signs for "libation" and "favor," and between them is the upper part of a hooked *was*-scepter ("power"), which continued below the mat. The plant atop the figure's head is conventionally identified as a sedge, used to represent Upper Egypt. This image might be either from a frieze of such figures, or from a pair; in either case, facing it there would have been another figure crowned by the papyrus plant emblematic of Lower Egypt, to encompass the productivity of the whole land.

The long striated wig and thin false beard with curved end are both divine attributes, yet the figure's eye does not have the wedge-shaped artificial "cosmetic line" and extended eyebrow that denotes deities and kings. Embodying the divinely created fertility of the Nile, these images of the Nile flood are appropriately lo-cated along the lower parts of temple walls and the seat of thrones. Scenes of the king adoring Min and other gods would probably have occupied the walls above him.

The inscriptions give no clue as to the date of the block, but the delicacy of the raised relief carving, and the detail of the incised pupil of the eye, are closest to the reliefs of Amenemhet I and Senusret I of the Twelfth Dynasty, also found reused in the foundations of the later temples at Koptos.[49]   TH

46 During his work at the temple of Min at Koptos in 1893–4, Petrie found that the oldest standing part of the temple, built in the reign of Thutmose III, included blocks from earlier buildings in its foundations.

47 W. M. F. Petrie, *Koptos* (London, 1896) 11, pl. 11.

48 John Baines, *Fecundity Figures: Egyptian personification and the iconology of a genre* (Warminster, 1985).

49 An incised pupil can be seen in Cairo JE 30770 bis, a raised relief block of Senusret I before the goddess Bastet, from the same site: Petrie, *Koptos*, pl. X 2.

17. Head of Amenemhet III

Dynasty 12, reign of Amenemhet III,
1831–1786 BC
Diorite
H. 15.9 cm., w. 19.3 cm; d. 11.8 cm
UC 14363

THE VEINING and granular surface of
the stone may initially conceal from
the viewer the subtle modeling of the
features on this powerful depiction of
King Amenemhet III. In the reign of
his father Senusret III, the royal sculptors produced images of unprecedented character, in which the traditional gentle smile and smooth, young
skin are replaced by a horizontal or
downturned mouth and the furrows
of older age (compare with cat. no.
20). Under Amenemhet III, images
may be less starkly lined, with a variety of portrayals from youth to elder.

In this example, the mouthline
between the prominent lips undulates
to a downward turn, echoing the style
of the previous reign. Although the
cheekbones are clearly modeled, between cheek and nose is a gently con-
cave dip instead of the deep lines seen
on other products of late Twelfth
Dynasty royal sculpture workshops.
Ears and eyes have thick raised borders, and the eyes are set under deep
brows, the eyeballs prominent; the
inner ear areas are plain except for a
slight rise, and the earlobes are simi-
larly stylized as ovoid masses. The
king is depicted wearing a *nemes*, the
kingship-headcloth, with forehead
strip from which parallel lines radiate
out in clusters of narrow bands separated by broader bands. The cobra to
protect the king is partly eroded, as is
the tip of the nose. The piece was the
highlight of the collection of Amelia
Edwards, representing the core of
the present collections of the Petrie
Museum.[50]   SQ

50 Anthea Page, *Egyptian Sculpture*
(London, 1976) cat. no. 31.

**18. Upper part of a statuette
of a royal woman**

Dynasty 12, 1985–1773 BC
Hornblende diorite
H. 22.0 cm; w. 15.9 cm; d. 10.6 cm
UC 16657[51]

THE SUBJECT of this finely sculpted image is identified as a queen or princess by the cobra at her brow, now missing. The image has been broken away at the waist, probably in antiquity to judge from the eroded surface; from the partly preserved back pillar it seems most likely that she was depicted seated. Her eyes are set deep, with pronounced outer line, the eyebrows continuing round to the nose. The ears are sculpted as plain ovals within a raised border. Her lips protrude slightly from an otherwise smoothly rounded face, an incised line reinforcing her even smile. Parallel wavy lines indicate the tresses of her hair or wig, massed behind the ears and tapering to narrow braids above each breast, in the so-called "Hathor-style," with the hair below the parting falling in a centered block down the back. The straps and upper edge of the sleeveless dress are marked with incised lines.

Though securely Twelfth Dynasty in style, the figure is difficult to date more closely, for images of the royal women of the time are surprisingly rare, and few examples come from clearly datable contexts or bear inscriptions. Suggestions have ranged across the first half of the period, from the reign of Amenemhet I to that of Senusret II. The divinity of the king was considered to be shared by the women closest to him in life—his mother, wife, and daughters. Such images of the royal women guaranteed their eternal supply of offerings within the cult of the king at his burial place, reflecting their unique role in the ritual life of the royal court as emblems and enactors of the fertility of Egypt.   SQ

51 Anthea Page, *Egyptian Sculpture* (London, 1976) cat. no. 24; Janine Bourriau, *Pharaohs and Mortals* (Cambridge, 1988) cat. no. 14.

19. Statuette of Yaket, her husband, and son

Dynasty 12, 1985–1773 BC
Basalt
H. 11.4 cm; w. 11.4 cm; d. 5.9 cm
UC 16650[52]

DURING THE TWELFTH DYNASTY, basalt statuettes of women and men, singly, in pairs or, more rarely as here, in threes, were often placed in wealthier burials in Upper and Middle Egypt. The woman, with hair or wig in heavy "Hathor-style" and long garment, stands with her arms to her sides and feet together. She is flanked by two men with shoulder-length hair or wigs, and long kilts tied at the front; the man on her left stands with feet together, while the man on her right has his feet apart, as if striding. Both men are depicted with their hands flat on their kilts, a gesture of prayer.

The quality of the figural carving tends to be higher than that of the hieroglyphic inscription on these images, as if the inscriber was not adequately trained to cut the fine lines needed for the signs. Nevertheless, the scratched hieroglyphs fulfill a vital function of the image, preserving for eternity ancient individual identities by name. Here, the signs scratched on the back and front give the name of the woman as Yaket. The signs to her left give the funerary formula "an offering given by the king for the ka-spirit of Khentkhety," evidently; the line of hieroglyphs to her right reads "his son Kesh." Along the front is also a fourth name, Khentkhetyhotep, either a fuller name for her husband, or, following regular Egyptian practice, a second name, for either her husband or her son. Whereas the names

Khentkhety and Khentkhetyhotep are Egyptian, Yaket and Kesh appear foreign; the idealizing carving of the faces provides no clue as to whether the woman came from south (Nubia), west (Libyan desert) or northeast (Syria-Palestine), but these names hint at the cosmopolitan mixture of peoples in Egypt at that time.   SQ

52 Anthea Page, *Egyptian Sculpture* (London, 1976) cat. no. 23.

20. Upper part of a statue of an aged man

Thebes, Karnak, Mut Temple
Late Middle Kingdom,
1850–1650 BC[53]
Granodiorite
H. 17.9 cm; w. 21.3 cm; d. 18.4 cm
UC 16451

THE FEATURES of this sculpture offer a radical formulation of seniority in stone: the deeply modeled lines of brow, cheeks, and chin of the man contrast with his smooth shoulder-length wig or hair. In other respects, the facial features are conceived in similar manner to the slightly earlier sculpture of a royal woman (see cat. no. 18): each ear is depicted as a plain undifferentiated space bordered by a high rounded ridge from upper to side hairline, the edges to the eyes are sunk, and the eye area itself deeply set within the arch of the brows to the nose, while the lips are shown jutting out from an even smile.

This image of an elder must be read not only as an exception within Egyptian art history, but also against the practical experience of its time. Life was shorter in ancient Egypt, at an average expected span of only forty years, and old age was highly valued. For eternal life, a man or woman might usually be depicted in the prime of life, but at certain periods emphasis could be placed instead on advanced age and corpulence, physical signs of success in survival. In contrast to classical Greek and Roman depictions of aged individuals, the Egyptian tradition constructed the elderly face as a perfectly symmetrical image, the deep furrows idealizing the elder as systematically as the smooth skin of other sculptures idealized youth.　　SQ

53 As Dynasties 25–26 in Anthea Page, *Egyptian Sculpture* (London, 1976) cat. no. 105. On the date, see Bernard Bothmer, *Antiquities from the Collection of Christos Bastis* (New York, 1987) 94, cat. no 36.

21. Statue of Amenemopet holding a stela

Probably from Luxor
Dynasty 18, reign of Thutmose III
or Amenhotep II, 1479–1400 BC
Gabbro
H. 45.2 cm; w. 15.5 cm; d. 21.9 cm
UC 8446[54]

THE STATUE depicts a kneeling man with partly raised arms, his body hidden behind a round-topped stela containing a short hymn to the sun god Re. The back pillar gives the name and titles of the owner of the statue, the High Steward and royal scribe, Amenemopet, and records that the figure was dedicated by his brother Ahmose, a priest of the god Amun.

The pose of adoration adopted by Amenemopet was difficult to render in sculpture, because the upraised arms needed to be supported by unsightly struts. Transforming these supports into a stela gave a more visually satisfactory result, and the presence of a hymn on the stela further amplified the meaning of the gesture. Contemporary depictions of tombs show these statues occupying niches in the small brick pyramids above the entrances.[55] As most tombs faced east towards the rising sun, this placement would have enabled the deceased to greet the sun god every morning, as the hymn states. This statue-type is a creation of the Eighteenth Dynasty, and a date in the middle of this period is suggested by Amenemopet's striated wig and conspicuously banded eyes.

TH

54 Gift of the Trustees of the Wellcome Collection, formerly Wellcome A.400019, previously in the collection of Lady Meux. See W. Budge, *Some Account of the Collection of Egyptian Antiquities in the Possession of Lady Meux* (London, 1896) 148–9, pl. 15, no. 64. See also Anthea Page, *Egyptian Sculpture* (London, 1976) cat. no. 72. This sculpture, together with several other monuments of the same man, is the subject of a forthcoming study by V. A. Donohue and S. Woodhouse.

55 An example inscribed for a man named Min-mes was discovered by Petrie *in situ* in a chapel at Sedment. The statue stood before a stela and altar, all of which are now in Cairo. The group likely dates to the reigns of Amenhotep I, Thutmose I, and Thutmose II (1525–1479 BC). W. M. F. Petrie and Guy Brunton, *Sedment* II (London, 1924) 23–4, pl. 1.

22. Torso of a princess

Dynasty 18, reign of Amenhotep III,
1390–1352 BC[56]
Steatite
H. 3.8 cm; w. 3.0 cm; d. 2.4 cm
UC 16486

THIS DIMINUTIVE TORSO likely represents a daughter of Amenhotep III and his primary queen, Tiye, and probably belonged to a group statue depicting the royal family.[57] The princess wears a lotus filet with single uraeus, and a vulture headdress with traces of a modius, or platform, crown. Her voluminous wig frames a plump, delicate face with the large, almond-shaped eyes and rounded cheeks characteristic of the statuary of Amenhotep III.

Amenhotep III frequently appears with both Tiye and one of their daughters. In such compositions, the princess assumes the role of a secondary queen, with regalia differing from that of her mother, and at a smaller scale. One example designates the princess as "the consort...the king's daughter."[58]   BTT

56 Dated to Dynasty 19 and attributed to the deified Ahmose-Nefertari in Anthea Page, *Egyptian Sculpture* (London, 1976) cat. no. 96.
57 Betsy Bryan has proposed a possible join with a fragmentary statuette of the royal couple now in the Louvre (E 25493, N 2312), suggesting that the UCL torso is appropriately scaled as a minor third figure. Arielle Kozloff and Betsy Bryan, *Egypt's Dazzling Sun: Amenhotep III and his World* (Cleveland, 1992) 203, fig. 22b. As further evidence, Bryan points to the unusual modeling of the eyelids found on both figures. Bryan, "Striding Glazed Steatite Figures of Amenhotep III: an Example of the Purposes of Minor Arts," in Elizabeth Goring, Nicholas Reeves, and John Ruffle eds., *Chief of Seers* (London, 1997) 60–75.
58 JE 33906. A colossal figure of princess Henuttaneb from Thebes. It should be noted that Henuttaneb wears the same set of headdresses as the UCL princess.

23. **Princess Sitamen**

Thebes, Temple of Amenhotep II[59]
Dynasty 18, reign of Amenhotep III,
1390–1352 BC
Sandstone
H. 57.9 cm; w. 52.1 cm; d. 10.9
UC 14373

DURING THE REIGN of Amenhotep III, royal women, most notably the Great Royal Wife, Tiye, achieved an unprecedented level of prominence and visibility. The daughters of the king and queen are frequently depicted in statuary and relief, in both royal and private contexts. Found in the temple of Amenhotep II at Thebes, this fragment depicts one of the royal princesses, Sitamen, identified by the traces of her cartouche at the upper left edge of the block.

Sitamen, who was elevated to the position of Great Royal Wife late in her father's reign, holds a lily scepter, an attribute carried by royal women. Her vulture headdress, worn by both queens and goddesses, emphasizes her child-bearing potential. Associated with mother goddesses, especially Mut, consort of Amun, the king of the gods, the vulture headdress in this instance underscores Sitamen's role as consort of the king.   BTT

59 W. M. F. Petrie, *Six Temples at Thebes* (London, 1897) 6, pl. 6.

24. Head and torso of a man from a dyad

Bubastis, Great Temple[60]
Dynasty 18, reign of Amenhotep III,
1390–1352 BC
Granodiorite
H. 37.4 cm; w. 25.6 cm; d. 17.8 cm
UC 14632

ONLY THE UPPER LEFT QUARTER of the original group is preserved. To the man's right once stood or sat a female figure, probably his wife, whose hand rests on his left shoulder; his missing right arm probably embraced her in turn. The remains of the inscription carved on the back slab do not preserve the names or titles of either figure, but describe how the man enjoyed especial favor at court—the cartouches of Amenhotep III on his chest supplying the name of the king this now nameless official served. The name of the god Amun in one cartouche was erased in the reign of Amenhotep's successor Akhenaten, as part of his rejection of the old pantheon in favor of the sun disk, Aten.

While the man's curled echeloned wig and almond-shaped eyes are characteristic of the whole reign of Amenhotep III, the elegant, elongated, pointed ends of the eyebrows and cosmetic lines are encountered in private sculptures datable to the end of his 38-year reign, and the first years of his son's rule.[61] Amenhotep's three rejuvenating *sed*-festivals, held in years 30, 34, and 37, necessitated vast building projects throughout Egypt. Little remains of the pharaoh's own works in Bubastis, but the importance of the site in this period is attested by the quantity—and quality—of private sculpture found there.[62] In his excavation report, Édouard Naville describ-

ed the bust as a "head of a woman," possibly influenced by the figure's fancy wig and softly modeled torso. He was not the only Egyptologist to be confused by the art of this period; a fine limestone bust of another official of Amenhotep III was celebrated as "the Mona Lisa of Ancient Egypt" until the First World War.[63]   TH

60 EEF excavations 1887–9; bequeathed by Amelia Edwards.
61 Datable examples of the elongated eyebrows include an unprovenanced, life-size granodiorite head of an official wearing a *sed*-festival ribbon, in a private collection in 1992; Arielle Kozloff and Betsy Bryan, *Egypt's Dazzling Sun: Amenhotep III and his World* (Cleveland, 1992) 252–3, cat. no. 45. Ashmolean Museum 1896–1908 E.4472f, schistose steatite head of the overseer of the

treasury, Panehesy, datable to regnal year 36, from Serabeit el-Khadim, Sinai: unpublished. From the reign of Amenhotep IV, comes Brooklyn Museum 60.96, a granodiorite bust.
62 Including two large statues of Amenhotep, Vizier in the last years of the king's reign. Further excavations in the 1940s by Labib Habachi uncovered two statues of Khaemwaset, Overseer of Foreign Lands and a participant in Amenhotep's first *sed*-festival. One of these is the lower part of a granodiorite dyad showing him seated, with his wife on his right. The material and scale of the two pieces are very similar, as is the line of the break; further investigation of the two fragments is necessary, but if they do not join, they derive from closely related monuments.
63 Birmingham City Museum 69'96; John Ruffle, "Four Egyptian Pieces in Birmingham City Museum," *JEA* 53 (1967): 39–41, pl. v.

25. Dyad

Late Dynasty 18, 1352–1292 BC
Limestone, pigment
H. 14.5 cm; w. 27.5 cm; d. 8.5 cm
UC 15513

WE SEE A RETURN to high quality private tomb sculpture at the apex of the New Kingdom, just as it had been in the glory days of the Old and Middle Kingdoms. In Dynasty 18, the sculpture often takes the form of a seated pair statue depicting the tomb owner and his wife in wood, hard stone, or most commonly, painted limestone.

This example preserves much of its original color. As was fashionable at the end of the Eighteenth Dynasty, the man has pierced ears and wears a full, elaborately curled wig and an open-necked linen shirt with pleated sleeves. His wife, whose voluminous wig is crowned with a band of lotus petals, has a broad collar at her neck and wears a filmy, finely pleated linen dress that exposes one breast, a style periodically found in women's costume.

The lower half of the sculpture is now missing, but probably would have depicted the pair seated. The flat back is inscribed with a hieroglyphic text that reads:

An offering that the king gives to Osiris, foremost of westerners, and to [...] that they may give every good and pure thing, a libation...water (?) and vegetables (?) in Heliopolis...to the *ka* of the uniquely excellent one who is praised by [...].

An offering that the king gives to Osiris, foremost of westerners, and to [...] that they may give glory in heaven, power (on earth...) each time (the sun) rises [...] to the throat on the day of the festival of perfuming the god, to the *ka* of [...].

The pair would have stood at the focal point in the tomb chapel, to be viewed by visitors to the tomb who would leave offerings and say prayers for the eternal well being of the couple.

PL

U.C 15513.

26. Head of the God Min-Amun

Koptos[64]
Dynasty 18, reign of Tutankhamen,
1333–1323 BC
Crystalline limestone
H. 14.9 cm; w. 5.8 cm; d. 7.0 cm
UC 34503

THE NINE-YEAR REIGN of Akhenaten's successor Tutankhaten saw the royal court leave Amarna and return to the old royal residences of Thebes and Memphis. This was matched by a return to religious orthodoxy, and the cults of the old deities were restored. Tutankhaten's name—"the living image of Aten"—was changed to Tutankhamen, honoring the king of the gods Amun instead. In a number of inscriptions from his reign, Tutankhamen describes how the temples had fallen into disrepair; the gods had forsaken the land and no longer heeded peoples' prayers. To rectify the situation, he ordered the renovation of the temples and increased their endowments and personnel. The cult images of the gods were made anew, that of Amun being made of "electrum, lapis-lazuli, turquoise, and every august and precious stone."[65]

In material and size, this small limestone head is far removed from the costly statues described above, but it comes from the same milieu. It represents the god Min-Amun wearing his typical slightly domed cap surmounted by two feathers. The god's heavily lidded eyes, full drooping lips, and small chin copy the features of Tutankhamen, and reflect the style of the preceding Amarna period. Although he only reigned for nine years, Tutankhamen's face—if not always his name—can be recognized on a large number of divine statues made to replace those destroyed in the reign of Akhenaten. This task must have been carried out in haste and have stretched the country's resources. Some of the images are of very high quality, but others are less carefully made: in some cases statues damaged during the Amarna period simply had new heads or torsos attached.[66]   TH

64 A notation on the underside reads "Koptos 94," indicating that the piece was found during Petrie's 1894 season at that site. See also B. Adams and R. Jaeschke, "A Silver Plume from a Statue of Min," *Discussions in Egyptology* 4 (1986): 12.

65 The "Restoration Stela" from Karnak, now in Cairo CG 34183; for an English translation, see B. Davies, *Egyptian Historical Records of the Later Eighteenth Dynasty* VI (Warminster, 1995) 31–2.

66 Examples of restored statues include Cairo CG 42065, a dyad of Thutmose III and Amun from Karnak, the head of Amun restored; Cairo CG 42052, seated group of Thutmose I, his wife Ahmose, and Amun from Karnak, upper part restored; Adel A. Mahmoud, in Rita E. Freed, Yvonne Markowitz, and Sue D'Auria, eds., *Pharaohs of the Sun: Akhenaten, Nefertiti, Tutankhamen* (Boston, 1999) 275, cat. no. 224.

27. Head and torso of a queen or goddess

Late Dynasty 18-early Dynasty 19,
ca. 1320–1279 BC
Biotite diorite
H. 18.0 cm; w. 10.7 cm; d. 10.4 cm
UC 16675

DESPITE THE LOSS of her arms and lower body, the woman represented in this fragment preserves her unruffled countenance. A uraeus serpent rises from under her striated wig, and above this is a cylindrical modius—a platform that would have supported another element, now broken off. She wears a broad necklace made of nine strands of beads, and traces of a bracelet are visible on what remains of her right arm. She may not be bare-breasted, as appears to be the case; women in Egypt are rarely shown topless, and the straps of a close-fitting dress may have been painted over, or to one side of, her breasts.

Who does the statue represent? Wigs and jewelry are worn by women from all ranks, but the uraeus protects only queens and goddesses. No traces of an inscription are visible on the back pillar, so no further identification can be made. This division may not have seemed especially important to an Egyptian; the boundaries between divinity and royalty were fluid. Just as the king was the living embodiment of the god Horus, so his queen could be identified with Hathor or Isis, respectively Horus' consort and mother.

The three-dimensional rendering of the eyelids reflects the influence of sculpture from the Amarna period. The face is fuller than representations usually assigned to the reign of Tutankhamen (see cat. no. 26) and is likely to be a little later.[67]   TH

67 M. Müller provides a catalog of female royal or divine sculpture from the post-Amarna period. "Über die Büste 23725 in Berlin," *Jahrbuch der Berliner Museen* 31 (1989): 22, figs. 8–9.

28. Block statue of Yey with a *naos*

Dynasty 19, reign of Ramesses II,
1279–1213 BC
Sandstone
H. 45.2 cm; w. 23.0 cm (at shoulders); d. 27.4 cm
UC 8739[68]

THE "BLOCK STATUE" is one of the most recognizable Egyptian statue types. It represents the owner seated on the ground and swathed in a cloak, his legs drawn up to his chest and his arms folded on top of his knees—a pose of submissive waiting especially suited for images destined to be placed in a temple. Yey's titles identify him as a priest of Ptah, the creator god of Memphis. His devotion to this particular god is put beyond doubt by the *naos* (shrine) in front of him, which contains a figure of Ptah, shown in his characteristic form wrapped like a mummy and wearing a close-fitting cap.

The geometric simplicity of the block statue can be visually satisfying, and the physical awkwardness of Yey's pose, with the deep *naos* somehow vanishing into his knees, is hardly noticeable. Scholars have traced the development of the block statue,[69] and variations in poses and accessories can be used as dating criteria; Yey's dainty cushion and sandals are encountered from the Eighteenth Dynasty onwards. His broad flat face with its pierced ears and slab-like lips takes as its model the sculptures of Ramesses II, whose cartouches are inscribed on his upper arms. TH

68 Most of the objects in the Petrie Museum come from documented excavations or were acquired by Petrie in Egypt, and few have had such a long history out of Egypt as this statue. It is first known in the collection of Jean-Francois Mimaut, a French diplomat who served in Egypt in the 1830s, and later in the collection of Sir Henry Wellcome (R4642–1937).

69 The most detailed study is by R. Schulz, *Die Entwicklung und Bedeutung des Kuboiden Statuentypus* (2 Vols., Hildesheim Ägyptologische Beiträge 33–4, 1992).

29. Tomb relief

Dynasty 30, 381–343 BC
Limestone
H. 14.5 cm; w. 21.8 cm; d. 5.1 cm
UC 14294

THE SCENE DEPICTED on this masterfully carved relief represents the end of one of the most ancient traditions in Egyptian art. A man and wife, now just indicated by her hand on her spouse's shoulder, sit together before a table of offerings under an awning. The man holds a long staff and sniffs a lotus in a traditional pose. Much as an eighteenth century European gentleman would hold a perfumed handkerchief to his nose, Egyptians were shown smelling a fragrant lotus.

Although this pose dates back to the Old Kingdom, here, the fine, rounded, low relief and the orientalizing abstractness of the plant bespeaks the beginning of Greek influence on Egyptian sculpture that appears just before the conquest of Alexander the Great (332 BC).

This style, known as neo-Memphite, is characterized by the "exaggerated plumpness" seen in the bouquet.[70] Few examples of this late and particularly fine relief carving survive, the most notable example being the tomb of Petosiris at Tuna el-Gebel.[71] This relief is related in style and quality to that last great monument of the Dynastic Age.　　　PL

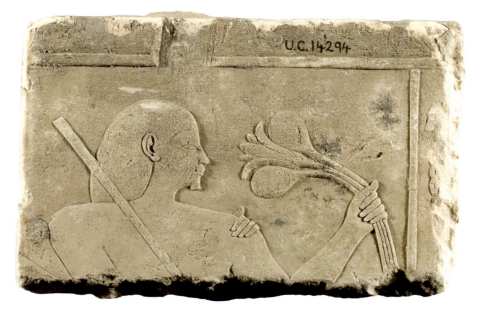

70 W. S. Smith, "Three Late Egyptian Reliefs," *BMFA* vol. 48/ no. 268 (June, 1949): 21–9.

71 Petosiris was High Priest of Thoth at Hermopolis during the late fourth century BC. His tomb was constructed jointly with his son, Tachos, who succeeded him as High Priest. See G. Lefebvre, *Le tombeau de Petosiris* (Paris, 1924).

30. Figurine of a queen

Memphis
Early Ptolemaic Period,
Third century BC
Terracotta
H. 4.6 cm; w. 3.0 cm; d. 3.2 cm
UC 48248

A GREAT NUMBER of terracotta figurines were unearthed at Memphis, representing both Egyptian and Graeco-Roman styles and subjects. This solid, mold-made figure depicting a royal woman with corkscrew curls and bangs, modeled by hand, would undoubtedly have been covered with plaster and then painted. Her face is long and oval-shaped, with heavily drooping eyelids and a small, slightly pursed mouth. The woman's features correspond to those found on images of Berenike II, queen of Ptolemy III Euergetes I (reigned 246–221 BC). Although the corkscrew hairstyle characterizes images of the queen as Isis during the Roman Period, Sally-Ann Ashton points out that there is nothing to support such an association for Ptolemaic queens. Rather, her coiffure suggests that this is likely to be a posthumous representation, depicting the queen after her deification in the royal cult.[72]   BTT

72 Sally-Ann Ashton, *The Last Queens of Egypt* (London, 2003) 88.

31. Torso of a queen

Early Ptolemaic Period,
Third century BC
Limestone
H. 11.6 cm; w. 6.5 cm; d. 4.4 cm
UC 16674

THIS TORSO depicts a Ptolemaic queen in the Egyptian style typical of the early years of that dynasty. She wears an echeloned tripartite wig with traces of a single uraeus and a modius crown, a low platform encircled with uraeus cobras, with a tenon for the attachment of an additional attribute. The brows are indicated in relief above almond-shaped eyes with elongated cosmetic lines. Her face is fleshy and the flat nose flares out at the nostrils. The smiling mouth protrudes slightly, giving the lips an almost pursed appearance. Her form-fitting dress covers a full, rounded figure, and she wears a single strand of beads at her throat. An uninscribed back pillar extends to the lower edge of her wig. BTT

32. Face of a Ptolemaic king

Probably from Memphis
Ptolemaic Period, 305–30 BC
Plaster
H. 19.2 cm; W. 14.4 cm; D. 4.4 cm
UC 28711

PLASTER SCULPTURES such as this one are among an unusual group of objects often described as votives or sculptors' models. Some of these objects were discovered in sculptors' workshops; this does not, however, conclusively demonstrate that the figures were models or trial pieces.[73] These objects are typically made of limestone or plaster, and may take the form of sculptures in the round or plaques, modeled on front and flat in back. It is possible that the plaster figures were cast from existing monuments, possibly metal repoussé reliefs.

This face is almost certainly an Egyptian-style representation of a king, based on the lower edge of a headdress visible along the side of the forehead. The fleshy features, the slightly smiling lips, and the shape of the eye all suggest that the figure depicts one of the later Ptolemaic rulers, possibly Ptolemy IX or X. The shape of the mouth and nose, in particular, resemble those of a gypsum face in Munich and a basalt head in Paris.[74] Although the Munich and Paris pieces are widely accepted to depict the same king, which king remains a point of debate.[75]   BTT

73 Scholarly debate regarding the function of such objects has flourished for decades, with convincing arguments in favor of both hypotheses. The use of non-durable materials, the occasional presence of gridlines, and the unfinished state of many of the pieces supports the sculptors' model theory. The presence of holes in the back of some plaques suggests that they were displayed hanging, perhaps as votives in the Ptolemaic dynastic cult.

74 Munich, Ägyptische Sammlung 5339; Paris, Louvre E8061.

75 Suggested attributions include: Nectanebo I, Karol Mysliwiec, *Royal Portraiture of the Dynasties XXI–XXX* (Mainz, 1988) 71, 79, 91. Ptolemy IX (second reign), Paul Stanwick, *Portraits of the Ptolemies: Greek Kings as Egyptian Pharaohs* (Austin, 2002) 120. Ptolemy X, Jack Josephson, *Egyptian Royal Sculpture of the Late Period 400–246 B.C.* (Mainz, 1997) 45, pls. 4c, 5b; Sally-Ann Ashton, *Ptolemaic Royal Sculpture from Egypt* (Oxford, 2001) 86, nos. 9–10.

33. Caricature figurine of Ptolemy VIII Euergetes II

Memphis
Mid-Ptolemaic Period, 170–116 BC
Terracotta
H. 9.4 cm; w. 7.0 cm; d. 4.3 cm
UC 47632

THIS TERRACOTTA FIGURINE, depicting an obese man in a chariot, most likely represents Ptolemy VIII Euergetes II. The man sits with legs splayed in a large seat, wearing a diaphanous garment that emphasizes his bloated form. Ptolemy VIII was nicknamed Physkon, meaning "fatty" or "potbelly," by his subjects. Athenaeus of Naukratis claimed that the king had "a belly of such a size that it would have been hard to measure it with one's arms" (*Deipnosophistai* XII.549e).

BTT

34. Head of a Ptolemaic king

Late Ptolemaic Period,
First century BC
Steatite
H. 4.4 cm; w. 2.8 cm; d. 3.5 cm
UC 49930

THIS HEAD depicts a young man with short hair combed forward framing his face. A twisted diadem, often associated with representations of athletes, encircles the head. Three small-scale royal figures sculpted of hard stone in Brooklyn and Bologna, and the example here, wear a comparable diadem, and have been attributed on stylistic grounds to Ptolemy XV Caesarion.[76] The similarities between the features of the figures in Brooklyn and Bologna and those of the Petrie head, allow a tentative identification of the latter as Caesarion, son of Cleopatra VII and Julius Caesar.

The dynastic cult flourished during the Ptolemaic Period, centered around both the dynasty in its entirety and individual rulers. These cults were celebrated through a variety of festivals and ceremonies. Furthermore, images of the royal family were installed alongside those of the gods by decree.[77] Small-scale images of the ruler such as this were likely fashioned as votives for the royal cult. BTT

76 Two examples are in the Brooklyn Museum of Art (70.91.3; 54.117) and the third in Bologna (Museo Civico Archeologico KS 1803). The Caesarion portrait-type was established by means of clay sealings, which, though uninscribed, were found in association with coins of Cleopatra VII. Sally-Ann Ashton, *Ptolemaic Royal Sculpture from Egypt* (Oxford, 2001) 98–9, cat. no. 32.
77 A series of decrees was issued by clerical synods from the beginning of the dynasty, often inscribed in hieroglyphs, demotic, and Greek, and copied at temples throughout Egypt. These decrees, of which the Rosetta Stone is best known, mandated the appearance, placement, purpose, and production of the royal image. See Günther Hölbl, *A History of the Ptolemaic Empire* (London, 2001) 105–11; Paul Stanwick, *Portraits of the Ptolemies: Greek Kings as Egyptian Pharaohs* (Austin, 2002) 6–8, 45.

35. Head of a man

Roman Period, 30 BC–AD 395
Limestone, plaster
H. 22.1 cm; w. 12.2 cm; d. 14.7 cm
UC 16493

THIS LIMESTONE HEAD, hollowed out in back, expressively depicts the face of a man, who, according to Petrie, "evidently imitated Caesar, and dissatisfied with scanty hair, had it amended with plaster."[78] Whomever the image was intended to replicate, the face remains strikingly individualistic, with its arresting gaze, prominent nose, broad mouth, and strong jawline.

Possibly used as a sculptor's model, the head clearly exhibits the more realistic style of the later years of Egyptian history. In contrast to their Dynastic predecessors, artists of the Roman Period favored more idiosyncratic, less idealized representations that are much closer to the modern concept of portraiture.   BTT

78 W. M. F. Petrie, *Handbook of Egyptian Antiquities exhibited at University College* (London, 1915) 23.

U.C.16493.

ARCHÆOLOGY

PYRAMIDS   SERIATION   TOMB GROUPS

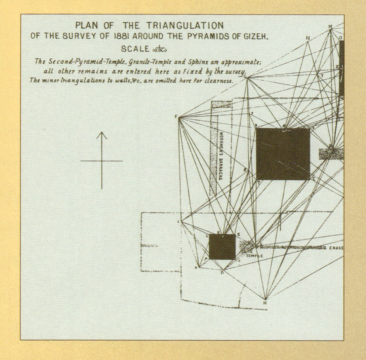

36. Model mason's tools

Sedment, tomb 1845
Dynasties 9–10, ca. 2160–2125 BC
Wood

A. Square
L. 27.0 cm; w. 20.0 cm; d. 1.0 cm
UC 16166

B. Plumb-bob
L. 15.0 cm; w. 1.8 cm; d. 1.0 cm
UC 16165

GIVEN HIS INTEREST in surveying, it must have delighted Petrie to find these model tools, remarkably similar to modern versions, in a tomb at Sedment. Just as today, incredible precision could be obtained with the naked eye and instruments as simple as these. Petrie noted

> the setting out of the orientation of the sides [of the pyramid to the points of the compass]. If a pile of masonry... was built up with a vertical side from North to South, a plumb line could be hung from its top, and observations could be made, to find the places on the ground where the pole star was seen to transit...on this scale [a deviation of just] 15 seconds of angle would...[read as] 1/10 inch, and [be] therefore quite perceptible.[79]

The mason's square, still used by masons and carpenters today, was handy for determining both a right and a 45° angle. The tool was even to become an amulet in the Late Period, undoubtedly to keep the departed on the "straight and narrow."[80]   PL

79 W. M. F. Petrie, *The Pyramids and Temples of Gizeh* (London, 1883) 84.
80 Carol Andrews, *Ancient Egyptian Jewelry* (London, 1990) 44.

37. Pyramid

Hawara
Middle Kingdom, 2055–1650 BC
Limestone
H. 14.1 cm; w. 21.6 cm; d. 23.2 cm
UC 14793

PETRIE DISCOVERED this small pyramid at the site of the large mud-brick pyramid of Amenemhet III at Hawara, and suggested that it was a model of that monument. Although the brick pyramids of the Middle Kingdom were capped with stone pyramidions, it is unlikely that this object is that of Amenemhet III's pyramid. Those that have been identified are far larger and elaborately carved.[81]

The sides of this miniature pyramid slope at an angle of roughly 50°, approximating the ideal height of a pyramid. It is not inconceivable that Petrie's identification could be correct.   PL

81 Mark Lehner, *The Complete Pyramids* (London, 1997) 180.

38. Drill core

Giza
Old Kingdom, 2686–2125 BC
Red granite
L. 11.0 cm; diam. 5.0 cm
UC 16036

ONE OF THE FIRST OBJECTS discovered by Petrie, this drill core held a particular fascination for him.[82] Having originally journeyed to Egypt to study the construction of the Giza pyramids, Petrie analyzed every scrap of evidence to deduce the building methods of the ancients. This core was the by-product of a copper drill, a tool that was only able to cut through granite with the use of quartz sand abrasives.

The striations on the sides of the core illustrate the cutting action of the grains of sand. Petrie examined these marks with the concentration of a forensic scientist, noting that:

firstly, the grooves which run around it form a regular spiral, with no more interruption or waviness than is necessarily produced by the component crystals; this spiral is truly symmetrical with the axis of the core. In one part a groove can be traced, scarcely without interruption, for a length of four turns. Secondly, the grooves are as deep in the quartz as in the adjacent feldspar, and even rather deeper. If these were in any way produced by loose powder, they would be shallower in a harder substance—quartz, whereas a fixed jewel point would be compelled to plough to the same depth in all the components....[83]

Tubular drills were used sporadically during the Old Kingdom, mostly for hollowing out stone vases, boring plug-holes for sarcophagi, and even carving sculptures.   PL

82 W. M. F. Petrie, *Ten Years' Digging in Egypt 1881–1891* (London, 1892) 26–7.
83 W. M. F. Petrie, *The Pyramids and Temples of Gizeh* (London, 1883) 175.

39. **Vessels**

A. Wavy-handled jar
Naqada
Naqada II (Gerzean) Period,
3700–3250 BC
Ceramic
H. 27.0 cm; rim diam. 12.0 cm
UC 4341

B. Wavy-handled jar
Naqada II (Gerzean) Period,
3700–3250 BC
Marl clay ceramic
H. 23.5 cm; rim diam. 10.2 cm
UC 6176

C. Jar with scalloped border
Naqada III (Late Gerzean/Dynasty 0)
Period, 3250–3100 BC
Marl clay ceramic
H. 27.9 cm; rim diam. 10.5 cm
UC 13404

D. Cylinder jar inscribed for King Ka
Tarkhan
Dynasty 1, 3000–2890 BC
Marl clay ceramic
H. 25.0 cm; rim diam. 11.5 cm
UC 16072

ONE OF PETRIE'S greatest contributions to the study of archaeology was the development of seriation, or as he termed it, "sequence dating." When Petrie initially discovered graves dating to the Predynastic Period, he was at a loss to properly place them in time. He thought that the occupants of the graves represented a "new race" that had migrated to Egypt at the end of the Old Kingdom.[84] Petrie was soon corrected by Jacques de Morgan, Director of the Antiquities Service, who accurately identified the deceased as prehistoric ancestors of the Egyptians.[85] However, without any historical records it was impossible to place the mass of new material in chronological order.

Petrie noted that some of the vessels resembled early ledge-handled jars from Syria-Palestine and theorized that they were Egyptian imitations of the form. He surmised that subtle changes in style in the Egyptian copies might signal stylistic development over time. He then placed paper strips with drawings of each pot type on them in a logical progression, from the wide-bodied vases that were clos-est in form to the actual imports, and graduating to more slender examples. He noticed that the protruding ledge handles became less prominent over time, evolving into a vestigial wavy band below the neck. Eventually, the wavy band disappears altogether and the pot becomes a slender cylinder. Some of the cylinder vases bore the names of kings of the First Dynasty, making a historical anchor for one end of the sequence. PL

84 W. M. F. Petrie and James E. Quibell, *Naqada and Ballas* (London, 1896) 14–8.
85 W. M. F. Petrie, *Prehistoric Egypt* (London, 1920) 1–6.

40. Hawara, Tomb 58

Middle Kingdom, 2055–1650 BC

A. Hemispherical bowl
Nile clay ceramic
H. 6.8 cm; diam. 12.3 cm
UC 16138a

B. Doll
Wood
H. 18.7 cm; w. 6.7 cm; d. 4.3 cm
UC 16148

C. Bell-mouth jar
Nile clay ceramic
H. 20.0 cm; diam. 14.0 cm
UC 16137

D. Hemispherical bowl
Nile clay ceramic
H. 5.7 cm; diam. 12.3 cm
UC 16138b

E. Scarab
Glazed steatite
L. 1.3 cm; w. 0.9 cm; d. 0.4 cm
UC 16142

F. Cylinder bead
Glazed steatite
L. 2.9 cm; w. 0.9 cm; d. 1.0 cm
UC 16143

G. Box
Wood
H. 7.2 cm; w. 8.5 cm; d. 12.5 cm
UC 16140

THESE OBJECTS all come from the tomb of a girl named Satrenenutet, excavated by Petrie in a cemetery north of the pyramid of Amenemhet III at Hawara.[86] The tomb contained a yellow and blue coffin of Middle Kingdom type; although, Petrie recorded that it was too decayed to save, it preserved the name of the owner who had been buried inside, wrapped in approximately twenty yards of linen. At her feet, was the small jewelry box containing a bracelet made of small seeds, a blue glazed scarab, a faience figure of a dove, a wood model vase, and the blue glazed lobed cylinder bead. Beneath the box was a shell necklace. Beside her left foot was the wooden doll with some mud and faience beads, and above it, a finely crafted model bed.[87]

The doll with no feet is paralleled by a number of figures known from this period, both in wood and faience.[88] The "doll" is less likely a toy than a symbol of rebirth like the so-called concubine figurines of the New Kingdom, to which this doll and the bed with which it is associated, may be ancestral. The loose mud and faience beads also may have been linked with the figurine, since some later versions of similar figures in clay were adorned with beads.

What we might consider jewelry boxes are occasionally found in Egyptian tombs, and often contain quite disparate items, as in this case. Some of the non-jewelry items may have been keepsakes or offerings placed with the adornments.

The pottery from the tomb is typical of the Middle Kingdom in its elegantly simple shapes. Both the bell-mouth beaker[89] and the hemispherical cups[90] are important forms for understanding the chronology of the Middle Kingdom.   PL

86 W. M. F. Petrie, *The Labyrinth, Gerzeh and Mazghuneh* (London, 1912) 35–6.
87 The model bed is a rare example of a bed from this period. The style of the inward curving legs with rounded feet is reminiscent of furniture found in contemporary tombs at Jericho. Kathleen Kenyon, *Digging up Jericho: the Results of the Jericho Excavations* (New York, 1957) 240–44, fig. 15.
88 Examples in Janine Bourriau, *Pharaohs and Mortals* (Cambridge, 1988) nos. 118–9 (faience), 120 (clay), 121 (wood).
89 B. J. Kemp and R. Merrillees, *Minoan Pottery in Second Millennium Egypt* (Mainz, 1981) 23–57.
90 Dorothea Arnold in Dieter Arnold, *The Pyramid of Senwosret I* (New York, 1988) 140–1.

41. Kafr Ammar, Tomb 99
Roman Period, Second century AD

A–C. Alabastra
Calcite ("Egyptian alabaster")
H. 10.8 cm; rim diam. 3.7
H. 12.9 cm; rim diam. 5.6
H. 14.1 cm; rim diam. 2.0
UC 37097-8, 37174

D. Necklace
Gold
L. 27.7 cm; w. 0.8 cm
UC 37095

E. Ring with incised figure
Gold
H. 1.9 cm; w. 2.3 cm
UC 8707

F. Bead
Silver, marble?
L. 1.8 cm; w. 1.8 cm
UC 37096

PETRIE excavated the cemeteries of Kafr Ammar, ranging in date from the Third Dynasty to the Roman Period, from 1911–13.

These objects accompanied the undisturbed burial of a woman, who lay on her back with her hands placed below her hips and her head oriented to the west.[91] The necklace and bead were both around her neck, and the ring lay close to her left hand. The necklace consists of hollow beads with impressed decoration, fashioned in separate halves that were soldered together. The ring, which shows signs of wear, depicts a woman presenting an offering at an altar.[92] Alabastra typically contained perfumes or fragrant oils, and were frequently buried with an individual, that they might continue to enjoy those products in the afterlife. BTT

91 W. M. F. Petrie, *Heliopolis, Kafr Ammar, and Shurafa* (London, 1915) 38. The burial also included an ivory disk with incised decoration and possibly two faience rings bearing the image of a mummiform falcon deity.
92 W. M. F. Petrie, *Objects of Daily Use* (London, 1927) 3, 9.

A   B   C

D   E   F

47

SITES

HIERAKONPOLIS ABYDOS LAHUN AMARNA
GUROB SAQQARA NAUKRATIS HAWARA MEROE

HIERAKONPOLIS

93 James E. Quibell, *Hierakonpolis* I (London, 1900).

ONCOMITANT WITH PETRIE'S WORK at the tombs of the First Dynasties at Abydos, excavations at the site of Hierakonpolis, were being undertaken by J. E. Quibell and F. W. Green on behalf of University College and the Egyptian Research Account. So astounding were their discoveries, that a volume of plates was rushed into print with a note by Petrie before the actual publication.[93]

Like Abydos, Hierakonpolis was distinguished by a large, mud-brick monument, built by the Second Dynasty pharaoh Khasekhemwy, that seemed to be modeled after an enclosed royal estate. Unlike Abydos, however, Hierakonpolis was not a major site after the Archaic Period and most of its cemeteries and monuments belong to that era or earlier. The site is situated on the desert edge, on the west bank of the Nile, with the cemeteries arranged along a great wadi, running out into the desert and along the border of the cultivation. A sacred area close to the cultivation was the site of a temple and royal palace of this early period. Later temples were built over the earliest one, and, as in many Egyptian temples and later in Catholic churches, sacred statues and images, once broken or out of style, were ritually buried in sacred ground.

At Hierakonpolis, a large pit filled with cult images, known as the "Main Deposit," was discovered, that appears to have been assembled during the New Kingdom. Many of the most significant objects we have from the beginning of Dynastic history come from here, including the Narmer Palette, now a highlight of the Egyptian Museum, Cairo. Like a number of votive objects found here, this was an oversize version of a familiar object, in this case, a cosmetic palette, decorated with commemorative relief. The Narmer Palette is the earliest monument to show the same king wearing the Red and White Crowns, and therefore taken as emblematic of unification by the reign of Narmer.

94 James E. Quibell and Frederick W. Green, *Hierakonpolis* II (London, 1902) 40, pl. XXVIb

Similar votive objects uncovered at Hierakonpolis included giant flint knives, far too heavy to use, and enormous stone vessels. Three gigantic versions of pear-shaped mace-heads were also found in the deposit, one decorated with a scene of King Scorpion of Dynasty O, enacting a foundation ceremony, perhaps for a new canal. Another depicts what appears to be a royal wedding of the pharaoh Narmer, perhaps to secure his control over Upper and Lower Egypt, as celebrated on the palette, and the third mace has a similar scene of an enthroned pharaoh and his court.[94] Also from the Main Deposit came many smaller votive images in ivory and faience of animal figures, including lions, baboons, and scorpions, human figures, and cult objects.

95 Ibid., 20–1, pl. LXVII. Tomb 100 possibly belonged to an early ruler.

In the desert cemeteries, the expedition discovered a tomb, painted with a depiction of battles, ships, and motifs derived from Mesopotamian art, which remains the most important surviving monument of the Predynastic Period.[95]

96 Vivian Davies and Renée Friedman, *Egypt Uncovered* (London, 1998) 23–8.

More recent and ongoing investigations of the site have revealed the wealth of the Predynastic cemeteries, and the association of the town with a palace with a Mesopotamian-style, niched, brick entrance gate. Additional cemeteries of Nubian populations and decorated, rock-cut tombs of the Dynastic Period are currently being conserved and explored under the direction of Renée Friedman.[96]

PL

42. Scorpion figure

Hierakonpolis
Archaic Period, 3000–2686 BC
Faience
H. 6.0 cm; w. 4.5 cm; l. 7.5 cm
UC 11000

THIS SMALL VOTIVE was one of many such figures that came from the early Archaic Period temple site at Hierakonpolis. A variety of animal figures, as well as miniature offering vessels, hieroglyphic symbols and pieces of composite sculptures were uncovered there. The scorpion may have had significance as an invocation of "King Scorpion," who reigned before the First Dynasty and is memorialized on the large Scorpion Macehead from the Main Deposit.[97] The figurines were hand-made in molds out of a glazed, crushed quartz ceramic that was mislabeled "faience" by early explorers, who confused it with the Italian pottery of the same name. While Hierakonpolis is the source of many of these early faience pieces, they have also been found at other Archaic Period sites such as Elephantine. As some of the earliest examples of three-dimensional faience objects, the technique was still rather primitive, as evidenced by the coarse grey core, pitted surface, and the uneven, thin, pale glaze layer.[98]

PL

97 James E. Quibell, *Hierakonpolis* I (London, 1900) pls. 25; 26 a, b, c.
98 Florence Friedman, "Scorpion," in Florence Friedman, ed., *Gifts of the Nile: Ancient Egyptian Faience* (RISD, 1998) 68, 178, cat. nos. 8–9.

43. Ceremonial mace-head fragments
Hierakonpolis, from the Early
Dynastic Period temple platform
Dynasty 1, ca. 3000 BC
Limestone
H. 20.0 cm; width 21.0 cm (14898);
H. 2.2 cm; diameter 2.4 cm
(14898A)
UC 14898 (fragment with king),
14898A (fragment with dancers)

AROUND THE LATER temple sanctuary at Hierakonpolis, F. W. Green recorded a rounded stone revetment, evidently for a great flat-topped platform, similar to an Early Dynastic monument at Medamud. Presumably, the platform once supported the early religious focus of the city, later overlaid by newer, more rectilinear temple structures.[99] Other early kingship

offerings were found elsewhere across the site, some on the other side of the platform area. According to the excavation report published in 1902, these two ceremonial mace-head fragments were "not from the main deposit, but found among a lot of limestone chips at a high level near the west end of the five chambers at the N. of the temple."[100] Evidently, in

the complex settlement history of the city, the Early Dynastic offerings had been moved at different times from their probable original destination in the sanctuary of the late Predynastic or First Dynasty temple, some buried in large groups as sacred material, others dislodged, broken into fragments, and eventually discarded in the strata closer to the modern surface. Together, they provide the most substantial assembly of evidence for belief in kingship and the gods at the formative moment in ancient Egyptian history. Quibell and Green retrieved several mace-heads distinguished from the great number of weapons of this type by their considerably larger size and by the relief carving of the surfaces, on themes of kingship.

It is not certain whether or not the two fragments come from a single mace-head. The larger fragment preserves part of a scene with, at left, an image of the king enthroned under an arching pavilion roof with double frontal pillar. He wears the short cloak characteristic of the *sed*, or periodic kingship festival, and the Red Crown later associated with Lower Egypt, though first attested in the Naqada Period at Naqada itself. The delaminated surface in front of the king has been interpreted as remnants of a name of king or deity, but, from closer inspection, it seems likely that all original surface at this point has been eroded. Facing and to the right of the king and pavilion, there is depicted a falcon, emblem of the deity of kingship, Horus, with tail stretched out horizontally at the back. The falcon's legs separated to, it appears, rounded claws, the left perhaps holding the end of a rope which reappears

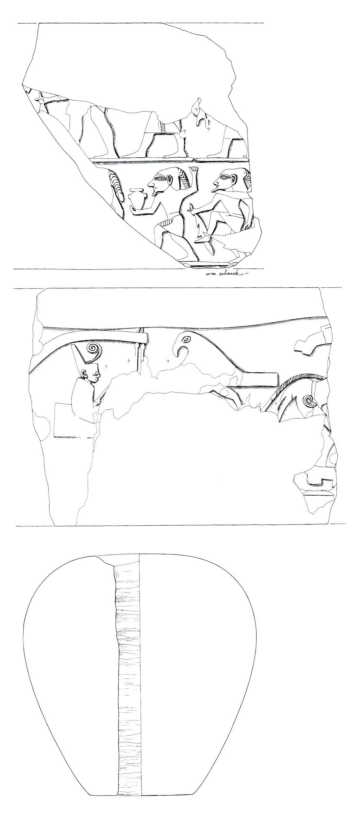

behind the falcon, curving around over the headgear and ear that remain from a human figure on a larger scale. Since scale is a compositional determinant in Egyptian formal art, it seems unthinkable that this smaller figure of a captive or enemy be larger than the king: presumably there was a larger image of the king to the right. Above and below the roped man can be seen the ends of an enclosing wall with bastions, depicted as if from the air, as on late Predynastic and Early Dynastic images of cities.[101] This may then be the remnant of a scene in which a victorious king was depicted at larger scale to the right of a destroyed city with its inhabitants or ruler shown captive, the cord held by the falcon deity as mediator between this scene and the image of the king in the pavilion of the *sed*-festival.

The smaller mace-head fragment preserves parts of two registers showing people moving towards the left. If part of the same object as the larger, these would be attendants behind the lost figure of the victorious king. The front figure in the upper register holds a tail or skin-like object, followed by two individuals wearing longer garments; below are three figures with hair or headgear bunched at the back into a pigtail. The two rear figures on the lower register both have bearded face and short kilt; the central man proffers a lugged vessel, his rear arm raised with clenched fist, his knees bent, while the man behind him holds a tail or skin-like object in his front hand, his rear hand down towards the ground at the back, and his front foot raised off the ground, as if the group is intended to be shown dancing, with each figure in a different posture. Human forms on this scale are rare in late Predynastic and Early Dynastic art, making it difficult to find parallels and contexts to explain this scene. At the present state of our knowledge, it can be only one guess among many that the two fragments together preserve a single depiction of a kingship festival combining the destruction of an enemy city and the dance of offering-bearers.   SQ

99 Cf. Barry Kemp, *Ancient Egypt: Anatomy of a Civilization* (London and New York, 1989) 65–107; Barbara Adams, "Early Temples at Hierakonpolis and Beyond," in *Centenary of Mediterranean Archaeology at the Jagiellonian University 1897–1997* (Krakow, 1999) 15–28.

100 James E. Quibell and Frederick W. Green, *Hierakonpolis* II (London, 1902) 39–40.

101 Compare the composition on the lower part of the Narmer Palette, beneath the large depiction of the king, showing a figure within a partial enclosure, overpowered by a bull.

ABYDOS

102 W. M. F. Petrie,
The Tombs of the Courtiers
(London, 1925) 1–9.

ONE OF PETRIE'S GREATEST ACHIEVEMENTS as an excavator was recovering the remains of the royal tombs of the First and Second Dynasties at Abydos, located in southern Middle Egypt on the west bank of the Nile. The site stretches along the desert edge and back towards the high limestone cliffs; the remains of the royal tombs lie far out in the desert. Associated with the royal tombs, but closer to the Nile, are vast enclosures built in conjunction with the burial of each king, modeled on the royal palace city. They were surrounded by burials of servants, some later excavated by Petrie.[102]

Émile Amélineau, a French priest and Coptic scholar, had been given permission to work at the site in 1894, but his efforts were less than satisfactory. Petrie noted:

103 W. M. F. Petrie,
Seventy Years in Archaeology
(New York, 1932) 185.

> no plans were kept (a few incorrect ones were made [by Amélineau] later), there was no record of where things were found, no useful publication. He boasted that he had reduced to chips the pieces of stone vases he did not wish to remove, and burnt up the remains of the woodwork of the 1st Dynasty in his kitchen.[103]

Gaston Maspero, head of the Antiquities Service, immediately turned the site over to Petrie, who meticulously re-cleared and drew plans of all the tombs and the subsidiary burials surrounding them. He carefully recovered tiny slips of ivory and vessel fragments with inscriptions and royal names on them, in order to establish the framework for the chronology of the kings of the earliest dynasties.[104] In addition to what he unearthed, Petrie was able to buy back some pieces taken from the site by local villagers.

104 W. M. F. Petrie, *The Royal Tombs of the First Dynasty* I (London, 1900)

Although between robbers in antiquity and Amélineau, the tombs were seriously looted, Petrie nevertheless made some spectacular discoveries. In the tomb of King Djer were the remains of a mummified arm, probably of the King himself, still wearing a group of exquisite bracelets. Hilda Petrie restrung them after painstakingly recording the position of each bead, but after this great find was presented to the Cairo Museum, the Petries were appalled to learn that the bracelets had been kept without the arm.

It was particularly amazing that the arm had survived, as in later years that tomb, associated with the burial place of Osiris, Lord of the Dead and mythical first king of Egypt, had become a favorite pilgrimage spot. The site was known as Umm el Ga'ab— "the mother of pots"—on account of the thousands of offering cups littering the ground, brought by pilgrims to the "Tomb of Osiris." The connection with Egypt's earliest monarchs gave the location singular importance, prompting everyone who was anyone to build a tomb or memorial there.

105 EA 37996, gift of the EEF. See Edna R. Russmann, *Eternal Egypt: Masterworks of Ancient Art from the British Museum* (London, 2001) 66–7, cat. no. 1.
106 W. M. F. Petrie, *Seventy Years in Archaeology* (New York, 1932) 195.

Also linked with the cult of Osiris was a large temple, even closer to the cultivation and surrounded by a vast enclosure wall. Petrie excavated this area, uncovering the earliest levels of the sacred structure, which yielded an ivory statue of one of the early kings dressed in a long cloak and white crown, now in the British Museum.[105] His greatest find here, however, was a tiny ivory statue with the name of Khufu, the only known image of the builder of the Great Pyramid. When it was first unearthed, its head was missing, but Petrie noticed that the break was fresh and had his workmen scour the site, sifting all of the dirt for three weeks until the head was located.[106]

107 E. Naville et al., *Cemeteries of Abydos* I (London, 1914); T. Eric Peet, *Cemeteries of Abydos* II (London, 1914); T. Eric Peet and W. L. Loat, *Cemeteries of Abydos* III (London, 1913).
108 A. Calverley, *The Cenotaph of Seti* I vols I–II (London, 1933).
109 David O'Connor, *The Sacred Landscape of Abydos: Royal Cults and the Mysteries of Osiris* (London, forthcoming).
110 T. Wilkinson, *Genesis of the Pharaohs: Dramatic New Discoveries Rewrite the Origins of Ancient Egypt* (London, 2003) 76–77.

South of this area lies a string of temples, cemeteries, and monuments of many of the great kings, ranging in date from the Old Kingdom to the Ptolemaic Period, and including a city and cenotaph of Senusret III and the last royal pyramid built in Egypt for Ahmose at the beginning of Dynasty 18. Petrie and the Egypt Exploration Society worked in many of these places, including the vast series of cemeteries,[107] the monuments of Senusret III and Ahmose, the beautiful temple dedicated by Seti for his funeral cult,[108] and a mysterious crypt temple, known as the Osireion.

Recent years have seen a return to the site by the Egyptian Antiquities Service, to restore and stabilize many of the monuments, and by the University of Pennsylvania under the direction of David O'Connor, to carefully map and systematically explore many of the most important features.[109] In addition, Gunther Dryer of the German Archaeological Institute has been re-clearing the tombs at Umm el-Ga'ab, to further Petrie's critical salvage work there.[110]

PL

44. Dish in the shape of a fig leaf

Abydos

Archaic Period, Dynasties 1–2,
3000–2686 BC

Slate

L. 32.6 cm; w. 26.1 cm; d. 4.7 cm

UC 35653

DESPITE HAVING BEEN plundered in antiquity and poorly excavated by Amélineau, the early royal tombs at Umm el-Ga'ab held great treasures. The graves of Egypt's first pharaohs were stocked with hundreds of stone vessels, a conspicuous reminder of the great wealth and power of these early rulers. Many of these vessels appear to have been especially made for the burial and ritually smashed as part of the funeral ceremony. Among the debris Petrie sifted through, were the remains of vessels elaborately carved in fantastic forms. The example here, reconstructed from numerous fragments, represents a fig leaf, perhaps imitating an actual one used for serving food. The remarkably thin walls and raised veins of the leaf demonstrate that this was the creation of a master artisan. PL

45. Stela

Abydos
Dynasty 1, 3000–2890 BC
Limestone
H. 50.5 cm; w. 17.5 cm; d. 4.5 cm
UC 14275

PERHAPS THE MOST astonishing discovery Petrie made in his work at the royal tombs at Umm el-Ga'ab at Abydos were the burials of people (and in some cases, dogs) that surrounded the graves of the kings. From a careful study of the construction history of the graves, Petrie concluded that many, if not all, of the individuals were members of the royal court who were killed in order to accompany the king into the next life.[111] This practice does not seem to have lasted in Egypt beyond the Second Dynasty (2890–2686 BC), although it does continue throughout much of Nubian history.

This is one of the largest and best-preserved gravestones found by Petrie at Abydos and comes from the area around the tomb of King Djet of the First Dynasty. It is inscribed for a man named Wedjka in the rather crude hieroglyphs characteristic of this early period. The round top became standard for stelae for the remainder of Egyptian history.   PL

111 W. M. F. Petrie, *Tombs of the Courtiers and Oxyrhynkhos* (London, 1925) 1–9.

LAHUN

LAHUN TODAY is a small town about 100 kilometers south of modern Cairo, on the north side of the Bahr Yusef waterway at the point where it veers west from the main Nile valley to drain into a desert depression as Lake Fayum. Just west of the village, a medieval earthenwork dyke cuts across the fields from south to north, where a range of ancient sites testify to the importance of this area at various periods throughout Egyptian history. The greatest of these sites, dominating the landscape, is the limestone skeleton walls with mud-brick core to a pyramid, constructed over the burial chamber for Senusret II, fourth king of the Twelfth Dynasty. Around the pyramid lie the tomb chapels and burial places of his courtiers and family. Along the fields are cemeteries both earlier and later; those to the west date predominantly to the Early Dynastic Period, while nearer the pyramid are numerous burials of the mid- to late Twenty-second Dynasty.

To the east, aligned with the pyramid itself, a new town was constructed in the Twelfth Dynasty, presumably when the pyramid was built. Half of the town lies buried under the fields and probably eroded to below its Twelfth Dynasty level, but half survives above the water table and the fields, on rocky and dry desert ground perfect for preserving the materials of life. For this reason, the town site at Lahun remains an archaeological exception as miraculous in its survival as the New Kingdom residence city of Akhenaten at Amarna. At these two sites Petrie searched for the full spectrum of life in two particular moments of Egyptian history, seeking to uncover the specific ways in which every aspect of living might change or be the same in comparison with the earlier and later periods. Although the picture is complicated by reuse of sites in later periods, notably in the late Roman Period, the general material retrieved from his early quest remains one of the richest treasuries of information on life and society in second millennium BC Egypt.

From his two seasons of a few weeks in spring and autumn 1889, Petrie recovered the street plan of late Middle Kingdom Lahun, revealing a rectangular walled town on a grid system of housing.[112] The north wall measures 384 meters, and the west wall 335 meters, though the town may have continued to the south of the pyramid axis. In the area cleared, there were eleven palatial mansions occupying the prestigious, and, with a prevailing northerly wind, fresher, northern sector. To the south of these, with the exception of one chambered building of unknown function in an empty square, the houses are packed more tightly, and a supplementary strip of housing at a lower level covers a western sector, giving altogether a total of 250 smaller dwellings. The difference between the largest and the small houses reflects strikingly the social gap between elite and general population. However, the small houses vary between the minimal three-chamber home of the poorest families, to more comfortable dwellings for a middle-ranking population group. Detailed study of these houses and the social lives behind them remains to be pursued. From the number of dwellings in the preserved portion, and reconstruction of the original town as a rectangle, it has been estimated that the ancient population might have reached five thousand or more at its height. The most densely packed area and the busiest economic zone

112 W. M. F. Petrie, *Illahun, Kahun and Gurob* (London, 1891) pl. 14.

113 Joseph Wegner, "Excavations at the Town of Enduring-are-the-Places of Khakaure-Maa-Kheru-in-Abydos: A Preliminary Report on the 1994 and 1997 Seasons." *JARCE* 35 (1998): 1–44.

114 M. Collier and S. Quirke, *The UCL Lahun Papyri: Letters* (Oxford, 2002).

115 Ludwig Borchardt, "Der zweite Papyrusfund von Kahun und die zeitliche Fixierung des Mittleren Reiches der agyptischen Geschichte," *ZÄS* (1899): 89–103.

116 W. M. F. Petrie and Guy Brunton, *Lahun* 2 vols. (London, 1920–3).

would probably have been alongside the river or canal, essential for transport as well as drinking water. As at Amarna, the absence of the embankment and dockyards on the archaeological map deprives us of a vital element in the overall picture of life in the town. Nevertheless, Lahun remains the only large Middle Kingdom settlement site for which we have such a complete plan, and recent excavations by Joseph Wegner at a similar planned town in Abydos South now help to complete many of the gaps in our knowledge from the nineteenth century archaeological record.[113]

Among the harvest of finds in 1889, Petrie obtained around eighty groups of papyrus fragments, preserving the full range of Middle Kingdom writing, from legal documents and treatises for good health, to literary compositions and personal letters, all now in the Petrie Museum.[114] These manuscript fragments complement the evidence of other objects found, giving voice in the Egyptian language to the original inhabitants of the town. A decade after the Petrie excavations, a new batch of papyri was discovered, this time a more tightly knit mass of business letters and accountancy documents, all from the rubbish heap beside the Valley Temple of the Senusret II pyramid complex; these discarded temple business files are now preserved in the Egyptian Museums of Cairo and Berlin, and contribute greatly to our understanding of the ancient management of estates, in this case the temple for the eternal cult of the king.[115] Twenty-five years after his first excavation here, Petrie returned with Guy Brunton and investigated more intensively the areas around the pyramid.[116] Here, their major discovery was the treasure of the king's daughter Sathathoriunet, today among the highlights of the Egyptian Museum, Cairo and The Metropolitan Museum of Art, New York. Thus, Lahun brings to us across the four millennia a wide-ranging picture of ancient society from rich to poor.

SQ

46. Relief fragment depicting Senusret II

Lahun, Pyramid Temple of Senusret II
Dynasty 12, reign of Senusret II,
1877–1870 BC
Limestone, pigment
H. 10.0 cm; w. 6.2 cm; d. 5.2 cm
UC 16149[117]

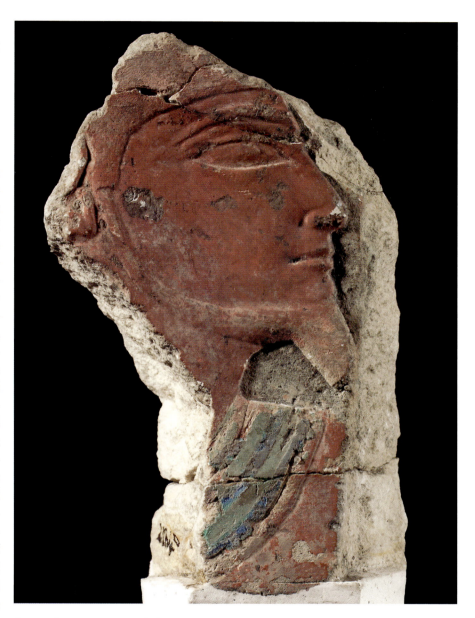

THIS FRAGMENT from a wall-block preserves a depiction of the king facing right, wearing a broad collar, with the stylized short wig and side-beard or wig-strap characteristic of elite men. The sculptor has delicately rendered in lightly raised relief the cheekbones, chin, and noseline, with slightly deeper carving for the lips, gently arching mouthline, eye-border, eyebrow, and hairline. Red-brown ochre covers both skin and hair areas. The rows of the broad collar are also carved in varying depth, and each row distinguished by alternating green-blue and deep blue pigment. Images of Senusret II are extremely rare, this being perhaps the only surviving example from the place where the king was buried and his cult maintained. The surviving color hints at the original overwhelming polychromatic impact of sacred architecture, in which each field of color stood sharply demarcated against the next, bringing to life the rhythmic sequences of scenes of king, gods, and offerings.

In contrast to other pyramid-complexes, the burial place of this king was not connected by a covered stone causeway to the other main temple for his cult at the edge of the fields and river; instead, the excavators uncovered in 1914 a line of tree-pits around the outer of two perimeter walls of the pyramid. Within the inner perimeter wall, on the east face of the pyramid base, there once stood the sanctuary with the altar for offerings to sustain the spirit of the king in life and after death, and this fragment of relief comes from that "Pyramid Temple," being the most sacred offering place, as nearest to the body of the king. The temples of the pyramid complex had been destroyed already by the end of the Eighteenth Dynasty, and the sites were being used as a quarry in the reigns of Tutankhamen and Ramesses II. The surviving fragments of the wall decoration suffice, though, to demonstrate the perfection attained by the Twelfth Dynasty sculptors.   SQ

117 W. M. F. Petrie and Guy Brunton, *Lahun* II (London, 1923) 5, pl. 18.

47. Boundary marker

Lahun
Middle Kingdom or later,
after 2055 BC
Limestone
H. 14.0 cm; w. 8.9 cm; d. 3.5 cm
UC 16047

THE INSCRIPTION on this small,
round-topped stela reads *mery ankh*,
though it is unclear to what this refers
and whether it is a person or property.
A similar stela from Kahun refers to a
block of houses, and is inscribed: "a
four house block 20 x 30 [cubits]."[118]
This seems to be a forerunner of the
Amarna boundary stelae.[119] This
example could come from an individual house and bear the name of the
owner, like the inscribed jambs found
on New Kingdom houses at Tell el-
Amarna, Deir el-Medina, and Luxor.
It is also possible, however, that this
marker refers to a plot of land. After
each inundation, the fields had to be
measured and laid out again, and
must have had such monuments as
their survey markers.[120]   PL

118 Peter Lacovara, *The New Kingdom Royal
City* (London, 1997) 77–8.
119 These round-topped stelae, presumably
set up in front of a house, would echo the
placement of stelae outside a tomb and again
form a connection between the architecture
of life and death, a theme running throughout
the history of Egyptian building design.
A similar round-topped stela from the "house
of Senet," dating to the Middle Kingdom,
is now in the British Museum (EA 59205).
W. M. F. Petrie, *Illahun, Kahun and Gurob*
(London, 1891) 8.
120 Sally Katary, *Land Tenure in the
Ramesside Period* (London and New York,
1989) 10.

48. Upper part of a lamp

Lahun
Late Middle Kingdom,
ca. 1850–1750 BC
Limestone, pigment
H. 13.5 cm; w. 13.2 cm; d. 11.2 cm
UC 16522

THIS LIMESTONE HEAD and bowl, with supporting hands partly preserved at the sides, are the surviving portion of a lamp, probably found in one of the late Middle Kingdom houses at the large town-site near Lahun. The deeply set eyes have raised borders, and brow and cheeks are furrowed. The lips jut out, with plain incised horizontal mouth-line, and another deep furrow between lips and chin. Areas of the original paint survive, black over the hair and pupils, white for the whites of the eyes, and yellow for the skin area with black stippling to indicate stubble.

The 1889 Petrie excavations at Lahun yielded several such lamps, varying in quality and form from finer sculpted faces such as this, to rougher figures, sometimes double back-to-back, and in some instances, an outstretched arm alone holding the lamp bowl.[121] From the darkened substance in the bowl, Petrie identified them as bread-altars,[122] but similar staining occurs in limestone altar lamps, for example from the Valley Temple of King Senusret II at Lahun,[123] and therefore it seems more likely that the residues represent the remains of fatty matter used to fuel the flame. However, the identification as household altar equipment seems plausible, and may rest on undocumented observation by Petrie in the field.

Although at first sight the faces and bodies may seem far from the repertoire of ancient Egyptian sculpture, in fact the motif of dwarf body with chondrodystrophic skull does occur throughout the dynastic period. Precisely in the late Middle Kingdom, dwarf figures in faience and ivory are known from both burials and settlements, such as the town at Lahun and the nearby cemeteries of Harageh (see cat. no. 50). The faience examples in particular belong within a visual vocabulary for the depiction of forces in defense of life at its most vulnerable moment, childbirth. As a different human form, the dwarf evoked forces of divinity capable of protecting mother and child, essential in a land of high maternal and infant mortality. In the Late Period, the human-divine dwarf motif becomes more widespread in a form of the Memphite god Ptah named as "Ptah-the-dwarf" in Egyptian sources, and called "pataikos" in ancient Greek sources. For the late Middle Kingdom, there is no known association with any one deity, but the same image evidently conveyed similar notions of powers capable of saving human life.

SQ

121 Selected examples illustrated in W. M. F. Petrie, *Illahun, Kahun and Gurob* (London, 1891) pl. 6.
122 Ibid., 11.
123 For example, UC 16794, in W. M. F. Petrie and Guy Brunton, *Lahun* I (London, 1920) 13, pl. 20, 4, 6.

49. Rat-trap
Kahun
Middle Kingdom, 2055–1650 BC
Marl clay ceramic
H. 13.7 cm; l. 27.0 cm; w. 12.3 cm
UC 16773

RODENTS AND VERMIN must have been a problem in the town of Kahun, since Petrie remarked that "nearly every room has its corners tunneled by the rats, and the holes stuffed with stones and rubbish to keep them back."[124] This object may have been an early version of a "live trap," where a slab of wood or ceramic would close off the entrance. The handle would allow the whole to be picked up and the pesky varmint whisked away. The design of the door is reminiscent of the portcullis slabs used to seal the entrances to the burial chambers in many tombs and pyramids.   PL

124 W. M. F. Petrie, *Illahun, Kahun and Gurob* (London, 1891) 8.

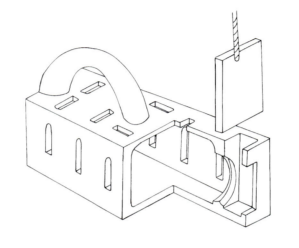

50. Dwarf playing a double pipe

Lahun

Middle Kingdom, 2055–1650 BC

Faience

H. 3.5 cm; w. 2.2 cm; d. 2.7 cm

UC 16684

A NUMBER OF IMAGES of dwarfs are known from the Middle Kingdom, including an ivory toy depicting a series of dancing pygmies.[125] Dwarfs, midgets, and pygmies held a special fascination for the ancient Egyptians, perhaps because of their exoticism or the magical belief in the mutability of size. These small people were associated with entertainment, an idea reinforced by this image of a musician playing a double-reed pipe.   PL

125 Mohamed Saleh and Hourig Sourouzian, *Official Catalogue: The Egyptian Museum, Cairo* (Mainz, 1987) no. 90.

51. Animal figures

Kahun
Middle Kingdom, 2055–1650 BC
Wood

A. Lion
H. 3.2 cm; l. 7.9 cm; w. 2.2 cm
UC 16647

B. Crocodile
H. 1.6 cm; l. 9.4 cm; w. 1.9 cm
UC 16741

THESE TWO enigmatic figures from Petrie's excavations in the town of Kahun are carved with great delicacy. In Petrie's words, "...they are about as fine as they can be."[126] There are peg holes on the bottom of the figures, one for the crocodile and two for the lion. Coming from the town debris, their purpose remains unclear, since their small size, fragility, and exceptional quality would argue against a function as either furniture fittings or toys.

Other crocodile figurines are known, including one from the fort at Semna,[127] and a blue, glassy faience crocodile excavated by The Metropolitan Museum at Lisht.[128] It is possible that these diminutive represen-

tations of fierce creatures were intended to protect the household. Figures of crocodiles and felines are found on the protective "magic wands" of the Middle Kingdom,[129] as well as a steatite rod now in The Metropolitan Museum.[130] It is possible that these carvings could have come from a wooden version of the latter piece.   PL

126 W. M. F. Petrie, *Illahun, Kahun and Gurob* (London, 1891) 11.
127 Dows Dunham and J. Janssen, *Second Cataract Forts I: Semna-Kumma* (Boston, 1960) pl. 127.
128 W. C. Hayes, *The Scepter of Egypt* I (New York, 1953) 248–9, fig. 159.
129 Ibid., 248–9 fig. 143.
130 Ibid., 227–8. See also Janine Bourriau, *Pharaohs and Mortals* (Cambridge, 1988) 115–6, cat. no. 104; 117–8, cat. no. 109 (for the crocodile individually).

AMARNA

WHILE THE SITE OF TELL EL-AMARNA is familiar to all those interested in the field of Egyptology, little was known about it prior to Petrie's pioneering work there. The ephemeral capital of the "heretic" pharaoh Akhenaten and his beautiful wife Nefertiti, and the boyhood home of Tutankhamen, Amarna was the scene of an unprecedented religious and artistic revolution. Having proscribed the worship of the traditional pantheon, the king who began his reign as Amenhotep IV, changed his name to Akhenaten, "the spirit of the Aten," and promulgated a new, monotheistic religion with the Aten as the sole deity and himself as the divine representative on earth. Tell el-Amarna, 200 miles north of the Theban heartland, was the location chosen for the new capital, named Akhetaten, "the horizon of the Aten." Conceived as a showplace for the cult of the Aten and the radical new art style created for its glorification, the city was built on virgin ground at the desert edge of the green fields bordering the Nile in the remote region of Middle Egypt.

Although the tombs of Akhenaten and his officials, cut into the cliffs adjacent to the town, and the boundary stelae set up around it were well known, there was little interest in the settlement until 1887, when local farmers digging for mud brick to use as fertilizer stumbled upon a cache of cuneiform tablets. These documents, the diplomatic correspondence of the royal court, generated much interest in the site.[131]

Although working independently with a very limited budget, Petrie made many important discoveries and helped articulate the plan of the town. He was able to locate the "Records Office" where the famous tablets had come from, as well as the Great Temple of the Aten, the King's House, and the Great Palace. He found the remains of beautiful plaster floors and wall paintings that he carefully conserved and recorded by his own hand in watercolor.[132] Petrie was especially fascinated by "the large waste ground of the palace, and of the glaze workers, we turned over a great quantity of glaze and glass (now in University College), which showed the products and methods of that age. Hundreds of pottery moulds, for making the glazed ornaments were found."[133]

Petrie's maps of the site were the first to provide an understanding of the urban plan of an ancient Egyptian settlement.[134] The main royal palaces and temples first excavated by Petrie were positioned in the city center. The rest of the site extends for about eight miles and is about three miles wide at its midpoint. Clusters of houses, great and small, were located to the north and south of the central city, along with planned residences for the workmen engaged in the construction projects and offices for the bureaucracy associated with the royal court. The city appears to have been inhabited for only about fourteen years, until the death of Akhenaten. Soon after, the site was abandoned and the capital returned to Thebes, where the old religion was reinstated by the "boy-king," Tutankhamen.

Subsequent excavations have included the German Archaeological Institute's work begun in 1907, which concentrated on the hundreds of houses spread out to the north and south of the central city.[135] The most important of these belonged to the sculptor Thutmose, in whose workshop was discovered the renowned bust of Queen Nefertiti.[136] With the out-

131 Cyril Aldred, "El-Amarna," in T. G. H. James, ed., *Excavating in Egypt: The Egypt Exploration Society: 1882–1982* (London and Chicago, 1982) 95; William Moran, *The Amarna Letters* (Baltimore, 1992).

132 W. M. F. Petrie, *Tell el-Amarna* (London, 1894).

133 W. M. F. Petrie, *Seventy Years in Archaeology* (New York, 1932) 152.

134 Peter Lacovara, "The City of Amarna," in Rita Freed, Yvonne Markowitz, and Sue D'Auria, eds., *Pharaohs of the Sun: Akhenaten, Nefertiti, Tutankhamen* (Boston, 1999) 61–71.

135 Ludwig Borchardt and Herbert Ricke, *Die Wohnhäuser in Tell el-Amarna* (Berlin, 1980).

136 Now in Berlin,
Ägyptisches Museum und
Papyrussammlung, Staatliche
Museen zu Berlin, inv. no. 21
300.
137 T. Eric Peet and Leonard
Woolley, *The City of Akhenaten* I (London, 1923).
138 Henri Frankfort and J.
D. S Pendlebury, *The City of Akhenaten* II (London, 1933).
J. D. S Pendlebury, *The City of Akhenaten* III, 2 vols.
(London, 1951).
139 B. J. Kemp, *Amarna Reports* I–VI (London, 1984–95).

break of the First World War, the German mission's work at the site ended and permission to excavate was given to the Egypt Exploration Society in 1921, under T. E. Peet and Leonard Woolley.[137] The excavations were continued after Peet's death by Henri Frankfort and later by John Pendlebury.[138] Work at Amarna ceased with the Second World War, but resumed in 1976, again by a team from the Egypt Exploration Society in London. The ongoing excavations, under the direction of Barry J. Kemp, are a model of archaeological reporting and have added much to our knowledge of the site and this pivotal period in Egyptian history.[139]   PL

52. Balustrade depicting the royal family

Tell el-Amarna,
from the Great Palace[140]
Dynasty 18, early reign of
Akhenaten, ca. 1352–1344 BC
Calcite ("Egyptian alabaster")
H. 53.7 cm; w. 52.4 cm; d. 13.6 cm
UC 401

THE SCENE on this calcite block typifies the art of the Amarna era, depicting the king, queen, and a princess worshipping the Aten. Akhenaten, followed by Nefertiti and Meretaten, their eldest daughter, stands before an offering table holding three vessels. The queen holds a similar vessel in her uplifted hands, proffering its contents to the Aten, no doubt replicating the gesture of the king, whose head and forearms are missing. Meretaten, her hair arranged in the customary sidelock of childhood, stands behind her parents, playing a sistrum. Mother and daughter both wear long pleated dresses of transparent fabric. Nefertiti wears the *khat*, or bag, wig with uraeus; only the streamers of Akhenaten's crown remain, trailing across his right shoulder. The family and the libation vessels are all blessed by the rays of the Aten, one of which extends an *ankh* to the uraeus of the queen.

The style and content of this block are remarkably similar to a more complete balustrade, now in the Cairo Museum,[141] both of which date to the first years of residence at Amarna. Sculpture produced at the beginning of Akhenaten's reign is distinguished by an extreme deviation from artistic tradition, resulting in figures that appear almost deformed in contrast to both preceding and succeeding representations. In this relief, the proportions of the bodies, with high waists and elongated limbs, and the exaggerated fullness of the hips, thighs, and buttocks all point to an early date for the block. The king bears incised cartouches on his upper arm, chest, and torso, containing the names of the Aten, in the form adopted at the beginning of the reign. Furthermore, the queen appears significantly smaller than the king, according to the Egyptian convention that required the king specifically and men in general to be depicted larger than other figures. Although artists continue to follow this precedent at the start of Akhenaten's reign, soon after the move to Amarna, images of Nefertiti begin to be rendered at the same scale as the king.

In all likelihood, this block decorated the balustrade of a ramp in the Great Palace. The ground line on which the royal family stands slopes upward slightly, in opposition to that on the Cairo relief described above.[142] The offering scenes in the reliefs would have echoed the actions of the king, queen, and their daughters, as they moved in ritual procession along the ramps and passages of the palace.

BTT

140 Discovered between the open court and first side hall, in the entrance on the east, along with another similar block.
141 Cairo JT 30/10/26/12. See cat. no. 72, in Rita Freed, Yvonne Markowitz, and Sue D'Auria, eds., *Pharaohs of the Sun: Akhenaten, Nefertiti, Tutankhamen* (Boston, 1999) 226.
142 The angled ground line is a diagnostic feature of the balustrades excavated at Amarna, typically counterbalanced by a rolled edge at the top, missing in this example. See Ian Shaw, "Balustrades, Stairs and Altars in the Cult of the Aten at el-Amarna," *JEA* 80 (1994): 110.

53. Relief depicting Nefertiti

Tell el-Amarna,
probably from the Great Palace[143]
Dynasty 18, early reign of
Akhenaten, ca. 1352–1344 BC
Indurated limestone
H. 12.3 cm; w. 4.2 cm; d. 2.7 cm
UC 038

THE TEMPLE and palace complex that Akhenaten constructed at Amarna was lavishly adorned with reliefs carved from a variety of stones, including limestone, quartzite, and calcite. This sliver of indurated limestone depicts Nefertiti in the extreme style that characterized the first years at Amarna, initially seen in the decoration of the Aten temples Akhenaten erected at Karnak. This early sculptural style is evidenced here by the queen's almost gaunt appearance, knobby chin, slitted eyes placed unnaturally high on the face, and overly large ear with pronounced piercing.

The crown is another indicator of the early date of the relief. In the nascent phase of the Aten theology, Nefertiti retained many of the traditional attributes of queenship, such as the modius, solar disk, double plumes and cow horns that she wears here, associating her with Isis or Hathor. She also wears a tripartite wig, in which she rarely appears following the move to Amarna,[144] when the Nubian wig, *khat* headdress, or tall crown become her preferred accessories.   BTT

143 Dorothea Arnold has suggested that this might be a fragment of one of the many balustrades or columns embellishing the palace. *The Royal Women of Amarna: Images of Beauty from Ancient Egypt* (New York, 1996) 22.
144 Ibid., 9–10.

54. Trial piece depicting Nefertiti

Tell el-Amarna
Dynasty 18, later reign of
Akhenaten, ca. 1344–1336 BC
Limestone, pigment
H. 8.2 cm; w. 7.6 cm; d. 1.6 cm
UC 011

AROUND HIS FIFTH YEAR on the throne, after changing his name from Amenhotep IV to Akhenaten, the king moved the Royal Residence to a new location in Middle Egypt, which he named Akhetaten, now known as Tell el-Amarna. While the move to Amarna provided Akhenaten with an empty canvas upon which he could create the visual expression of his new religion, it also required the construction and ornamentation of an entire city within an extremely compressed time frame. The scope of the project was compounded by Akhenaten's radical departure from artistic convention, necessitating the participation and training of an enormous number of artisans. One by-product of the artistic process at Amarna was the multitude of trial pieces, such as this one, discovered throughout the city.

The example here is a preliminary sketch of Nefertiti wearing her distinctive tall crown, with a uraeus faintly visible at her brow. The upper, lower, and right edges of the piece have been worked, although the left edge is broken. Even in the earliest stage of production, the mastery of the Amarna artists is clearly demonstrated in the graceful sweep of the queen's profile and the elegant almond shape of her eye, enhanced by a cosmetic line and arching brow. Carving was begun around the mouth, chin, ear, and tab of the crown.

This piece likely dates to the middle of Akhenaten's reign, after the exaggerated style of the early years had relaxed somewhat, illustrated here by the less angular features, wider, less slanted eye, and the wrinkles on the neck.   BTT

55. Torso of a princess

Tell el-Amarna
Dynasty 18, later reign of
Akhenaten, ca. 1344–1336 BC
Quartzite
H. 13.6 cm; w. 7.6 cm; d. 12.3 cm
UC 002

SCULPTURE OF THE Amarna Period was innovative in its manipulation of space, light, and composition, all exemplified by this diminutive torso of a princess. The figure is that of a prepubescent girl, depicted naked, and originally part of a group that most likely included Akhenaten, Nefertiti, and at least one other daughter. On the right side of the figure, the surface is rough and the arm bent at the elbow, with the now-missing forearm raised. Another figure or carved block must have been contiguous to this princess, probably portraying her parents or an older sister, upon whom she rested her right hand. The left arm, which is broken away, extended down and backward, clasping the hand of an even smaller child, of which only traces remain. The gap between the two girls has a finished surface, indicating that the figures were not free-standing, but rather, carved in extremely high relief.

The royal family was frequently depicted in complex arrangements of this sort at Amarna, most notably on the statues adjoining the Boundary Stelae that delineated the city, but also on much smaller statuettes.[145] In this instance, the figures did not stand in line beside or behind one another, but were separately recessed. While this arrangement adhered to Egyptian artistic convention, showing the children both behind and at a smaller scale than Akhenaten and Nefertiti, it also placed each figure within its own space, emphasizing the central role played by the royal daughters at Amarna.

Furthermore, the depth of the relief, the choice of the richly-hued quartzite, and the angular juxtaposition of multiple carved blocks would have heightened the all-important effect of sunlight on the sculpture. The fundamental visual element of the new religion was the royal family blessed by the rays of the Aten, an image repeatedly rendered in two dimensions (see cat. nos. 52, 56). The group to which this princess belonged would have brought that image to vivid reality, with each family member touched and enlivened by the rays of the god.

Although it has been suggested that the Petrie torso depicts Nefertiti, it is far more likely to represent one of her daughters.[146] The proportions and rounded forms of the body of the Petrie princess suggest a representation of a pre-adolescent girl, as seen later in the reign of Akhenaten. Her thighs are less full and breasts less developed and wider spaced than contemporary depictions of older women, not yet fully focusing on her reproductive capacity. In addition, her stance, protectively surrounded by her family, is tentative, perfectly embodying the awkwardness of a young girl adjusting to her developing body, in sharp contrast to the poised, authoritative elegance seen in representations of Nefertiti. BTT

145 For example, on Boundary Stelae A and N, the King and Queen appear with at least two princesses to the side and slightly behind them. See Norman de Garis Davies, *The Rock Tombs of el Amarna* vol. 5 (London, 1903–8) pl. 43. A statuette of the royal family using a similar composition is also in the Petrie Collection (UC 004).

146 By Julia Samson in *Amarna: City of Akhenaten and Nefertiti. Key Pieces from the Petrie Collection* (London, 1972) 27, pl. 9. Cyril Aldred has countered this hypothesis by pointing to the absence of representations of Nefertiti completely nude in *Akhenaten and Nefertiti* (Brooklyn, 1973) 163, cat. no. 90.

56. Relief depicting Nefertiti

Tell el-Amarna, possibly from
the Great Aten Temple
Dynasty 18, later reign of
Akhenaten, ca. 1344–1336 BC
Quartzite
H. 16.2 cm; w. 10.5 cm; d. 13.0 cm
UC 040

THIS RELIEF FRAGMENT, carved from a purplish-red quartzite, depicts Nefertiti presenting an offering to the Aten. The queen, wearing a Nubian wig and uraeus, cups a spouted vessel between her elongated hands. Two cartouches that would have contained the names of the Aten are incised on her right forearm. A ray from the Aten extends a hand toward the uraeus at her brow, while another ray passes behind her head. In the original composition, Nefertiti would have followed Akhenaten, most certainly performing the same action. Only the ball of the king's shoulder and the streamers of his crown remain, at the left edge of the fragment.

The large number of scenes in which Nefertiti is depicted offering to the Aten underscores her political and religious stature. In ceremonial representations, Nefertiti typically mimics the gestures of her husband, holding the same objects. Nefertiti is a primary participant in the state cult, unlike her queenly predecessors who were, for the most part, limited to specific rituals or cults, especially in association with goddesses. Yet, Nefertiti was not the only royal woman at Amarna depicted in this context. Both Kiya, a secondary wife, and Meretaten, Akhenaten and Nefertiti's eldest daughter, appear in similar scenes. Dorothea Arnold has surmised that these portrayals of Nefertiti and the other royal women were not necessarily indicative of their own authority, but may rather have arisen from a desire to inject the Aten cult with a female element "to counteract the exclusively male character of its single deity."[147]

BTT

147 Dorothea Arnold, *The Royal Women of Amarna: Images of Beauty from Ancient Egypt* (New York, 1996) 86.

57. Inlay head

Tell el-Amarna
Dynasty 18, reign of Akhenaten,
1352–1336 BC
Quartzite
H. 9.7 cm; w. 11.7 cm; d. 6.2 cm
UC 103

THOUGH NOW BROKEN and fragmentary, this head, most certainly representing Nefertiti and intended to fit into a larger composition, clearly illustrates the lush patterns and deep colors surrounding the residents of Amarna. Modeled from a reddish-brown quartzite, the head would have been completed by the addition of a headdress in a different material. The upper and rear edges have been carved for the attachment of a crown, most likely the tall crown so closely associated with the queen.

The gently arched brow and almond-shaped eye with a slight cosmetic line would have been inlaid in another material, enhancing the rich polychrome appearance of the composition. Two small furrows curve around the inner canthus of the eye. The ear is pierced, though not with the exaggerated hole characteristic of early representations of Akhenaten and Nefertiti (see cat. no. 54). The elegant expanse of the profile, the modeling around the nostril, and the pronounced, yet still graceful chin are strongly reminiscent of the sketch of the queen described above (cat. no. 54). Like the trial piece, this inlay, with its restrained features, probably dates to the later years of Akhenaten's reign.   BTT

58. Trial piece depicting a Nubian

Tell el-Amarna
Dynasty 18, later reign of
Akhenaten, ca. 1340–1336 BC
Limestone
H. 7.8 cm; w. 8.1 cm; d. 1.3 cm
UC 009

THIS TRIAL PIECE depicts the head of a Nubian wearing a round wig and large hoop earring. The surface of the sculpture remains rough and unfinished; only the lips and nostril have been fully modeled. Although it has been suggested that this face is an inlay, to be inserted into a larger relief composition, it more likely served as a sculptor's prototype. Cyril Aldred points out the improbability of an Egyptian artist representing a dark-skinned individual using such a light-colored stone, even if pigment was to be applied to the final product.[148] Despite the unfinished state of the piece, the technical proficiency and sensitivity of the Amarna sculptors is clearly apparent.   BTT

148 Aldred, *Akhenaten and Nefertiti* (New York, 1973) 199, cat. no. 134.

59. Jar fragment with inscription

Tell el-Amarna
Dynasty 18, reign of Akhenaten,
ca. 1336 BC
Marl clay ceramic, pigment
L. 15.3 cm; w. 10.2 cm
UC 32931

MUCH AS MODERN sommeliers keep an album of wine labels for favorite vintages, the dockets inscribed on ancient wine jars seem to have been saved in the palace cities of the New Kingdom. This potsherd came from a large, two-handled amphora, a type of vessel that originated in Canaan and became the standard container for estate wines in Egypt, both imported and locally made.[149]

The hieratic inscription, written in black ink on the shoulder of the jar, reads: "Year 17, sweet wine of the domain of Shetep-A[ten]...." Many of the wine-producing estates were the property of the king or of various temples and wine was shipped along the river when called for.[150] The year date, referring to the reign of Akhenaten, is the highest recorded for the "heretic" pharaoh. Soon after this, Akhenaten died and the court returned to Thebes.

PL

149 Leonard Lesko, *King Tut's Wine Cellar* (Berkeley, 1977).
150 W. C. Hayes, "Inscriptions from the Palace of Amenhotep III," *JNES* 10 (1951): 35–7, no. 1.

60. Head of a shabti of Akhenaten

Tell el-Amarna[151]
Dynasty 18, reign of Akhenaten,
ca. 1344–1336 BC
Granite
H. 6.4 cm; w. 5.6 cm; d. 5.2 cm
UC 007

DESPITE THE RADICAL theological changes enacted during the reign of the "heretic" king, many traditional elements of burial equipment were retained, though slightly tailored to fit the new religious scheme.

Over two hundred fragments of funerary figurines were found in the Royal Tomb at Amarna.[152] In accordance with the new doctrine, the shabti spell taken from the *Book of the Dead*, with its Osirian focus, was omitted (see cat. nos. 137 a–c) in favor of the names and titles of the king, inscribed in a column on the front of the figure.[153] The shabtis of Akhenaten are otherwise comparable to those of both his predecessors and successors, especially Tutankhamen. Like the array of figurines provided for Tutankhamen, Akhenaten was accompanied into the afterlife by shabtis ranging widely in quality, features, and material.[154]

This shabti head wears the *khat*, or bag, headdress, with pigtail at the back, uraeus at the brow, and the remains of a beard. The deeply modeled eyes protrude slightly, underneath well-defined brows, and the full lips are gently pursed, giving the mouth a sensuous appearance. The features, softer and more rounded than early representations of Akhenaten, foreshadow those seen in the sculpture of his successor, Tutankhamen.   BTT

151 Supposedly found "near the palace." W. M. F. Petrie, *Tell el Amarna* (London, 1894) 17.
152 Only one intact example is known, currently in The Metropolitan Museum of Art (1982.50).
153 In contrast to the Amun cult, there seems to have been no animosity directed at that of Osiris; rather, the god of the underworld is simply absent from the religion of Akhenaten.
154 Figurines for Akhenaten were manufactured from calcite, granite, faience, limestone, sandstone, and quartzite, wearing a variety of headdresses, including the *khat* and *nemes*, and carrying an assortment of attributes.

GUROB

155 W. M. F. Petrie, *Ten Years' Digging in Egypt* (London, 1892) 128–137.

THE SITE OF GUROB consists of a palace, settlement, and cemeteries grouped along the desert edge near the modern town of el-Lahun. While Petrie was working at Hawara in 1888–9, some artifacts from the site were brought to him and he journeyed there to investigate. Realizing that it was largely a New Kingdom site, without later occupation, that could well repay investigation, Petrie put his assistant, W. O. Hughes-Hughes, in charge of the project.[155] Many very fine objects ranging in date from the reigns of Thutmose III to Ramesses II were discovered in the ruins of the palace, the surrounding settlement, and the associated graves. Petrie was particularly intrigued by the large quantities of foreign pottery and other imports, as well as the representations of non-Egyptians at the site. Regrettably, Hughes-Hughes left the field of archaeology soon after, leaving no records of his work.

156 The wonderful head suggested to be Queen Tiye, now in the Berlin Museum, is said to have come from Gurob; Ägyptisches Museum und Papyrussammlung, Berlin 21834 (head), 17852 (headdress). See cat. no. 39 in Rita Freed, Yvonne Markowitz, and Sue D'Auria, eds., *Pharaohs of the Sun: Akhenaten, Nefertiti, Tutankhamen* (Boston, 1999) 215.
157 W. L. Loat, "Gurob," in M. A. Murray, *Saqqara Mastabas* I (London, 1904).
158 Guy Brunton and Reginald Engelbach, *Gurob* (London, 1927).
159 Peter Lacovara, "Gurob and the New Kingdom 'Harim' Palace," in Jacke Phillips, ed., *Ancient Egypt, the Aegean, and the Near East: Studies in Honor of Martha Rhoads Bell* (San Antonio, 1997) 297–306.
160 Angela P. Thomas, *Gurob* I (Warminster, 1981) 17.

Once this rich site was revealed, it unfortunately attracted many looters who mined the area for antiquities to sell on the art market.[156] W. L. Loat returned briefly to the site, under Petrie's direction in 1905, but as an amateur ichthyologist, he was most interested in a cemetery of fish mummies.[157] With Petrie's help, the British School of Archaeology revisited Gurob in 1920 to re-survey the area, since the notes and plans of the first season were missing.[158] The British School concentrated on cemetery excavation, finding some earlier graves, ranging in date from the Archaic Period to the First Intermediate Period.

The most important feature at Gurob is a large, twinned building that has now been identified as a *harim* palace, dating to the Eighteenth Dynasty.[159] In all likelihood, this was not only a court settlement, but also the residence of some of the pharaohs' foreign-born wives and their retinues, which would explain the presence of so many imports and high status goods. Maathorneferura, the Hittite wife of Ramesses II, appears to have resided here.[160]

Although Petrie noted the excellent state of preservation of the houses in the town, his survey data has yet to be fully checked and plotted. It is to be hoped that in the future, this important site can be more completely published and interpreted.   PL

61. Stirrup vases

Gurob

A. Mycenaean IIIB1,
ca. 1340/30–1260/50 BC
Ceramic
H. 8.6 cm; max diam. 11.1 cm
UC 16631

B. Dynasty 18, 1550–1069 BC
Faience
H. 6.2 cm; max diam. 6.7 cm
UC 16630

FOREIGN POTTERY has been found in most of the palace cities of the New Kingdom, verifying the appetite of the royal court for exotic products. The stirrup jar is so-named for its distinctive handle, evoking the shape of a stirrup; it would have been used to pour precious oils or perfumes from the spout jutting up from the side.[161] Jars such as these were exported from Mycenaean Greece throughout the Mediterranean world and into Egypt.[162] Not only are actual imported vessels found in Egypt, but they are also depicted in tomb paintings,[163] and reproduced by Egyptian artisans in pottery or faience,[164] such as the example illustrated here. In Egypt, these imports seem to have remained in use even after their original contents were exhausted, probably prized as curiosities. PL

161 Janine Bourriau, *Umm el-Ga'ab, Pottery from the Nile Valley before the Arab Conquest* (Cambridge, 1981) 137.
162 M. Bell, "Preliminary Report on the Mycenaean Pottery from Deir el Medina," *ASAE* 68 (1982): 143–63.
163 Cf. tomb of Ramesses III.
164 Emily Vermeule, "Stirrup jar," in Edward Brovarski, Susan K. Doll, and Rita E. Freed, eds. *Egypt's Golden Age: the Art of Living in the New Kingdom* (Boston, 1982) 155–6, cat. nos. 163–6.

62. Bowl

Gurob
Dynasty 19, 1292–1185 BC
Faience
H. 3.8 cm; rim diam. 10.5 cm
UC 16049

LIKE FAIENCE CHALICES (see cat. no. 154), bowls of this type were not functional, but were made as funerary offerings. As such, they were replete with symbolism of rebirth, beginning with the lotus blue color, and including images of women, marsh scenes, or cows. This bowl combines several of these elements, portraying a nude woman transporting a calf in a papyrus skiff through a papyrus marsh. The style of the bowl, shallow with plain exterior and a dotted rim, is similar to examples dating to the later Eighteenth Dynasty.[165]

The surface of the bowl is darkened from burning; indeed, much of the Gurob material seems to have sustained damage from fire. It has been postulated that this may have resulted from cremation burials, though Martha Bell has suggested that it is more likely due to the destruction of the palace by fire.[166]   PL

165 Angela Milward, "Bowl," in Edward Brovarski, Susan K. Doll, and Rita E. Freed, eds. *Egypt's Golden Age: the Art of Living in the New Kingdom* (Boston, 1982) 144–5, cat. nos. 143–4.
166 Martha Bell, *The Tutankhamun Burnt Group from Gurob, Egypt: Bases for the Absolute Chronology of* LHIII A *and* B (Ann Arbor, 1991) 188–91.

63. Strap-handled amphora inscribed for Tutankhamen

Gurob

Dynasty 18, reign of Tutankhamen,
1333–1323 BC
Calcite ("Egyptian alabaster"),
pigment
H. 25.0 cm; max. diam. 28.0 cm
UC 16021[167]

INCREASED FOREIGN TRADE and conquest flooded New Kingdom Egypt with exotic products, including precious oils and ointments. Even the containers of these prized materials were valued, reused, and copied by Egyptian artisans. The elegant, strap-handled amphora was derived from prototypes imported from Cyprus.[168] Commodities such as perfumed oils and unguents were contained in vessels such as these because the non-porous material, in contrast to pottery, prevented valuable liquids from leeching out over time.

This vase is inscribed with the names of Tutankhamen and his wife, Ankhesenamen, incised in a square on the middle of the vase and filled in with Egyptian blue pigment. Similar vessels were found in Tutankhamen's tomb,[169] and according to Petrie, this broken and now partially restored example was also found in a burial. However, it had probably been used in daily life or a festival at the palace, before it was deposited in the ground. Perhaps, along with the return to Thebes following the reign of Akhenaten, this is evidence of the restoration of the other royal residences, including Gurob.   PL

U.C. 16021.

167 Identified by Petrie as fragments "found in a tomb" at Gurob. *Kahun, Gurob, Hawara* (London, 1890) 35.
168 R. Amiran, *Ancient Pottery of the Holy Land* (Jerusalem, 1969) pl. 57.
169 Ali el-Khouly, *Stone Vessels, Pottery and Sealings from the Tomb of Tutankhamun* (Oxford, 1993) 185.

64. Figure of a harpist

Gurob

New Kingdom, 1550–1069 BC

Wood

H. 4.4 cm; w. 1.6 cm; d. 1.6 cm

UC 16670

THIS SMALL FIGURE from the *harim* palace at Gurob represents a woman with a long braid playing a tall, stringed instrument, probably a lyre or lute. The broad, simple style of the face is reminiscent of a Hittite silver figure found at Amarna.[170] There is evidence that foreigners were living at Gurob, possibly even foreign wives from diplomatic marriages of the king.[171] Perhaps this little figure was a reminder of home in far-off Anatolia. The peg on the bottom of the piece suggests it was attached to another object, such as a box, cosmetic implement, or perhaps as a finial on an instrument similar to that depicted.

PL

170 Martha Bell, "A Hittite pendant from Amarna," *AJA* 90, no. 2 (April, 1986): 145–51.
171 Angela P. Thomas, *Gurob* 1 (Warminster, 1981) 6.

65. Figure of a mother and child on a bed
Gurob
New Kingdom, 1550–1069 BC
Limestone, pigment
L. 14.3 cm; w. 6.2 cm; d. 3.8 cm
UC 16758

THIS SMALL SCULPTURE depicts a woman lying on a bed, naked except for a broad collar and beaded girdle. She wears a full wig framed by fronds or a garland. Painted on the bed beside her is a diminutive figure representing a child wearing a long, pleated tunic.

These enigmatic figures, usually of females, are found both in tombs and domestic contexts.[172] Although they have been described as "concubines of the dead," children are sometimes portrayed alongside the woman, as in this case; furthermore, the figures are found in the graves of women and children. It is more likely that they symbolized fertility and rebirth, common themes in funerary goods. Examples found in settlements may have been kept in household shrines or even functioned as children's toys, exactly the type of object one might expect to find in a palace of royal women.　PL

172 Sue D'Auria, "Female figure on a bed," in Sue D'Auria, Peter Lacovara, and Catharine Roehrig, eds. *Mummies and Magic: the Funerary Arts of Ancient Egypt* (Boston, 1988) 137, cat. no. 74.

SAQQARA

173 J.-P. Lauer, *Saqqara, the Royal Cemetery of Memphis* (London, 1976).

SAQQARA IS THE NAME of the great necropolis west of the ancient city of Memphis, throughout ancient Egyptian history the centerpoint of the country.[173] Here, in the twenty-seventh century BC, the first monumental complex entirely in stone was created as the eternal place for cult and burial of King Netjerkhet. Later Egyptians knew him by the name of Djoser, and revered Imhotep, the head of his administration, as a god of knowledge and healing, the son of Ptah, chief god of Memphis. The focus of the complex was the first known Step Pyramid, beneath which lay the burial chamber with the body of the king. Although this was disturbed in antiquity, decades of meticulous work by Jean-Philippe Lauer have revealed and restored much of the surrounding architecture. Solid masonry buildings with facades of engaged columns surround open courts with rounded boundary-markers, around which a king must run after thirty years of reign to regenerate himself and the country—the *sed*-festival. On the north side of the pyramid, a chapel enclosed a life-size limestone statue of the king. Farther north, in later times and perhaps already from the Early Dynastic Period, the sacred bull named the Apis was interred with ceremonies fit for a king. The origin of the Apis cult, central to Egyptian kingship, is shrouded in mystery, but in Pharaonic times the bull is named as herald of Ptah. There was only one Apis at any one time, distinguished by special markings that enabled the temple staff to identify the next Apis after his death; from the Late Period, the dead Apis was called Osiris-Apis, and would become the Ptolemaic Sarapis, still a god of fertility but in Hellenistic form.

Beyond the enclosure, other Old Kingdom kings built their pyramids; from the end of the Fifth Dynasty, the walls of the inner chambers were inscribed with spells from the mummification, funeral, and regenerative rites—"Pyramid Texts"—the oldest religious literature to survive from Egypt. Two thousand years later, Memphis remained a central city of Egypt, and earlier rock-cut tombs were reused as catacombs for a new religious practice—the mummification of select species as divine offerings. For the god of embalming, Anubis, jackals and dogs were mummified; and for Bastet, goddess of sacred ointment and protection, cats were given; while Thoth, the god of wisdom, was honored with baboons and ibis, literally by the million. By mummification, the Egyptians gave eternal life to these animals and birds, often farmed and even culled for the rites, about which we know little in detail. On the escarpment overlooking the fields towards the city of Memphis, new terraced temples were built in the Late and Ptolemaic Periods, one for Anubis, another for Bastet.[174] Behind them toward the desert, the other side of the same rocky hill faced west onto the Serapeum valley, where temples were built for the worship and mummification of the sacred animals and birds, with catacombs freshly cut, perhaps by royal decree.[175] The flat hilltop in between is covered with tombs of courtiers and officials from the First Dynasty to the later Old Kingdom. Here, during the 1960s, Petrie's successor W. B. Emery pursued the quest for the lost tomb of Imhotep. Although he died without discovering where Imhotep had been buried, he and his successor, H. S. Smith, excavated a wealth of material of both the third millennium BC tomb-monuments, and the animal cults of the late first millennium BC. These are among the highlights of the Petrie Museum today. SQ

174 D. Jeffreys and H. S. Smith, *The Anubeion at Saqqara, Volume 1, the Settlement and the Temple Precinct* (London, 1988).
175 H. S. Smith, *A Visit to Ancient Egypt: Life at Memphis and Saqqara 500–30 BC* (Warminster, 1974).

66. Anubis shrine

Saqqara
Dynasty 26, 664–525 BC
Limestone
H. 49.5 cm; w. 15.5 cm; l. 46.5 cm
UC 30565

ANUBIS, who played a crucial role in protecting the dead and helping them achieve a good afterlife, was typically portrayed in the form of a recumbent jackal, an image derived from an epithet describing him as being "on his booth." Figures of the deity often adorned the tops of wooden funerary shrines and coffins, as well as architectural elements such as this example, one of a group found at Saqqara,[176] the site of a temple complex dedicated to Anubis.[177] Although the date of the group of statues is uncertain, they seem to belong to the Saite, or more generally, Late Period. This date is further supported by a fragmentary snout of a similar Anubis, found in association with other Late Period sculptures at the Anubieion.[178] This piece is similar to the shrine-shaped, gilded chest found in the tomb of Tutankhamen.[179] PL

176 E. A. Hastings, *The Sculpture from the Sacred Animal Necropolis at Saqqara* (London, 1997) 42–3.
177 D. G. Jeffreys and H. S. Smith, *The Anubeion at Saqqara. Volume 1, the Settlement and the Temple Precinct* (London, 1988).
178 Ibid., 62–3.
179 C. N. Reeves, *The Complete Tutankhamun* (London, 1990) 133–4.

67. Censer

Saqqara
Dynasty 30-Ptolemaic Period,
381–30 BC
Bronze
L. 51.0 cm; h. 6.5 cm; diam. (bowl)
7.2 cm
UC 30663

EGYPTIAN CENSERS took the form of an arm with outstretched hand that was also the hieroglyphic symbol for presenting an offering. In the middle, a small basin, usually cartouche-shaped, contained the incense pellets. The incense was burned in a small bowl resting in the open palm of the hand, which the officiant held up to the object or image being venerated.

This example was hollow-cast in three parts: a central tube with the pellet box, and the two end sections. The cup is riveted onto the hand that projects from a bound papyrus flower. The falcon finial at the opposite end is finely modeled with a detailed face and tripartite wig. Found in a deposit of temple equipment, this censer was almost certainly used in ritual performances within the sacred animal necropolis of Saqqara.[180]

BTT

180 The deposit was uncovered in gallery 1b of the falcon necropolis at North Saqqara, a subterranean maze filled with tens of thousands of pots containing mummified falcons. W. B. Emery, "Preliminary Report on the Excavations at North Saqqâra, 1969–70." *JEA* 57 (1971): 6.

68. Situla

Saqqara[181]
Dynasty 26, 664–525 BC
Bronze
H. 18.7 cm; diam. 5.4 cm
UC 30657

A VARIETY OF LIQUIDS, including milk, water, and wine, were poured during divine and funerary rituals, and were also presented as offerings to the deceased or the gods. Numerous scenes in both tombs and temples show ritual vessels, such as the situla, being carried in procession or used to pour libations. Situlae were usually cast of bronze, in a distinctive teardrop shape, with a handle attached to the rim.

This vessel is decorated with three registers of incised relief. In the upper register, a floral frieze tops an image of two jackals pulling a boat, and a second boat bearing an enshrined deity. The middle register depicts a standing figure pouring a libation over a laden offering table. A line of deities stand behind the table, including Amun, Isis, Nephthys, and Neith, along with another figure of Isis, nursing Horus in a papyrus thicket. A procession of deities fills the bottom register, including Amun, Neith, Anubis, Sakhmet, and Nephthys.   BTT

181 Excavated in Hawk Gallery 1b.
W. B. Emery, "Preliminary Report on the Excavations at North Saqqâra, 1969–70." *JEA* 57 (1971): pl. VII, 2.

69. Figurine of a goddess

Saqqara[182]
Dynasty 30-Ptolemaic Period,
381–30 BC
Bronze, gilt
H. 23.5 cm; w. (base) 7.0 cm;
d. (base) 15.5 cm
UC 30489

THIS FIGURINE most likely depicts a composite of the goddesses Isis and Mehet-Weret. The name of the ancient bovine deity Mehet-Weret means "great flood," in reference to her supposed origins, rising from the primeval waters at the time of creation. In their combined form, Mehet-Weret and Isis represent the mother of the Apis bull. Considered the physical manifestation of the god Ptah and identified by distinctive markings, the Apis bull lived a luxurious lifestyle within a sacred precinct. At its death, each bull was mummified just as a human would have been and interred in a necropolis known as the Serapeum, located at Saqqara.

A figure such as this, celebrating the creative force of the goddess and her role as divine mother, would probably have been a votive offering in one of the shrines at the Serapeum. She wears a uraeus and modius crown, surmounted by double plumes, with a solar disk between her horns, symbolizing her role as the mother of the sun-god, Re. Both hands are pierced to hold implements, now lost. The goddess' gracefully modeled body is accented with gilding on the eyes, collar, and wig. The hieroglyphic inscription around the base is well-executed, with incised details, invoking Isis and Anubis, requesting health and long life on behalf of Wah-ib-re, son of Qen-her.[183]

BTT

182 The figure was excavated by W. B. Emery in 1968–9, in a chapel within the small temple of Nectanebo. The chapel contained numerous bronze figurines, a wooden statue of Osiris, and three wooden shrines, each holding additional bronze statuettes. Emery, "Preliminary Report on the Excavations at North Saqqâra, 1968–9." *JEA* 56 (1970): 6.
183 The figure and base do not belong together, as indicated by the larger space around the feet, filled in after insertion of the figure.

70. Aegis of Isis

Saqqara[184]
Dynasty 30-Ptolemaic Period,
381–30 BC
Bronze
H. 21.0 cm; w. 20.3 cm; d. 23.2 cm
UC 30479 (aegis), 30482 (*menat*)

THE AEGIS is a ceremonial ornament usually associated with certain goddesses, including Bastet, Sakhmet, and, as seen in this instance, Isis. In its most basic form, the aegis consisted of two elements: a beaded broad collar, or *wesekh*, and the head of a deity. Here, the finely modeled head of the goddess wears a tripartite wig and uraeus, surmounted by a modius, a platform crown composed of twelve uraei. A pair of falcons flanks Isis, facing outward with one wing spread in a protective gesture.

As an amulet, the aegis provided the protective force of the divinity depicted, in addition to the power of regeneration and rebirth. This sizable bronze example reinforces those blessings by incorporating a *menat*, or counterpoise, on the back of the aegis. A massive aegis would have adorned both the prow and stern of the sacred barque in which the cult image of a deity was carried during religious processions. An ornament of this scale, far too large to be a personal amulet, may have been presented as a votive offering, a miniature version of the divine figurehead.   BTT

184 Sector H5-228, no. 900. W. B. Emery, "Preliminary Report on the Excavations at North Saqqâra, 1966–7." *JEA* 53 (1967): 143, pl. 24

71. Statue of Imhotep

Late Period, 664–332 BC
Limestone
H. 34.2 cm; w. (base) 10.8 cm; d. (base) 21.3 cm
UC 8709

IMHOTEP, the fabled architect of the Step Pyramid, was so revered by later generations of Egyptians, not only as a patron of architecture, but of medicine and writing as well, that he was deified. Votive images of Imhotep usually depict him with shaven head, in the customary guise of a priest, seated with a papyrus roll opened up in his lap.

While numerous small figures of Imhotep were cast in bronze, this unusually large stone image may have been a particularly sacred representation of the man. An inscription of Imhotep, found at Saqqara and dating to the reign of Djoser, indicates that the great architect was not merely a mythical character. Given the importance of the cult of Imhotep at Saqqara, Walter Bryan Emery of University College excavated there for many years in hopes of finding his tomb. Although no tomb has yet been discovered for the renowned architect, Emery did unearth a vast necropolis of sacred animals buried in celebration of the cult of Imhotep.　PL

NAUKRATIS

185 Herodotus (*The Histories*, II.135), Strabo (*Geography*, XVII.I.33), and Athenaeus (*Deipnosophistai* XIII. 596b) all mention Charaxus' sojourns in Naukratis in the early sixth century. Both Herodotus and Strabo refer to Sappho's derision of her brother and Rhodopis.

IN 1883, working under the auspices of the Egypt Exploration Fund in one of his first seasons of independent fieldwork, Petrie came across a wealth of Greek potsherds scattered atop a settlement mound in the vicinity of the villages of el-Nebira, el-Niqrash, and el-Ge'eif. It was not until the following season, when he spotted an inscribed block outside his dig-house, that Petrie realized the identity of the site.

The block contained a civic decree of Naukratis, a Greek enclave long sought by explorers and archaeologists, including Heinrich Schliemann, excavator of Troy. Scholars were drawn to the search by the numerous Classical references, most notably Herodotus, by the role of the city as a linchpin of the Hellenistic economy, and by its unique status as an essentially foreign city existing within Egypt.

According to Herodotus in *The Histories*, "[Amasis] gave [the Greeks] Naukratis as a commercial headquarters for any who wished to settle in the country" (II 178). Yet, archaeological evidence as well as Herodotus' own words indicate that a city inhabited by Greeks existed on the site prior to the reign of Amasis (570–526 BC). Other sources attest that the brother of the poet Sappho, Charaxus, frequently traveled to Naukratis, where he mixed his business as a wine merchant with the pleasure offered by the notorious courtesan Rhodopis.[185] There was a Greek presence at Naukratis, probably then known by a local name, as early as the late seventh century BC, possibly consisting of mercenaries hired by Psamtek I and granted land in return for their service.

In all likelihood, Amasis merely formalized an existing situation by officially granting the residents of Naukratis a monopoly on the marketing of Greek products in Egypt. Silver, olive oil, and wine were exchanged for linen, papyrus, and Egypt's most important export—grain. Herodotus, again, sheds some light on the situation, stating:

> In old days, Naukratis was the only port in Egypt, and anyone who brought a ship into any of the other mouths of the Nile was bound to state on oath that he did so of necessity, and then proceed to the Canopic mouth; should contrary winds prevent him from doing so, he had to carry his freight to Naukratis in barges all round the Delta, which shows the exclusive privilege the port enjoyed. (II.179)

Although the city's florescence came during the reign of Amasis, Naukratis continued to be a center of commerce and industry throughout the periods of Persian domination and the waning years of Egyptian rule.

Petrie's excavations at Naukratis focused largely on the sacred precincts of the city, many of which had been described in ancient literature. Remains of temples to Apollo, Hera, Aphrodite, and the Dioskouroi were discovered, each having been funded by one of the Greek city-states represented in Naukratis. Herodotus indicated that this privilege had been granted by Amasis, who "made grants of land upon which Greek traders might erect altars and sanctuaries" (II. 178). A later excavation conducted in 1899 by D. H. Hogarth revealed the ruins of the Hellenion, an enormous sanctuary constructed jointly by nine Greek cities. Herodotus described the sanctuary, sponsored by Mytilene, Cnidus,

Halicarnassus, Rhodes, Phaselis, Phocaea, Chios, Teos, and Clazomenae as "the best known...most used...and...largest" (11.178) in the city. One of the few industrial buildings unearthed at Naukratis was a facility for producing faience scarab seals, located near the Aphrodite temple.

The status of Naukratis changed with the advent of the Ptolemaic Dynasty, native Greek monarchs ruling from the newly established capital in Alexandria, which immediately became the Hellenistic city *par excellence*, the heart of art, literature, science, and philosophy of the ancient world. Yet, Naukratis retained some of her previous stature, as one of the three centers of Greek society in Egypt, along with Alexandria and Ptolemais. Despite the loss of exclusive control over Greek wares, Naukratis remained an important distribution point for Mediterranean trade.

Although it never achieved the magnitude or renown of Alexandria, Naukratis was a gathering spot for scholars, authors, and artists, even as late as the third century AD, when Athenaeus wrote the *Deipnosophistai*. Another indication of the enduring reputation of the city dates to AD 130, when Hadrian used its legal system as a model for that of the new city of Antinoöpolis. BTT

93

72. Gorgoneion

Naukratis
Early Ptolemaic Period,
Third century BC
Terracotta
H. 7.5 cm; w. 7.0 cm
UC 54628

TERRACOTTA ORNAMENTS such as this were dubbed "gorgoneia" by Ernest Gardner, a colleague of Petrie who excavated Naukratis. Discovered in burials of the early Ptolemaic Dynasty, the gorgoneia adorned wooden coffins, of which there were no extant remains.[186] Contemporary coffins found at other sites were architecturally styled, rectangular in shape with gabled lids and pediments at either end. The gorgoneia were attached, in the manner of an antefix, to the ends of the beams of the coffin.   BTT

186 The date was determined based on both style and coinage associated with the burials. Gardner, *Naukratis* II (London, 1888) 25–6.

73. Figure of a man

Naukratis
Dynasty 26, 664–525 BC
Limestone, pigment
H. 22.9 cm; w. 7.3 cm; d. 5.1 cm
UC 16469

THIS FIGURE, wearing a short kilt, stands with one leg advanced, and both arms held at the sides, in a characteristic representation of Egyptian males, both private and royal. Several features, however, highlight the increasing influence of Hellenistic culture in Egypt during the Saite Period.

The rendering of the body clearly differs from that of typical Egyptian figures, with arms that appear overly long, a slender torso, and sloping shoulders. Sculpture of the Late Period tends to combine an elegance of composition and technical proficiency not seen here. The overall lack of modeling produces a body that seems undefined and amorphous in comparison with contemporary sculptures. The absence of a back pillar, a standard feature on Late Period sculpture, and the open space between the body and arms are additional indicators of Greek influence.   BTT

74. Man bearing a ram

Naukratis
Late Period, 664–525 BC
Crystalline limestone
H. 9.5 cm; w. 6.0 cm; d. 3.5 cm
UC 16622

FIGURES OF THIS TYPE are not characteristic of Egyptian sculpture, but are found in the sculptural repertoire of the Greek community at Naukratis. In this instance, the figurine portrays a man wearing a headcloth, carrying a ram across his shoulders. One arm hangs at his side, while the other hand clasps the animal's hooves. The features of both man and beast are almost completely eroded.

While excavating the temple precincts of Naukratis, Flinders Petrie and his colleague Ernest Gardner found a multitude of broken statuettes, in both stone and terracottta. The statuettes were particularly numerous in the temple of Aphrodite, with the majority representing females wearing draped garments. Others, such as this one, probably depict a worshipper, bearing an offering for the deity.

BTT

75. Attic black-figure amphora fragment[187]
Probably from Naukratis
Mid-sixth century, ca. 540 BC
Ceramic, pigment
H. 11.7 cm; w. 12.1 cm
UC 19361

SHERDS SUCH AS THIS, scattered on the ground, first alerted Petrie to the location of Naukratis. Furthermore, Greek ceramics have allowed scholars to estimate the initial habitation date of the city.[188] As the sole point of entry for Greek goods into Egypt, the citizens of Naukratis would have imported vessels of all types, throughout the occupation of the city.

This fragment is particularly intriguing, since it depicts a soldier, wearing a crested Corinthian helmet and possibly a cuirass, and carrying a sword. The mane of the soldier's horse is visible along the right edge of the fragment. Although ancient sources, including Herodotus, indicate that Naukratis was founded by Amasis (reigned 570–526 BC) early in the sixth century, it is likely that a significant Greek population was already resident in Egypt, consisting of mercenaries employed by the Saite pharaohs. Given that mercenaries in Egyptian service retained their own distinctive arms, uniforms, and materiel, this sherd could well provide a "snapshot" of a Greek soldier living in the Egyptian Delta. BTT

187 Many thanks to Jasper Gaunt for his insights and commentary on this piece.
188 The earliest datable pottery fragments from the site are Corinthian, and suggest a Greek presence there as early as the mid-seventh century. John Boardman, *The Greeks Overseas: their early colonies and trade* (London, 1980) 121.

HAWARA

PETRIE BEGAN WORK at Hawara in 1888, intending to study the pyramid complex of Amenemhet III. His excavations in that season and a second in 1910–11 would far surpass his expectations, shedding light on one of antiquity's most renowned monuments, the Labyrinth, and unearthing some of the most evocative images produced in ancient Egypt, the so-called Fayum portraits. Situated near the entrance to the Fayum, Hawara was the site of the burial complex of Amenemhet III, the largest and most elaborate of the Middle Kingdom, and was first studied in 1843 by Richard Lepsius, who suggested that it was the ancient Labyrinth.

The forty-five year reign of Amenemhet III represented the economic apex of the Middle Kingdom, exploiting the agricultural potential of the Fayum, the stone quarries of Egypt, and the turquoise mines of Sinai. Amenemhet began preparations for his burial at the start of his reign, constructing a pyramid at Dahshur.[189] Structural and design flaws resulted in the near-collapse of the Dahshur pyramid, prompting Amenemhet to commission a second tomb in his fifteenth year on the throne. Though the king was not buried there, the Dahshur complex was not abandoned. The pyramid contained burial chambers for two queens; one, named Aat, was interred there around year 20 of Amenemhet's reign, at which time the pyramid was sealed.

The second pyramid at Hawara was built of mud-brick and originally faced with limestone. Innovations in the interior plan of the pyramid, such as sliding stone portcullises and dead-end passages, were likely designed in reaction to the violation of earlier royal burials and would become standard features in those of the succeeding dynasty. The design of the burial chamber was without precedent, consisting of a basin carved into a single piece of stone, estimated by Petrie to weigh 110 tons, and set into a trough near the center of the pyramid.

The excavation of the pyramid was a testament to Petrie's skill and tenacity, since the chambers were flooded by ground water. Despite the arduous conditions, Petrie discovered two sarcophagi and two canopic chests inside the burial chamber, and numerous items inscribed for Neferuptah, a daughter of Amenemhet, inside an antechamber.

The interment of royal women in the pyramid complex or the pyramid itself was common practice from the earliest dynasties, as attested by the aforementioned pyramid at Dahshur. Despite the presence of funerary equipment belonging to Neferuptah in her father's pyramid, a separate tomb for her, containing an inscribed sarcophagus and remnants of coffins and bandages, was discovered in 1956.[190] Given the construction of Amenemhet's burial chamber and the likelihood that he predeceased Neferuptah, it is doubtful that the body of the princess was moved to her own tomb at a later time. The royal vault could not have been re-opened: it was sealed with three enormous stone slabs, installed by means of the earliest attested sand-lowering mechanism, yet another innovation of Amenemhet's complex.[191]

Finding fragments of inscriptions and colossal statuary of Amenemhet III, Petrie identified the ruins to the south of the pyramid as the ancient Labyrinth, a building well known

189 Graffiti left by workers on the casing of the pyramid are dated as early as year 2 of the king's reign.

190 The contents of the tomb were damaged by ground water, yet otherwise undisturbed. N. Farag and Z. Iskander, *The Discovery of Neferwptah* (Cairo, 1971).
191 A construction method well-known in later periods, this process involved resting the roofing slabs on pillars supported by sand in shafts around the chamber. The sand was then released into adjacent compartments, allowing the slabs to descend into place.

192 In addition to Herodotus, the Labyrinth is mentioned, in varying degrees of detail, by five other authors including, in chronological order, Manetho, Diodorus Siculus, Strabo, Pliny the Elder, and Pomponius Mela.

193 W. M. F. Petrie, *Hawara, Biahmu, and Arsinoe* (London, 1889) 5.

194 Pietro della Valle, an Italian traveler, acquired two portrait mummies at Saqqara in 1615. The portraits came to the attention of the European art market in 1887, when Austrian dealer Theodor Graf purchased and exhibited all of the panels unearthed by the residents of el-Rubayat.

from numerous Classical sources. In his description of the monument, Herodotus stated that "no words can tell its wonders; were all that Greeks have built and wrought added together the whole would be seen to be a matter of less labor and cost than this Labyrinth" (II, 148).[192] Herodotus claimed that the Labyrinth contained dozens of courts roofed with stone, massive colonnades, and 3,000 rooms, half of which were subterranean. Petrie uncovered extensive ruins, measuring approximately 1,000 by 800 feet, and hypothesized that the expanse could hold "all of the temples on the east bank of Thebes, and one of the largest on the west."[193]

During his first season at Hawara, Petrie unearthed a Roman cemetery north of the pyramid. Although it was probably the necropolis of the nearby nome capital Arsinoe, the presence of the funerary complex of Amenemhet III made the site a desirable burial place from the Middle Kingdom through the Roman Period. Initially dismayed, Petrie planned to abandon the area "as not worth working," until the discovery of mummies bearing painted portrait panels. Although similar portraits had been acquired in Egypt as early as 1615, the Hawara excavations provided the first archaeological context for the panels.[194] The designation of the panels as "Fayum" portraits is inaccurate, despite the fact that the majority had been found there. Following Petrie's initial finds, portrait panels have been excavated at numerous sites, including Antinoöpolis, Akhmim, el-Hibeh, and most recently at Thebes and Marina el-Alamein.   BTT

76. Mummy trappings
Hawara

A. Mask
Early Roman Period, AD 40–60
Cartonnage, gilt, bronze, glass
H. 50.0 cm; w. 40.0 cm; d. 0.1 cm
UC 28084

B. Foot Case
Early Roman Period, 30 BC–AD 149
Plaster, linen, gilt
L. 13.1 cm; w. 20.0 cm; d. 1.0 cm
UC 28085

THIS GILDED mummy mask depicts a woman with elaborately styled hair, arranged in tiers of ringlets. She wears a veil edged in dark red and a tunic with a dark red stripe at the right shoulder.[195] Only one original eye is preserved, made of glass and calcite with bronze fitting and eyelashes, set into a slightly plump face. Her ornate jewelry, including a pair of snake bracelets, armbands, and a pectoral with figures of Isis, Harpocrates, and Serapis, suggests a date during the reigns of Claudius or Nero.

Cartonnage covers such as this would have protected the feet of the mummy. Sandal straps and possibly the hem of a garment are indicated in black and red paint. The gilded surface, like that of the mask, associated the deceased with the sun-god, whose flesh was thought to be covered with gold.   BTT

195 The band of color, usually purple in Rome and an indication of rank, is referred to as a *clavus*. In Egypt, the insignia marks an association with Rome. Susan Walker and Morris Bierbrier, *Ancient Faces: Mummy Portraits from Roman Egypt* (London, 1997) 80.

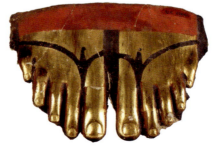

77. Mummy portrait

Hawara
Roman Period,
early second century AD[196]
Wood, encaustic
H. 41.0 cm; w. 27.2 cm
UC 79360

THIS MUMMY PORTRAIT is the most recent addition to the collection of the Petrie Museum, despite the fact that it was excavated by Petrie during his 1888 season at Hawara.[197] According to his usual practice, Petrie presented a group of objects, including the portrait, to one of his financial backers, Jesse Haworth, who gave it in turn to the Victoria & Albert Museum.[198] Archival material at the Victoria & Albert indicates that the Museum approached both Haworth and Martyn Kennard, Petrie's other primary financier, requesting gifts from the Hawara divisions. It remains unclear to which benefactor the portrait originally belonged. The objects, stored in a crate at the Victoria & Albert, were identified as part of an inventory in 2003[199] and transferred to the Petrie Museum the following year.

The portrait depicts a mature man with no garment visible at his shoulders. His hair is dark and receding at the forehead, resulting in a slight widow's peak; no other details of the treatment of the hair are perceptible. His beard and mustache are closely trimmed, highlighting full lips painted in dark red. The large eyes are deep-set and heavily shadowed, flanking a long, broad nose.

Representations of bare-chested youths and adult males with ruddy skin tone most likely indicate that they were trained in the *gymnasium* as an *ephebe*, in the traditional Greek manner emphasizing athletic and military prowess. During the early years of the Roman Period, the elite of the Fayum were educated in the *gymnasium* in preparation for entry into the upper levels of political service.[200] The depiction of the man as an *ephebe* in addition to the large scale of the portrait suggest that he was of high social status in the Fayum community.[201]   BTT

196 The date is suggested by the remaining traces of the hairstyle.
197 A field notation on the verso designates the portrait as "UU," in accordance with the identification system Petrie used during the 1888 season at Hawara. The piece will also be discussed by Susan Walker in a forthcoming publication of mummy portraits in the Petrie Collection, edited by Jan Picton, Stephen Quirke, and Paul Roberts.
198 Although the portrait was apparently acquired by the Victoria & Albert Museum on July 17, 1888, it was never officially accessioned. The bulk of Haworth's share of the Petrie excavations would later become the Egyptian collection at the Manchester Museum, which did not yet exist in 1888.
199 Conducted by Rebecca Naylor as part of a project to research the Egyptian holdings of the Victoria & Albert.
200 On the representation of the *ephebe* and the role of the *gymnasium* in Roman Egypt, see Susan Walker, "Mummy Portraits in their Roman Context," in M. L. Bierbrier, ed. *Portraits and Masks: Burial Customs in Roman Egypt* (London, 1997) 3–4; Idem., "Mummy Portraits and Roman Portraiture," in Susan Walker and Morris Bierbrier, eds. *Ancient Faces: Mummy Portraits from Roman Egypt* (London, 1997) 15.
201 The panel is split vertically into two pieces, with several other smaller cracks. Sections of the linen wrappings remain adhered to the lower edge and verso of the panel. Conservation of the portrait is currently being conducted by Renée Stein at the Michael C. Carlos Museum.

MEROE

ALTHOUGH THE ANCIENT CITY of Meroe was located by James Bruce in 1772, the site was not excavated until 1909, under the direction of John Garstang of the Liverpool University Institute of Archaeology.[202] The city, apparently covering a tremendous area of which only a small portion has been uncovered, was situated about halfway between the Fifth and Sixth Cataracts, on the eastern bank of the Nile.

Meroe was a residence of Kushite royalty as early as the sixth century BC, beginning under the Napatan kings who ruled Egypt as the Twenty-fifth Dynasty. Following their departure from Egypt, the Napatans continued to reign in Nubia for a thousand years.[203] At the beginning of the third century BC, the ruling dynasty relocated their necropolis from the Napata region to Meroe, greatly heightening the prestige of the city.

While Egyptian traditions remained influential, a distinctively Nubian culture came to the fore, centered in Meroe, and including not only much of Lower and Upper Nubia, but areas well south of modern Khartoum. Meroe was an ideal capital, advantageously situated for both commerce and agriculture. The city lay in a fertile area receiving annual rainfall, which facilitated horse and cattle breeding and cultivation of crops. In addition, Meroe was positioned in close proximity to important trade routes leading to the Red Sea, western desert, and central Africa.

The city's central district, enclosed by a stone wall, contained palaces, administrative buildings, an astronomical observatory, a water sanctuary, orchards of fruit trees, and royal baths. An enormous temple dedicated to the Egyptian god Amun, who was particularly venerated among the Nubians, lay at the end of an avenue lined with statues of rams. Royal workshops produced fine ceramics and faience, sophisticated metalworks, elegant jewelry, and colossal sculptures and stelae. Many of these monuments were inscribed, and after the second century BC, Egyptian was no longer the chosen script, as it had been in the Napatan Period.

The innovative nature of the Meroitic culture is perhaps best exemplified by the creation of a written form of the language spoken in Meroe. The scripts, hieroglyphic and cursive, that developed were loosely based on Egyptian hieroglyphs and demotic. Yet unlike Egyptian, Meroitic relied on a twenty-three sign alphabet that included vowels. The hieroglyphic form of Meroitic was primarily used in monumental settings, for wall texts in temples or tombs. A much wider variety of texts were written in cursive, including funerary stelae, graffiti, and ostraka. Despite the fact that the alphabetic values of the script were deciphered in the early twentieth century by F. Ll. Griffith, the Meroitic language remains an enigma.[204] No bilingual inscriptions have been found of sufficient length to determine the grammatical structure of the language or to assemble a working vocabulary. As a result, our knowledge of the religion and politics of ancient Meroe is limited and must be gathered from other sources.

Meroitic society was headed by a king and included a hereditary upper class, consisting primarily of officials and priests. The clergy of the god Amun, as in Egypt, seem to

202 Many of the artifacts excavated by Garstang were eventually acquired by Sir Henry Wellcome, whose extensive collection was transferred to University College in the 1960s. See above, p. xxv.

203 Modern scholars distinguish the kingdom of Napata, which existed until the start of the third century BC, from the subsequent kingdom of Meroe. There is not, however, a discernible break between the two kingdoms.

204 Griffith used a bilingual inscription on a sacred barque from Wad Ban Naga that listed the names of its dedicants in both Meroitic and Egyptian. This allowed him to determine the sound-values for Meroitic, but very little else.

205 Many representations of
the king include not only his
queen, but his mother as well.
In their titles, both the queen
and queen-mother emphasize
their status as "king's sister."
Insufficient evidence exists
to determine the rules of
succession, with convincing
arguments having been proposed for collateral, matrilin-
eal, and patrilineal systems.

have wielded considerable wealth and power. Women, especially the mother and sisters of the king, enjoyed great prestige in the kingdom.[205] In fact, the Roman historian Pliny claimed that Meroe was ruled by women named Kandake, a misinterpretation of a title held by royal women, possibly mothers of kings, whose meaning remains unclear.

The art and architecture of the Meroitic Kingdom were extremely innovative, combining Egyptian and Meroitic forms with elements from both Graeco-Roman and central African cultures. Relief decoration in funerary and religious contexts retained a strong Egyptian influence. While the king was portrayed in pharaonic regalia in certain settings, a distinctively Meroitic costume developed as well. Buildings frequently exhibited this cultural synthesis, such as the Graeco-Roman and Egyptian style of the so-called kiosk at Naga, and the elephant sculptures decorating the sacred precinct at Musawwarat es-Sufra, indicative of African inspiration.

Syncretism also distinguished the Meroitic pantheon, which contained numerous uniquely Nubian deities alongside Egyptian gods such as Amun and Isis. Pre-eminent in the pantheon, as in Egypt, was Amun, most often in his ram-headed incarnation.[206] Apedemak, a bellicose lion-god, occupied the second position in the divine hierarchy and was venerated in temples throughout the kingdom, most notably at Musawwarat es-Sufra and Naga. At the latter sanctuary, Apedemak seems to have been assimilated with Serapis, the Hellenistic god who was himself a combination of Osiris and Apis.

206 During the Napatan
Period, many distinct local
incarnations of Amun were
recognized, often differentiat-
ed by their crowns, although
Amun of Gebel Barkal was
paramount.

The erosion of Egyptian influence in Meroe is especially apparent in funerary practice. Some fifty pyramids, marking interments of kings, queens, and princes, were built along two desert ridges east of the city at Begarawiya.[207] The Meroitic pyramid, which evolved during the Napatan Kingdom, was based on the small monuments built by non-royal Egyptians at Thebes. Elite and royal burials at Meroe continued some Egyptian practices, notably interior tomb decoration and mummification. Other Egyptian funerary traditions, such as inclusion of shabti figures and canopic jars, were gradually abandoned in favor of Nubian customs, including the sacrificial burial of retainers along with the ruler.

207 In addition, four non-
royal cemeteries ranging from
the first century BC to the
post-Meroitic period have
been identified at Begarawiya.

The Meroitic Kingdom began a gradual decline initially evidenced in the first century AD by smaller, lower quality tombs in the royal necropolis and decreased construction of monumental buildings. Grave goods contained increasingly fewer foreign items, attesting to the growing isolation of the kingdom from its previous trading contacts. The cause of Meroe's final demise is not completely clear, as it certainly resulted from a number of factors, although the primary catalyst seems to have been the emergence of the kingdom of Axum, located in what is now northern Ethiopia. After AD 200, the trading ability of Meroe was severely compromised, with Axum blocking lucrative access to the Red Sea, and nomadic tribes on the northern and eastern peripheries rendering overland roads dangerous and commerce with Roman Egypt ever more difficult. Eventually, it appears that Meroe itself was invaded and destroyed by the armies of Axum, led by King Ezana around AD 350.   BTT

78. *Ankh* inscribed for King Aspelta

Meroe
Napatan Period, reign of Aspelta,
593–568 BC
Faience
H. 23.3 cm; w. 9.9 cm; d. 2.2 cm
UC 43949

THE ANKH, the hieroglyphic symbol for life, was a common amulet in both ancient Egypt and Nubia, frequently placed in burials to endow the deceased with renewed life. Based on its size and the absence of a suspension loop, this example was most likely not intended to be used as an amulet, but perhaps to be held during a religious ceremony or presented as a votive offering.

The inscriptions on each side list the names and titles of King Aspelta, in traditional Egyptian style. Although Nubian rule in Egypt ended decades before Aspelta took the throne, the influence of pharaonic culture remained strong, particularly among royalty and the elite. It is likely that this *ankh* and two others found at Meroe[208] came from one of the temples in the city and were intended to ensure the renewed, enduring life of the king.   BTT

208 Two fragmentary amulets are in the Liverpool Museum (49.47.845–6). All three were excavated by Garstang in 1911. Two more elaborate examples currently in the British Museum (EA 54412–3), acquired from Lord Kitchener, were reportedly from the Temple of Taharqa at Gebel Barkal. Janice W. Yellin, "Amulet combining *ankh*, *djed*, *heh*, and *was*-scepter signs," in Florence Friedman, ed., *Gifts of the Nile: Ancient Egyptian Faience* (RISD, 1998) 131, 226, cat. no. 119.

79. Figure of a lion

Meroe
Meroitic Period, 275 BC–AD 350
Sandstone
H. 13.0 cm; w. (base) 7.0 cm;
l. (base) 17.9 cm
UC 43982

IN ANCIENT EGYPT, the lion symbolized royal authority, most notably in the form of the sphinx. While the animal held the same significance for the Nubians, there seem to have been many more representations of lions, in relief and in the round, extant in Meroe. The lion was sacred not only to Amun, but also to the Meroitic deities Apedemak, typically portrayed with a leonine head, and Sebiumeker and Arsenuphis, who were often accompanied by lions.

Small-scale, stylized figures such as this one have been found at several sites, including Musawwarat es-Sufra, Basa, and Wad Ban Naga, although their function remains unclear. In some cases, the figures were found near *hafirs* (reservoirs), suggesting apotropaic or fertility connotations. Lion heads occasionally decorated waterspouts, a feature with Egyptian prototypes (see cat. no. 123).   BTT

80. Amun Temple seal

Meroe[209]
Meroitic Period, 275 BC–AD 350[210]
Bronze
H. 4.4 cm; w. 3.2 cm; d. 3.4 cm
UC 43960

THIS ELABORATE bronze seal, in the form of an openwork pyramid with suspension loop, contains figures of a crocodile and the ram manifestation of Amun. The finely modeled ram bears the customary attributes of the god, including solar disk with crowned uraeus, tripartite wig, and large, curled horns. The crocodile, also carefully detailed, is secondary to the ram in neither position nor size. Since crocodiles are not usually associated with Amun, it is likely that the combination was particular to the cult at Meroe.

The inscription on the base of the seal refers to the house, or temple, of Amun, but does not provide a specific name or title. A seal or official insignia was typically a very personal item, and the lack of individualization in this instance suggests that the seal was associated with the temple itself. BTT

209 Although some records indicate that the seal was discovered by John Garstang in 1911 in Palace 294 at Meroe, it is more likely that it was among a group of bronzes found in three rooms of Palace 924 in 1913. Frances Welsh, "A bronze seal from Meroe in the Petrie Museum, London," *JEA* 88 (2002): 244.
210 If the seal was, in fact, discovered in Palace 924, its deposition would date to the second century BC. The date of its manufacture remains uncertain.

81. Inscription fragment

Meroe
Meroitic Period, 275 BC–AD 350
Sandstone
H. 9.4 cm; w. 7.6 cm; d. 8.6 cm
UC 44174

THIS FRAGMENT of stone preserves a
portion of text inscribed in the Meroitic language, which existed solely in
a spoken form prior to the second century BC, when a distinctive writing
system was derived from the Egyptian
hieroglyphic and demotic scripts. The
Meroitic system differed dramatically
from the Egyptian with its multitude
of superfluous elements, representing
consonantal groups and determina-
tives, without any vowel signs. In contrast, Meroitic relied upon an alphabet consisting of twenty-three signs,
including vowels.

A wide variety of inscriptions in
Meroitic survive, including royal decrees, funerary texts, and captions in
decorative scenes. In spite of the wealth
of source material, translation of the
Meroitic language has eluded modern
scholars. The script was deciphered
early in the twentieth century by F. Ll.
Griffith, but with no bilingual inscription for comparison, with no Meroitic Rosetta Stone, the words themselves cannot be translated.   BTT

82. Thumb ring

Meroe
Meroitic Period, 275 BC–AD 350
Siltstone
H. 4.0 cm; diam. 4.2 cm
UC 43962

NUBIA WAS SO FAMED for its archers that it was called "the Land of the Bow." Representations of platoons of Nubian archers and individual bowmen are found not only in Egyptian art, but also in the art of the Aegean and Classical worlds.[211]

Bows were often strung so tightly that archers would wear stone rings over their thumbs so that they would not be cut while drawing the bowstring to shoot. These rings were often made of brightly colored or exotic stones, and may well have been marks of status; one is even depicted on the thumb of a king in a famous bronze statue from Tabo, now in Khartoum.[212]   PL

211 Ladislas Bugner, ed., *The Image of the Black in Western Art I: From the Pharaohs to the Fall of the Roman Empire* (Cambridge, 1976) 42–7, 136, 150, 275.
212 Khartoum, SNM 24705. D. Wildung, *Sudan: Ancient Kingdoms of the Nile* (Paris/New York, 1997) 244–5.

83. Ram pendant

Meroe
Meroitic Period, 275 BC–AD 350
Faience
H. 2.0 cm; w. 5.0 cm; l. 9.0 cm
UC 44593

THE RAM PENDANT has a long life in Nubia, first appearing as a royal insignia during the Twenty-fifth Dynasty, and continuing into the post-Meroitic, or X-group, Period. It is most frequently found as an element of royal regalia worn on a thick chain or cord, with one pendant at the base of the throat, flanked by two others on either side of the neck. Associated with the Nubian kings of Egypt, in some instances, it was erased by their Saite successors.[213] The combination of the sun disk and the ram of Amun clearly evokes Amun-Re, the chief deity of the Napatan Dynasty.

Other images of ram-headed sun disks were used as decorative elements in diadems, rings, amulets, and costume appliqués. This sizable example is composed of the pale blue-green, loosely cemented faience typical of the later Meroitic Period. Its large size and flat back suggest that it was an architectural inlay, rather than an amulet or personal ornament.[214] PL

213 Cf. a bronze figurine of Taharqa in the Carlos Collection, MCCM 2001.16.1.
214 For a similar example from Meroe, cf. Dietrich Wildung, *Sudan: Ancient Kingdoms of the Nile* (Paris and New York, 1997) 182.

84. Fragment of a zodiac

Meroe

Meroitic Period, 275 BC–AD 350

Faience

H. 8.9 cm; w. 9.8 cm; d. 1.8 cm

UC 43929

THIS WEDGE-SHAPED SECTION comes from a circular representation of the zodiac, with what appears to be a goat depicting Aries and a man holding an eel or large fish, standing for Pisces. The original disk would have been over eighteen centimeters in diameter, with all twelve signs of the Roman zodiac, the same that we use today, ranged around a central medallion. The fact that it is the Roman, rather than Egyptian, zodiac demonstrates the far-reaching impact of Roman astrology. Roman zodiacs have also been discovered in Syria-Palestine and Anatolia.[215]   PL

215 A. Ovadiah and S. Mucznik, "A Fragmentary Roman Zodiac and Horoscope from Caesarea Maritima." *LA* 46 (1996): 375–380.

85. Meroitic pottery

Meroe
Meroitic Period, 275 BC–AD 350
Marl clay ceramic, pigment

A. Cup
H. 18.0 cm; diam. 15.0 cm
UC 44417

B. Bowl
H. 11.7 cm; rim diam. 22.3 cm
UC 30224

THE POTTERY from late Meroitic Period Nubia is famed for its beautiful painting. In part, it was inspired by painted pottery imported from Greece and Rome. Some of the decorative elements in Meroitic ceramics, such as the vine leaf motif, were taken directly from Classical sources. Other motifs are of local Nubian or Egyptian origin, incorporated in inventive ways. The clay used to make these vessels is a very fine marl, porcelain-like clay which was thrown to such a thinness that the vessels are designated "eggshell ware."

The cup (A) even appears to derive its shape from an ostrich egg, which was frequently used as a drinking vessel in Nubia. Its exterior is decorated with the *ankh*, the Egyptian, and later, Nubian, symbol of life. The vines and grape leaves on the large bowl (B) recall those found on Classical ceramics, but are used here in a very different and aesthetically sophisticated way. Much of our knowledge of Meroitic painted pottery relates to provincial sites, which do not display the same degree of technical and artistic proficiency as these examples.[216]

PL

216 A. A. el-Hassan, *Religious Motifs and Meroitic Painted and Stamped Pottery* (Oxford, 2004).

WEIGHTS AND MEASURES

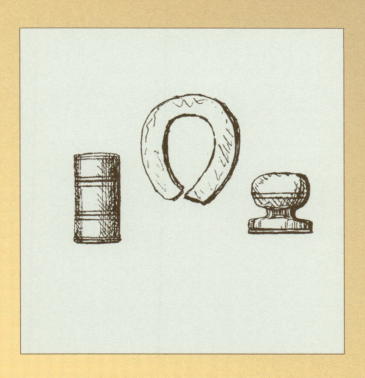

WEIGHTS and MEASURES

OF ALL THE MANY AREAS to which Petrie dedicated his life, measurements must rank among the first, though also as the one least alluring to his successors. The statistical crunch of massed tabulated data must have satisfied his computing brain as deeply as it mystifies and alienates historians trained for the verbal or the visual. Everywhere in his notes he left series of numbers and calculations, from reconstructing ancient standards of weight to paying his excavators a fair wage. In a sense, Petrie anticipates post-war sociological schools of history, with their emphasis on the quantifiable and the details of accountancy records. This mathematical attitude to life extends past the study of ancient times to the daily life of the excavator. Unwittingly or not, the Petrie notebooks would provide ideal material for a study of archaeological practice, the impact of excavating on local communities, the wage rates, and object valuations across five decades of archaeology in Egypt. Not surprisingly then, Petrie the computing wizard and pre-eminently practical worker, was the only archaeologist of Egypt to tackle in detail the ground where mathematics meets life, the systems used by accountants and traders in ancient societies to measure volume and weight.[217]

217 W. M. F. Petrie, *Ancient Weights and Measures* (London, 1926).

Without measuring standards, estate management and trade are vulnerable to fraud and injustice: rough measures are precisely rough justice, as, without some means of external control, the trader or accountant cannot know whether one batch of grain or metal or cloth is precisely the same as the last or the next. In turn, exact measurement is conceived as a metaphor for justice: judgement of the dead person is depicted as the weighing of the heart against the measure of truth, on the same scales that would have been used to weigh precious metal in the New Kingdom economy. In his focus on metrology, Petrie had identified the essential institution of any large-scale economy, and he prepared the ground for progress in this fundamental history, in which human society develops ever more accurate means of checking its own activities in space and time.

Although researchers today would not use the Petrie names for ancient weights, they have confirmed the essence of his conclusions.[218] In the Old and Middle Kingdom there was a weight standard equivalent to about 12.5 to 13.5 grams, for which inscriptions indicate the name *deben*, "ring," with the qualification "(for) gold." During the same periods, there is evidence for a heavier standard of just over double the gold ring, at about 27.5 grams: manuscripts refer to a "large ring," and this would presumably have been useful for metals such as copper, less precious than gold or silver but still of relatively high value.

218 See especially M.-A. Cour-Marty, "Les Poids Égyptiens, de Précieux Jalons Archéologiques" *CRIPEL* 12 (1990):17–55.

Under the Twelfth Dynasty, there is evidence for an alternative system, possibly adapted from exchange values in use abroad: units of 17.5 and just under 90 grams can be interpreted as double and tenfold multiples of a basic nine gram weight. By the mid-Eighteenth Dynasty, that newer standard has effectively replaced the earlier 13.5/27 gram system, and *deben* now refers to a weight of 90 grams, divided into ten sub-units, called *qedet*, of around nine grams each. The *deben/qedet* system seems to have remained in force down to the Twenty-sixth Dynasty, to judge from the weights retrieved by Petrie from the Greek colony of that date at Naukratis (see above, pp. 92–3).

Throughout this time-span, a different system seems to have operated in western Asia, based on eight grams rather than the Egyptian nine: wherever traders from both areas operated, there must have been calculations of exchange in daily economic life, but the intricacies of such practice remain to be studied. Other systems operated in other traditions, for example in ancient Greece and Italy, complicating transactions in these cosmopolitan market places. However, little research has yet been devoted to understanding how the Egyptian weight standards were created, enforced, and maintained across the thousand kilometers of the country for so many centuries. In many respects, in our economic history of Egypt, we remain at the point to which Petrie led us a hundred years ago.

86. Weight inscribed for the treasurer Herfu

Early Dynasty 13, ca. 1775 BC
Actinolite-tremolite schist
W. 7.9 cm; d. 4.6 cm; l. 13.4 cm
UC 16366[219]

IN UNION with the architecture of its time, this weight can be recognized as a microcosm of the geometric perfection and the deceptively simple union of curving and rectilinear lines and planes. Precisely this restraint and reduction to essentials can be felt in the burial chamber of the pyramid of King Senusret III at Dahshur. The upper surface is finely inscribed in carefully spaced hieroglyphs that preserve for us either the owner or the authority behind the weight: "the leader of nobility, foremost of action, sealbearer of the king, sole companion, the treasurer Herfu, repeating life."

At this period, the treasurer was an exceptionally powerful official, second only to the vizier or overall coordinator of the administration; the treasurer administered the economic aspect of palace life, the literal translation being "the overseer of sealed things" (i.e. of commodities of high enough value to be sealed). Weighing, and the control of measuring standards, might naturally have fallen within the duties of the treasurer. This magnificent example has been personalized by the addition of the name; in the absence of any documented context, it is not known whether it survived in a tomb, or as an object discarded or lost on a town site. The treasurer Herfu is also known from a block-statue in the Brooklyn Museum, and from scarab-shaped seal-amulets.[220]

SQ

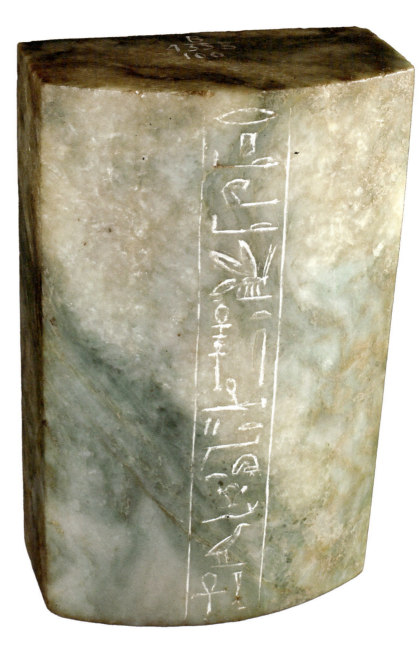

219 W. M. F. Petrie, *Ancient Weights and Measures* (London, 1926) 19, pl. 7, no. 4355. A photograph in the Petrie Museum archive confirms the evidence of a laconic note in the Petrie journals in Oxford that this weight was acquired during his 1908–9 winter season of excavation at Thebes.
220 Wolfram Grajetzki, *Die hochsten Beamten der ägyptischen Zentralverwaltung zur Zeit des mittleren Reiches* (Berlin, 2000) 55, no. II.18.

**87. Weight of six "rings"
on the gold standard**
Koptos
Middle Kingdom, 2025–1750 BC
Banded gneiss
W. 3.8 cm; d. 2.1 cm; l. 4.3 cm
UC 34793[221]

BEFORE THE NEW KINGDOM, the dominant form for the weight was a cuboid block with rounded upper surface, well illustrated here. The curving plane bears a deep-cut hieroglyphic inscription identifying it as "6 rings (for) gold(-weighing)." This is one of the relatively rare inscribed examples, confirming the "gold ring" as a unit of about 12.5–13.5 grams. Although the precise provenance is not recorded, it is significant that Petrie acquired this and other weights at Koptos, for that city has the Nile port that acted as western end of a trade-route through desert valleys such as the Wadi Hammamat and beyond to the Red Sea. In Ptolemaic and Roman times, the trade reached out to India, documented in finds along the way and in Greek ostraka found at Koptos. Already in prehistoric times this route to the Hammamat gold mines played a crucial role in the development of the Egyptian state, and, though more gold was obtained from Nubia farther south, the gold of Koptos remained a major asset into the Ramesside Period and beyond: the only surviving map from ancient Egypt is a Ramesside chart of key features in the Hammamat gold mines. It is likely that this Koptos weight was used literally as a measure for gold at the city nearest to the source of the precious metal.   SQ

221 W. M. F. Petrie, *Ancient Weights and Measures* (London, 1926) pl. 7, no. 4547.

88. *Deben*-weight in the form of a hippopotamus head

Naqada, Seth Temple
Dynasty 18, 1550–1292 BC
Haematite
H. 2.5 cm; w. 3.4 cm; l. 4.8 cm
UC 29019[222]

AMONG THE ANIMAL FORMS favored for weights in the Eighteenth Dynasty, the hippopotamus head is perhaps the most striking, as well as the hardest to explain: did the sheer bulk of the hippopotamus itself suggest the form? In that case, one might have expected the whole animal, not just the head to be represented, but other weights also take head alone, as part for whole. Perhaps, though, the Egyptian word for hippopotamus, *deb*, simply evoked the sound of the word for ring-weight, *deben*. The choice of hippopotamus for a weight might have been considered particularly apt at Naqada, center of the Seth cult, where this weight was found by Petrie, for the figure of the great beast was at various periods selected as the means of depicting the anarchic character of the god Seth. However, the same form can be found among depictions of weights in the tomb of the Eighteenth Dynasty vizier Rekhmire at Thebes, farther south, and so its use was evidently not restricted to the city of Seth.

Haematite is a dense mineral, and this makes it perfect for producing weights, a function for which it was often chosen in the Eighteenth Dynasty. This example weighs 90.6 grams, within the margin of accuracy for the *deben*, or "ring"-measure in the New Kingdom and later. Along the upper lip of the hippopotamus, signs are carved to indicate the presence of ten units, being the ten *qedet* into which the *deben* was divided in New Kingdom measuring: there are ten individual strokes, and at the center, to summarize the whole, the hieroglyph for "ten." SQ

222 W. M. F. Petrie, *Naqada and Ballas* (London, 1896) 67; Petrie, *Ancient Weights and Measures* (London, 1926) 15, pl. 33, no. 3218.

89. Weight in the form of a reclining calf
Dynasty 18, 1550–1292 BC
Copper alloy with lead (?) core
H. 2.9 cm; w. 2.8 cm; l. 7.1 cm
UC 2302[223]

DURING THE NEW KINGDOM, both in Egypt and across the Near East, weights often took the form of animals, in this example a reclining calf. In hieratic, the cursive script in daily use by accountants who would be involved in weighing, the sign for *shena*, "value-unit," is indistinguishable from the sign for "herd," and this might explain the preference for herded animals such as cattle among the animal forms chosen for weights. Most of the surviving weights in animal form are cast in copper alloy, perhaps usually with a lead core for heavier material. This calf is a typically finely molded and chased piece of the period, with details of legs, folds, face, and budding horns all clearly demarcated.   SQ

223 W. M. F. Petrie, *Ancient Weights and Measures* (London, 1926) pl. 9, no. 5253.

90. Scale-arm and pans
Roman Period, 30 BC–AD 395
Copper alloy, modern string
L. 10.1 cm (balance arm)
UC 69776

THE SCALES formed an essential part of the equipment for an estate accountant as for a trader. Balances varied in intricacy from simple hand-held devices to the complex New Kingdom standing balances, as seen in depictions of the judgment of the dead in the *Book of the Dead* and other visual sources. This plain balance and its weighing pans may be a late example of the simpler, still effective, portable kit.   SQ

91. Votive cubit rod inscribed for Bakennefu

Dynasty 26, 664–525 BC
Basalt
H. 4.0 cm; w. 3.2 cm; l. 6.8 cm
UC 16374[224]

THE ESSENTIAL ancient Egyptian unit of length was the royal cubit, corresponding to about 52.5 cm, divided into seven equal palms of four fingers each. From the late Eighteenth Dynasty to the Ptolemaic Period, sacred versions of the cubit were produced as royal gifts and temple offerings.[225] They take the form of long cuboid blocks with one side cut diagonally, giving five long sides, all of which were inscribed with hieroglyphs. This fragment belongs to the right end of a temple votive cubit, and the inscription on the underside contains a funerary formula requesting offerings to Thoth, god of wisdom and writing, for a man named Bakennefu.

The inscriptions on the other sides belong to a remarkable group of compositions that amount to a compendium of religious geographical knowledge, known from fourteen other votive cubit fragments, and from Roman Period papyri, notably the Geographical Papyrus discovered by Petrie at Tanis.[226] As the Egyptians read from right to left, the Bakennefu fragment preserves the start of the inscription for each side. The upper face gives the name and purpose of the object: "the cubit according to its formula of calculation, established as potent, calculator (?) as the incantation of [Thoth]." Beneath this, on the same face of the rod, each of the twenty-eight fingers of the cubit was assigned a particular deity, starting

with the Creator-god, the sun Re, and his offspring Shu and Tefnut, preserved here. On the slanting face of the rod, in compartments aligned with the deities above, and then continuing on the rear face, all the provinces of Egypt were listed, starting with the southernmost of Upper Egypt. The slanting face of this fragment preserves the first three: Bowland (province of Elephantine), Throne of Horus (province of Edfu), Nekhen (Hierakonpolis). The rear face here preserves, as on other sources, the phrase "division of the domain of the king," as a title of the province-list, and then the continuation of the list with the seventh and eighth provinces of Lower Egypt: "west harpoon-spur" (Wadi Natrun, west of the Delta) and "east harpoon-spur" (Wadi Tumilat, east of the Delta). For each province the same linear measurement is given, "1 cubit 3 palms," perhaps an ideal Nile flood height (compare with cat. no. 1). The short front side of the rod, under the sloping face, gave the names of sacred divisions of the cubit,

not found in practice in accountancy documents, starting with the whole unit as partly preserved here "royal [cubit];" under these, mathematical fractions are listed, here "1/2, 1/3, ..."

Votive cubits condense into a tight three-dimensional form a great array of exact, formalized knowledge, an ancient precursor to the Greek and Arabic astrolabe or the modern multi-function calculator. The Bakennefu cubit is the only known example with both the extended inscriptions of temple cubits and a funerary formula for a named individual. Like many officials before and after, he may have sought to secure his own identity for eternity through the mastery of the sacred sciences of Thoth.   SQ

224 W. M. F. Petrie, *Ancient Weights and Measures* (London, 1926) 40, pl. 24.
225 A. Schlott-Schwab, *Die Ausmasse Ägyptens nach altägyptischen Texten* (Wiesbaden, 1981).
226 F. Ll. Griffith and W. M. F. Petrie, *Two Hieroglyphic Papyri from Tanis* (London, 1889).

92. Shadow-clock inscribed for Senusheri

Probably from Koptos
Early Ptolemaic Period, ca. 275 BC
Basalt
H. 9.0 cm; w. 4.8 cm; l. 13.8 cm
UC 16376[227]

AS IN OTHER ANCIENT and more recent societies, the shadow-clock was used in ancient Egypt to measure time within the sunlit hours of a day, especially important in ritual. This fragment is one of the few surviving examples of a time-measuring device small enough to be portable. Although such moveable measurers may have been more convenient, relocation would raise problems, as each move would require a new positioning of the object: a sundial must be oriented in a certain way (normally east-west) and the sundial must be placed absolutely horizontal on its ground. In order to guarantee the level, the time-measurer needed to hang a plumb from a line attached to the plinth of the clock. For orientation, it might be more difficult to find a solution.

This example preserves the diagonal slope marked with the scale of hours, divided by vertical lines across the slope to distinguish between the seasons with their different day-lengths. At the top of the slope, there is a broad rectangular slot for another element; the complete clock would have included at the foot facing the slope a vertical column or slab from which the shadow would be cast.

The inscription around the base does not refer to the function of the object, but names instead its owner or donor, a man named Senusheri. On the preserved vertical face of the clock, he is shown worshipping a fal-con-headed deity identified in hiero-glyphs as "Horus son of Isis and son of Osiris." The same man is known from two statue fragments, one excavated by Petrie at Koptos (Cairo CG 70031), the other of unknown origin, probably from the nearby town of Qus (British Museum EA 1668).[228] From the inscriptions on the statues we know that Senusheri held high office in the reign of Ptolemy II, managing the estates of his queen, Arsinoe.[229] Beginning beneath the depiction of worship of Horus, the sequence of titles inscribed on the shadow-clock is almost identical to that on the Koptos statue, allowing the full set to be reconstructed as follows (with the parts restored from the Koptos statue in square brackets):

the revered, courtier unique in affection (of the king), god's servant of Osiris, Horus and Isis of the Temple of Offerings, servant of the gods of the Temple of Offerings, [of Isis, bringer of the Osiris-image amid the province of Koptos, of the southern lion] and the northern [lion], the twin lions, daughter and son of Re amid Qus, god's servant of Isis [the great,] mother of [the god], who is over the great place, god's servant of Ptah-Sokar-Osiris the great god amid the Secret Sanctuary, god's servant of Osiris foremost of the pavilion of the god, god's servant of Osiris of Koptos foremost of the Temple of Gold, Senusheri.

These titles reveal the Osiris cults at Koptos as the focus of activity for Senusheri. The main deity of the city was Min, but there was a place of worship for Osiris, named, as at other cities, the Temple of Offerings. According to inscriptions at Dendera, in each temple of Egypt, images of the funerary deities Osiris and Sokar were made every winter in a special temple area called the Temple of Gold, and the images from the previous year interred. The priestly titles of Senusheri suggest a role for this shadow-clock within his management of ritual and new constructions at Koptos for Horus and his parents, Isis and Osiris.   SQ

227 W. M. F. Petrie, *Ancient Weights and Measures* (London, 1926) 45, pl. 25.
228 P. Derchain, *Les Impondérables de l'Hellénisation* (Turnhout, 2000) 27–29.
229 According to Quaegebeur and Derchain, most probably Arsinoe II. Ibid.

DAILY LIFE

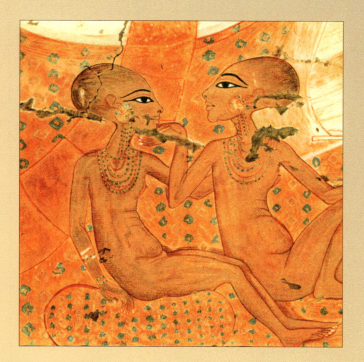

93. Chair leg
Gurob
New Kingdom, 1550–1069 BC
Wood
H. 28.5 cm; w. 6.7 cm; d. 3.7 cm
UC 7918

SINCE ALL GOOD TIMBER had to be imported into Egypt, wooden furniture, even in the homes of the wealthiest, was scarce. From the beginning of the Dynastic Era, beds and chairs often had legs imitating those of animals[230] that inspired later versions in the Classical age and in late eighteenth and early nineteenth century Europe and America. The lion-leg chair is familiar to us from numerous New Kingdom examples and representations, including those from the tombs of Yuya and Tuya[231] and Tutankhamen.[232]

This beautifully carved leg, depicting the hind leg of a feline, is extremely naturalistic, showing even the bulging tendons. It would have been one of a pair at the back of the chair, while the straight forelegs would have been in the front. The leg rests on a series of stacked pads that would have protected the feet from wear and damage. Representations occasionally show furniture legs standing on truncated stone pyramids for further protection. The tang at the top would have been pegged into the seat. Such a leg would have been fitting for the throne of one of the royal women living in the *harim*, located at Gurob during the New Kingdom. One side of the leg is badly burned, like many other artifacts excavated at Gurob, perhaps resulting from the destruction of the palace.   PL

230 G. Killen, *Egyptian Furniture*, vol. 1 (Warminster, 1980) 57.
231 Theodore Davis, *The Tomb of Iouiya and Touiyou* (London, 1907) pls. 33–6.
232 Howard Carter and Arthur Mace, *The Discovery of the Tomb of Tutankhamun* (London, 1923) 203–8.

94. Gaming-board
Possibly from Naqada
Early Dynastic Period, ca. 3000 BC
Limestone
H. 4.1 cm; diam. 29.5 cm
UC 20453

THIS BROAD LIMESTONE disk is sculpted on one side with a depiction of a snake, head at center, three coils to the body, and tail at the outside near a triangular protrusion pierced for suspension. Head and tail are incised with criss-cross lines. The body of the serpent is deeply incised at regular short intervals to create the "squares" for the board-game *mehen*, "the coiled." The circumstances of the find are not recorded; at least one other such gaming board was found during the work by Petrie and his col-league J. E. Quibell at Naqada and Ballas in 1894–5, with a two-coiled serpent, illustrated in the excavation report but without precise indication of find-spot.[223] Both may derive from late Predynastic or Early Dynastic burials in the area. The rules for the game are not known, and it seems not to have been used after the Old Kingdom; a depiction in a Late Period tomb chapel, copying Old Kingdom scenes, shows the serpent board apparently reinterpreted as a pot.[234]   SQ

233 W. M. F. Petrie and James *Quibell, Naqada and Ballas* (London, 1896) pl. 43.
234 K. Kuhlmann, *Das Grab des Ibi, Obergutsverwalters der Gottesgemahlin des Amun (thebanisches Grab Nr. 36)* (Wiesbaden, 1983) 81–2, pl. 28. Lower register, right end, painted yellow apparently without internal board-spacings.

95. Gaming-board squares

Qau, burial 7618[235]
Early to mid-Dynasty 18, ca. 1450 BC
Faience
Largest l. 3.4 cm; w. 2.9 cm
UC 26299

IN HIS LAST EXCAVATION in Egypt, Petrie supervised the recording of a cemetery near Qau, on the east bank in Upper Egypt. On January 2, 1924, the excavator Aly Omar uncovered a shaft tomb three meters deep, with a chamber that had been partly robbed in antiquity, though still with many of the original grave goods. The coffin did not survive the damp ground, with only fragments of faience inlay preserved. However, over the bones, so originally laid on the coffin or directly on the body itself, Aly Omar found these fifteen green glazed faience square plaques, and fragments of four more, evidently from a gaming-board, the wooden frame of which had long since decayed.[236]

Since only nineteen squares survive, it is not certain whether the gaming-board was for games of thirty squares, such as Egyptian *senet*, or a combination of that with the board for twenty squares on the underside. The low number might suggest that the board contained only one side, with just twenty squares, as reconstructed here, although the New Kingdom norm seems to have been single-sided thirty or double-sided thirty-and-twenty boards.[237] Evidence for twenty-square games first appears in Egypt during the Second Intermediate Period, varying in layout, with either a rectangle of 3x4 and a central line of the remaining 8, or a 3x3 block at one end, and one square either side of the central line, one short of the end.

No rules for games survive, and each board-type could have been used for many different games, much as the same board can be used for chess and draughts (checkers) today. Depic-tions indicate that games were for two players at a time, and some boards have sets of gaming-pieces in different shapes, usually one set of taller pieces and one set of squat cylinders (see cat. no. 96). Presumably the general object of each game was to move all of your own pieces along some route from one end of the board to the other ahead of your opponent. Although some dice have been found in New Kingdom contexts, the usual means of deciding how many squares to move a piece seems to have been by throwing a set of double-sided sticks of different lengths.

On thirty-square boards, certain squares sometimes bear depictions, presumably to indicate an advantage or disadvantage. As in medieval European depictions of chess, the games of chance took on a religious dimension as allegories for life and death as a game of fate for each individual: in the corpus of New Kingdom funerary compositions known as the *Book of the Dead*, the long title for Chapter 17 includes the aim of the deceased "taking the form of any form he wishes to take there, and to play *senet* and to dwell in the pavilion," and the corresponding illustration shows him seated in a pavilion and moving a gaming piece on a thirty-square board. This religious aspect might have been one reason for including gaming-boards among the daily life objects placed in the tomb during the Eighteenth Dynasty.   SQ

235 Not in the publication of the excavation; information from the tomb card in the Petrie Museum.
236 Other items in the chamber included fragments of a copper alloy dagger-blade, and pottery that allowed the group to be dated to the early New Kingdom, a period when more expensive objects of daily life were often placed in the burial of, presumably, their lifetime owners. The excavation team identified the body as that of a man.
237 *Jouer dans l'Antiquité* (Marseilles, 1991). In western Asia, fewer examples have survived, though other variations on the twenty-square layout can be seen among the finds from the Royal Treasures of Ur in Iraq, going back almost a thousand years earlier to 2400 BC, at a time when only thirty-square boards are known from Egypt.

96. Sets of gaming-pieces

Dynasty 18, 1550–1292 BC
Faience
H. 4.4 cm; diam. 2.9 cm
(set of nine); H. 2.2 cm; diam. 2.4 cm
(set of four)
UC 8681 (set of nine), 8682
(set of four)[238]

PETRIE ACQUIRED these two sets of gaming-pieces together, and it is possible that they belong to a single set. Where preserved, in undisturbed rich burials, board game equipment generally includes two sets of distinctly shaped pieces, one set for each player. The sets may be of different materials, heights (as here), or shapes. These tapering cylinders with flared base have the typical bulbous tip to make the pieces easier to hold when moving.   SQ

238 W. M. F. Petrie, *Objects of Daily Use* (London, 1927) 53, nos. 48–56, pl. 48.

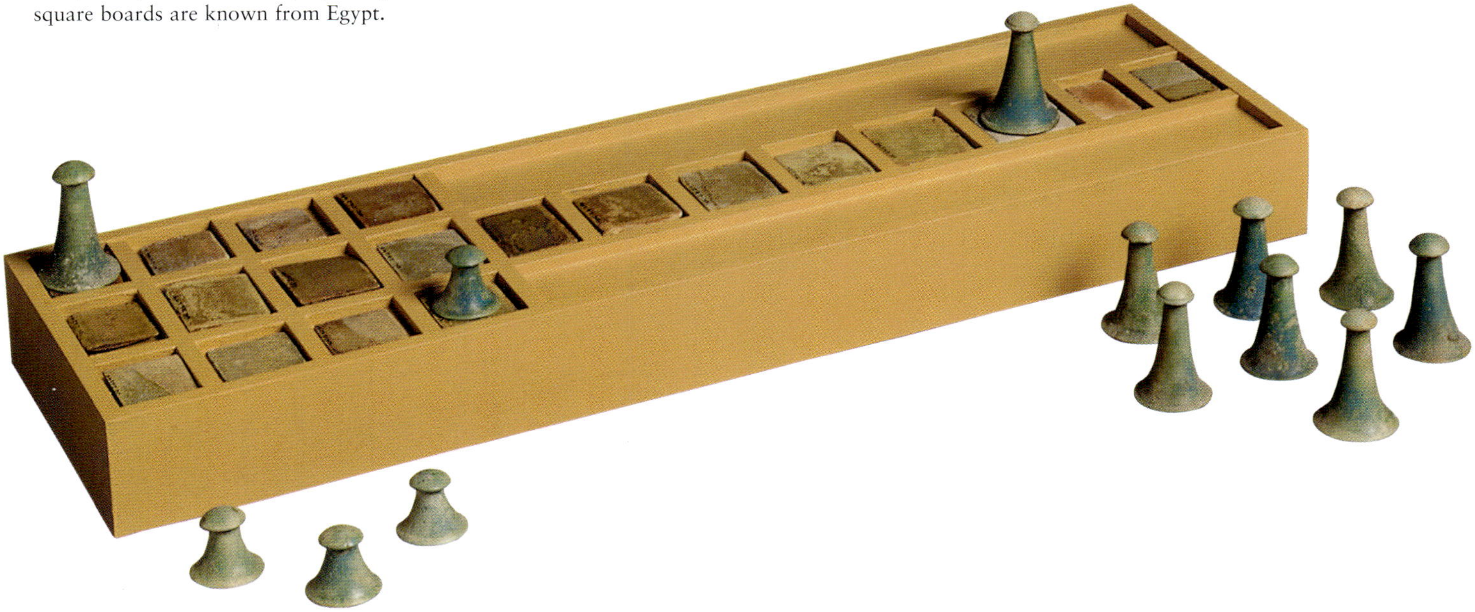

97. *Menat* amulet

Gurob

New Kingdom, 1550–1069 BC

Wood

H. 9.5 cm; w. 3.2 cm; d. 0.4 cm

UC 16759

MENATS, or counterweights, originally worn to keep heavy necklaces in place, eventually became more decorative than the necklaces themselves. They could also be rendered in miniature as amulets, or over-size, as in this example. Associated with the goddess Hathor, *menats* were often given by her priestesses as offerings to the deceased;[239] however, as one was found in the palace of Amenhotep III at Malkata, it is not surprising that one should turn up at Gurob.

This finely carved wooden example is similar to others known in bronze and faience. The goddess is shown wearing a beaded broad collar and choker, a curled wig, and vulture headdress. Atop her head is a sun disk, which is pierced by two holes through which the threads of the necklace would have been strung. PL

239 Peter Lacovara, "Counterpoise," in Sue D'Auria, Peter Lacovara, and Catharine Roehrig, eds. *Mummies and Magic: the Funerary Arts of Ancient Egypt* (Boston, 1988) 135–6, cat. no. 72.

128

98. Vessel in the shape of an ointment horn

Gerzeh, tomb 20
Naqada I (Amratian) Period,
4200–3700 BC
Nile clay ceramic
L. 17.4 cm; diam. 5.4 cm
UC 10736

BECAUSE OF THEIR SHAPE and impermeability, cow horns were often used as feeders, medicine droppers, and ointment vessels in the ancient world. This remarkable object imitates a horn in black-burnished pottery, with the addition of a cow's head with inlaid bead eyes at the tip. A hole with a ceramic plug lies just below the head, serving for both the introduction and dispensing of the contents. The plug is pierced and originally may have been threaded with a leather thong to keep it in place.

Petrie discovered this horn in a burial,[240] clasped in the hands of the deceased, close to the face. The placement might be a sign of hope that the medicinal power of the horn might heal the ailment of the deceased. The piece probably dates to the Naqada I Period, which saw the production of a number of these theriomorphic, or animal-shaped, vessels in fine, burnished, Nile-silt wares. Although horn vessels, both real and imitation, are found throughout the Dynastic Period, this early example illustrates the longevity of that tradition.   PL

240 W. M. F. Petrie, *The Labyrinth, Gerzeh and Mazghuneh* (London, 1912) 23.

99. Razor

Dynasty 18, 1550–1292 BC
Bronze
L. 9.4 cm; w. 2.7 cm; d. 0.4 cm
UC 30135

THIS FINELY CRAFTED RAZOR is embellished with a handle cast in the shape of a monkey that has just picked a cluster of dom palm nuts. The Egyptians often depicted monkeys trying to grab the sweet fruits of the branching palm. It is clearly an appropriate theme, since so many toilet articles seem to evoke exotic peoples and creatures. The crescent shaped blade of the razor has been hammered and sharpened, indicating that this exceptional piece was actually used for shaving.[241]

PL

241 W. Vivian Davies, "Razor," in Edward Brovarski, Susan K. Doll, and Rita E. Freed, eds. *Egypt's Golden Age: the Art of Living in the New Kingdom* (Boston, 1982) 192–3, cat. no. 224.

100. Cosmetic implement
Dynasty 18, 1550–1292 BC
Bronze
H. 3.5 cm; l. 5.4 cm
UC 26935

101.
Tweezers
Dynasty 18, 1550–1292 BC
Copper alloy, gold, silver
H. 1.9 cm; l. 6.4 cm; w. 1.8 cm
UC 8529

This pair of tweezers is cleverly fashioned in the form of a gazelle being chased by a hound. The figure of the dog gained ground or was outdistanced as the implement was opened and closed.[243] The dog wears a collar made of inlaid gold bands bordering silver circles.   PL

243 The exact function of the implement remains unclear. See Arielle Kozloff in Arielle Kozloff and Betsy Bryan, *Egypt's Dazzling Sun: Amenhotep III and his World* (Cleveland, 1992) 428, cat. no. 115.

THIS IMPLEMENT may have been used as tweezers or a curling iron, perhaps to arrange the tresses on a wig.[242] Horses were first imported into Egypt from western Asia at the beginning of the New Kingdom and were still quite a novelty when this item was produced. The horse here is adorned as one would be today for the most spectacular European coronation. It sports ostrich plumes atop its head and wears a lotus petal collar and spotted horse blanket. The front legs of the horse are outstretched in a full, flying gallop, resting in a pivoting sleeve that could have crimped hair or plucked something unwanted.

PL

242 Rita Freed, "Toilette implement in the shape of a horse," in Edward Brovarski, Susan K. Doll, and Rita E. Freed, eds. *Egypt's Golden Age: the Art of Living in the New Kingdom* (Boston, 1982) 195, cat. no. 227.

102. Cosmetic spoon with images of Bes

Sedment, tomb of Mena
Dynasty 18, 1550–1292 BC
Wood, pigment
L. 17.3 cm; w. 5.9 cm
UC 14366

THE HOUSEHOLD GOD BES was portrayed as a bandy-legged dwarf, with a large head, broad nose, furrowed brow, and leonine features, including a long mane, feline ears, and panting tongue. The fearsome aspects of his depiction served in his role as protector of the home and of women, though his comical aspects, such as the rotund belly emphasized on this example, made him quite appealing. Because of his association with women, the image of Bes frequently decorated cosmetic equipment.

This particular spoon, found in the tomb of Mena, mayor of Herakleopolis Magna,[244] was an appropriate funerary offering due to the association of cosmetics with renewal, the green coloring infilling the carved areas, and the overall shape of the piece, resembling the *ankh*, symbol of life. PL

244 Édouard Naville, *Ahnas el Medineh (Heracleopolis Magna)* (London, 1894) 12–3.

103. Cosmetic spoon with image of a Libyan

New Kingdom, 1550–1069 BC
Glass frit ("Egyptian blue")
H. 4.3 cm; w. 3.4 cm; d. 0.5 cm
UC 45371

ALTHOUGH ONLY FRAGMENTARY, the outstanding craftsmanship of this piece is clearly evident. As with many examples of cosmetic equipment, a foreign servant is depicted bearing the weight of the spoon on his shoulders (see cat. no. 104). His long hair, short beard, and cross-strapped, embroidered kilt identify him as a Libyan. Frit is a brittle and easily broken material suggesting that this object was not intended to be functional, but was specifically a grave or temple offering.

PL

104. **Cosmetic dish in the form of a Nubian girl**
Thebes
Dynasty 18, 1550–1292 BC
Wood
H. 15.5 cm; w. 4.3 cm; d. 8.7 cm
UC 14210

THIS EXQUISITE wooden sculpture is one of the prized pieces of the Petrie Museum collection and was one of Petrie's personal favorites. He remarked that "the detail of this statuette is better than any other such work; the perfect pose of the attitude, the poise of the head, the fullness of the muscles, the innocent gravity of the expression, are all excellent."[245] Indeed, the artist here certainly triumphed over the genre, representing the little Nubian girl, not as an exotic curiosity, but as an individual with great dignity. Such cosmetic vessels often depict nude girls to emphasize youth and beauty. The fine ebony wood, a product of Nubia, may have inspired the choice of the figure. Her head is shaven except for a number of circular tufts of hair, a coiffure associated with the Nubians, but also popular among young Egyptian women in the Eighteenth Dynasty.

The figure faces forward with both arms outstretched, holding a large, footed dish. Her feet are placed so that the left foot is very slightly in advance of the right. A monkey balances the dish on its head to provide stability, to evoke the lands of the south, and also, perhaps to contrast a little humor with the grave expression of the serving girl.   PL

245 W. M. F. Petrie, *The Arts and Crafts of Ancient Egypt* (London, 1909) 43.

105. Mirror

New Kingdom, 1550–1069 BC
Bronze
L. 19.0 cm; w. 10.2 cm
UC 58738

IN ADDITION to being functional, mirrors, which capture the likeness of an individual, were thought to be haunts of the soul, and so were frequently included in tombs. The word for mirror, *ankh*, is the same in Egyptian as that for life. Most mirror disks in the New Kingdom were of highly polished bronze, so perhaps the reflection would be a reminder of the transformation of the face into the golden skin of the god Osiris in the next life. Furthermore, the oval shape of the mirror evoked the orb of the rising sun, again, symbolizing the hope of resurrection.

In this instance, the tang of the mirror disk is set in a handle that terminates in a stylized papyrus umbel, yet another regenerative emblem. The braided handle occurred frequently in the early Eighteenth Dynasty, with a number of examples known from Nubia. They may represent mirror handles made of perishable materials or a covering placed over the mirror. In many cases, these mirrors have been found with traces of fabric over them in which they were wrapped for burial.   PL

106. Earring

New Kingdom, 1550–1069 BC
Gold
Diam. 3.5 cm; d. 0.8 cm
UC 38242

THIS FORM of ornament became popular in the New Kingdom, for adorning both hair and ears. Smaller versions of this shape in carnelian, jasper, faience, glass, and shell are often found in multiples of graduated sizes, and have been suggested to be "hairrings," strung along braids of hair.[246]

Larger gold examples, however, were worn as earrings, often in combination with other decorative elements. Earrings first appeared for men and women at the beginning of the New Kingdom, derived from jewelry worn by Nubians. This example is made of sheet gold, wrapped to form a tube, and capped on the ends, with two strands of gold wire braided around the circumference at the outermost edge. Earrings with a braided wire at the equator, as in this case, were imitated in other media.[247]   PL

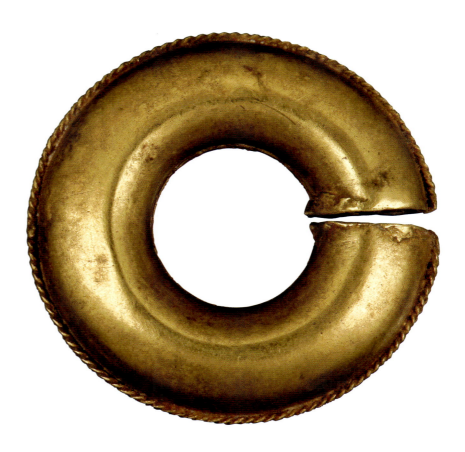

246 Cyril Aldred, *Jewels of the Pharaohs: Egyptian Jewelry of the Dynastic Period* (London, 1971) 142.
247 Carol Andrews, *Ancient Egyptian Jewelry* (London, 1990) 116–7.

107. Cylinder pendant

Harageh
Dynasty 12, reign of Amenemhet III,
1831–1786 BC
Gold, copper
L. 5.4 cm; diam. 1.2 cm
UC 6482

THE CYLINDER PENDANT is a unique type of amulet that first appears in the Middle Kingdom, having either a solid core composed of a single piece of stone, or stacks of alternating stone and gold bands. Other cases such as this, are hollow, with removable end caps.[248] While later cylinders seem to have held scraps of papyrus with prayers written on them,[249] there was no evidence of this in earlier specimens. This cylinder contained three copper balls and some organic residue, perhaps placed there to make a sound as the wearer moved.

The exterior of this tube is covered in granulation, a decorative technique often used on these pendants, which may have originally derived from Mesopotamia. In the process of granulation, tiny beads of gold are adhered to the surface with a copper flux and then fired, in order to fuse them to the underlying substrate.[250] It is still unclear how such minute and perfect gold balls were made.   PL

248 Carol Andrews, *Ancient Egyptian Jewelry* (London, 1990) 171–3.
249 Ibid., 173.
250 Christine Lilyquist, "Granulation and Glass: Chronological and Stylistic Investigations at Selected Sites, ca. 2500–1400 B. C. E." *BASOR* 290–291 (1993): 29–94.

108. Necklace

Dynasty 12, 1985–1773 BC
Gold, amethyst
L. 46.0 cm
UC 8971

THE GOLD COWROID that forms the central element of this reconstructed necklace was a motif found in a number of types of Egyptian jewelry. It was worn as an independent decorative element or in groups, as part of necklace clasps and frequently on girdles, in ornaments generally associated with women. The shape was derived from the shell of the cowrie, a mollusk found in the Red Sea. Examples of actual shells and imitations in faience, gold, and silver are known. There is even an instance, dating to the Middle Kingdom, of real shells that were covered with silver leaf.[251] The backs of the shells were usually cut off to form a flat open bead.

The fine quality amethyst here is of a type mined in the Wadi el-Hudi and predominantly used in the Middle Kingdom.[252] The deep purple of these beads was highly sought after, since most Egyptian amethyst is a rather pale, washed-out color. Given that amethyst is a particularly hard stone to carve, the small, amuletic beads on this strand in the shape of a falcon and sphinx are rendered in a rather summary way.   PL

251 Found in "Giza Pit 77625 on top of large wooden anthropoid coffin." Now in the Museum of Fine Arts, Boston (29-12-240, 29-12-240G).
252 Ashraf Sadek, *The Amethyst Mining Inscriptions of Wadi el-Hudi, Part I: Text* (Warminster, 1980).

109. Shell pendant and bracelet[253]

Middle Kingdom, 2055–1650 BC
Silver

A. Pendant
H. 4.3 cm; w. 3.7 cm; d. 0.9 cm
UC 25971a

B. Bracelet
Diam. 7.0 cm
UC 25971b

THESE ARE TWO classic forms of Middle Kingdom jewelry, notable for their streamlined elegance. Shell pendants, imitating freshwater oyster shells, were worn as jewelry at this time, occasionally inscribed with the king's cartouche.[254] Imitation gold and silver shells have been found worn singly as pendants, or in multiples on necklaces.

Another ornament popular at this time was the reef-knot bracelet. This remarkably simple concept consisted of two flattened loops of wire that are threaded through their wide ends. This not only made the bracelet adjustable, but also called to mind the knot representing the union of Egypt, the Two Lands. At first restricted to royal usage, this motif became popular on scarabs and jewelry from the First Intermediate Period (2160–2055 BC) onward, eventually evolving into the famous "knot of Heracles."[255]

PL

253 Identified as a single item in W. M. F. Petrie, *Objects of Daily Use* (London, 1927) 4, pl. 3, no. 32.
254 Cyril Aldred, "A Pearl-shell Disk of Ammenmes II," *JEA* 38 (1952): 130–2.
255 Yvonne Markowitz, "Reef Knot Bracelet," in Nancy Thomas, ed., *The American Discovery of Ancient Egypt* (Los Angeles, 1995) 142, cat. no. 50.

110. Burial equipment of a family
Abydos, tomb 817
Middle Kingdom, 2055–1650 BC

COSMETIC VESSELS AND IMPLEMENTS

A. Bowl
Anhydrite
H. 3.1 cm; diam. 11.3 cm
UC 16230

B. Kohl pot
Anhydrite
H. 4.0 cm; diam. 4.6 cm
UC 16231

C. Kohl stick
Copper
L. 5.4 cm; w. 0.4 cm
UC 16237

D. Lidded cylinder vessel
Anhydrite
H. 6.0 cm; max diam. 5.0 cm
UC 16232

E. Bottle
Calcite ("Egyptian alabaster")
H. 15.0 cm; max diam. 5.8 cm
UC 16235

F. Lid
Calcite ("Egyptian alabaster")
D. 0.7 cm; diam. 5.4 cm
UC 16233

G. Bowl
Archaic Period, ca. 3000–2686 BC
Ortho-quartzite
H. 7.4 cm; diam. 12.9 cm
UC 16240

H. Footed kohl pot
Calcite ("Egyptian alabaster")
H. 3.8 cm; diam. 2.9 cm
UC 16234

I. Model adze blade
Copper
L. 6.5 cm; w. 1.4 cm; d. 0.1 cm
UC 16238

J. Model saw blade
Copper
L. 3.1 cm; w. 1.8 cm; d. 0.1 cm
UC 16239

K. Pot
Nile clay ceramic
H. 8.0 cm; diam. 8.7 cm
UC 16236

A   B   C   D   E   F   G   H   I   J   K

ALL OF THIS MATERIAL came from the tomb of a man, woman, and child excavated by Petrie within the enclosure of Djer at Abydos.[256] A number of particularly rich tombs of the Middle Kingdom are known from Middle and northern Upper Egypt. These often comprise a variety of finely crafted, fancy stone cosmetic containers and jewelry items.[257] Particularly favored for stone vessels during this period was pale blue anhydrite, a type of gypsum sometimes erroneously called "blue marble."

Kohl pots are the most frequently encountered cosmetic container in graves of the Middle and New Kingdoms. Twelfth Dynasty examples, such as this one (B), generally have a wide shoulder, sharply tapering to a narrow foot. The rim of the vase was made separately and then fitted on, in a technique dating to the beginning of the Dynastic Period. It is unclear whether these separate rims were intended to showcase the skill of the carver, replace broken parts, or to aid in carving. In any event, great skill was required to match the body of the vessel so closely.

The alabaster cylinder vase (D) has a long history in Egypt, dating to the First Dynasty (3000–2890 BC), with even more ancient ceramic predecessors. The earliest examples were tubular with rounded rims, but by the Old Kingdom, these containers had developed their classic form, with a flat, square rim and flaring shape. They usually contained kohl, black eye paint, made from galena or simply black soot, which could be applied with an applicator, such as that seen here in copper with bulbous ends (C).

Sets of cosmetic vessels have been found in wooden boxes in tombs of the Old and Middle Kingdoms, and served as "make-up kits," containing a variety of precious oils and unguents. They were often fitted with round, flat, or slightly convex lids, that were sometimes secured with cloth tied around the top and sealed with mud.

The most commonly used stones for vessels, however, were forms of the mineral calcite, popularly known as "Egyptian alabaster" and quite a soft stone to carve. Its translucent quality and attractive banding made it a desirable material for decorative objects. The cylindrical, footed kohl pot and tall bottle (H, E) are Middle Kingdom forms. The large, deep bowl (G), though, is a type known from the First and Second Dynasties. Throughout Egyptian history, objects of earlier periods were reused in graves. These are less likely heirlooms than pieces turned up by tomb robbery or accident. The site of Abydos is so honeycombed with tombs that earlier

graves were probably turned up during construction of new ones, providing a potential source for this reinterred bowl. The small tools (I, J) may have been used for cosmetics, or like the bowl, removed from a set made as a foundation deposit and recycled.

The pottery vase (K) is covered with a burnished red slip and is characteristic of the elegant shapes and finely finished surfaces of Middle Kingdom stone and ceramic vessels.   PL

256 W. M. F. Petrie, *Tombs of the Courtiers and Oxyrhynkos* (London, 1925) 11; pls. XVI, XXX.
257 For a discussion of some of these, see B. J. Kemp and R. Merillees, *Minoan Pottery in Second Millennium Egypt* (Mainz, 1980) 215–9.

JEWELRY GROUP

L. Necklace or girdle of disk and barrel beads
Faience
L. 73.7 cm
UC 16228

M. Necklace of disk and cylinder beads with rhomboidal central pendant
Faience, carnelian, silver foil
L. 70.5 cm
UC 16226a

N. Necklace of ball, disk, barrel, and segmented beads
Carnelian, faience, steatite, quartz
L. 50.6 cm
UC 16227

O. Necklace of ball beads
Garnet
L. 44.0 cm
UC 16220

P. Necklace of barrel beads with ball beads and falcon pendants
Faience, microcline feldspar
L. 41.5 cm
UC 16225

Q. Necklace of ball beads
Amethyst
L. 33.9 cm
UC 16222

L   M   N   O   P   Q   R

S

U   W

V

T   X

142

R. Falcon pendant
Gold
H. 5.5 cm; w. 4.0 cm; d. 0.4 cm
UC 16229

S. Beads and jewelry elements
Carnelian
L. 55.8 cm
UC 16218

T. Bracelet of barrel beads
Garnet
L. 11.3 cm
UC 16221

U. Ball beads
Gold
L. 1.1 cm
UC 16219

V. Scarabs
Faience, carnelian, amethyst
L. 5.5 cm
UC 16224

W. Beads with falcon amulets
Amethyst
L. 3.8 cm
UC 16223

**X. Bracelet of ring beads
with falcon pendants**
Faience, copper alloy, microcline
feldspar
L. 15.7 cm.
UC 16226b

EVEN MODEST TOMBS of the late First Intermediate Period and Middle Kingdom contained sumptuous parures of jewels.[258] This group was found with the assembly of cosmetic equipment (cat. nos. 110 A–K) and a mirror at Abydos. Most of the jewelry from the tomb was found on the body of the woman. Although Petrie carefully noted the order in which they were found on the body and strung them in the field, there is some question as to how correct the order is. It is regrettable that so much Egyptian bead jewelry has been restrung in modern times according to contemporary tastes, that very few examples preserve their true order.

Regrettably, the record for this group is confusing. Petrie's notes read as follows:

> Round neck and in hair of female were large amethyst and carnelians with amulets. Round arms were smaller carnelians and amethysts. At waist were more carnelians and 2 plain amethyst scarabs. On child in North chamber were amethyst and carnelian strings round waist, a small blue round arms. There was nothing on the other [male] body but 1 amethyst, 1 carnelian and 1 green glazed scarab were picked up in the *radim*.

Some of the stringing that was done in the field does not seem correct, and it is impossible at this date to tell if the original order was not what we would have expected, if the material was disturbed during or after burial, or if it was misstrung in haste.

Strands of stone, faience, gold amulets, and beads, often of all the same material strung together, are characteristic of the Middle Kingdom. Such hard stones as amethyst, rock crystal, carnelian, microcline feldspar, and garnet were used for amulets as well as beaded necklaces, girdles, bracelets, and anklets.

The hard stones were often difficult to work with the copper tools generally used during this age, resulting in rather summary carving on many of the amulets. The large gilt falcon was fashioned from two sheets of hammered gold and soldered together. It is pierced horizontally, though it is unclear whether it was strung with beads or by itself on linen thread. The falcon was the earthly manifestation of the god Horus, embodied by the king, and its use in jewelry might be seen as an example of the "democratization of the afterlife," wherein private people appropriated the symbols and regalia that had been reserved for pharaohs in earlier periods.

The scarab, symbol of rebirth and renewal *par excellence*, also became a common amulet during this period, and was either strung with beads in necklaces, girdles, and bracelets, or on thread or wire as a finger-ring. Most hard-stone scarabs of the period were uninscribed, while the faience one has a typical scroll design on its base.

Claw amulets were generally worn as anklets, so their stringing here as elements in a girdle is questionable. A carnelian bracelet spacer with holes for very fine threads was also strung on the so-called girdle, again raising questions about the correct order of this group.   PL

258 Peter Lacovara, "Jewelry group and mirror," in Sue D'Auria, Peter Lacovara, and Catharine Roehrig, eds. *Mummies and Magic: the Funerary Arts of Ancient Egypt* (Boston, 1988) 117–8, cat. no. 44.

111. Fly necklace

Abydos, tomb 75
New Kingdom, 1550–1069 BC
Gold, silver, faience, frit
L. 45.0 cm
UC 51593

THIS NECKLACE comes from a disturbed grave excavated at Abydos in 1922. The seven fly pendants are made out of gilded silver sheet, with plain backs and chased fronts that have been joined. They are strung on a strand of glassy blue faience and blue frit beads. The surface was covered with copper corrosion, perhaps a result of the piece originally being contained in a copper vessel or in contact with a copper or bronze object when removed from the grave by robbers.

The fly first appeared as a jewelry element in Nubia during the Second Intermediate Period (1650–1550 BC).[259] It was initially a military decoration, presented to a soldier as persistent in battle as a fly in the face of an enemy. Such ornaments are found in the treasure of Queen Aahotep and become more commonplace as jewelry components in New Kingdom Egypt.[260]

PL

259 Cf. Charles Bonnet, *Kerma: Royaume de Nubie* (Geneva, 1990) 224, cat. no. 297.
260 Marianne Eaton-Krauss, "Fly pendants," in Edward Brovarski, Susan K. Doll, and Rita E. Freed, eds. *Egypt's Golden Age: the Art of Living in the New Kingdom* (Boston, 1982) 238–9, cat. no. 315.

112. Beads and scorpion pendant
Gurob
Dynasty 18, 1550–1292 BC
Carnelian, steatite, frit, gold, silver
L. 45.8 cm
UC 45602

THIS ELABORATE NECKLACE is composed of beads, scarabs, and amulets. The central pendant is made out of two sheets of gold joined together, with chased details on the top sheet depicting a scorpion. The scorpion figure would have been worn to protect the owner against the sting of that insect, a very real danger in the desert-edge settlement of Gurob.

Large scarabs were often made into swiveling rings, set in gold mounts similar to those seen here on some of the tiny steatite scarabs. The frog scaraboids, which have figures of scorpions on the base, symbolize fertility and magic, and are sacred to Hathor, protector of women, appropriate to a *harim* palace city, such as Gurob. The other scarabs are decorated with hieroglyphic signs including *nefer*, *kheper*, and *ma'at* feathers.

PL

113. Fish pendant

Nubia

Middle Kingdom-Second
Intermediate Period, 2055–1550 BC

Gold, feldspar

L. 3.9 cm; w. 2.3 cm

UC 25969

THIS PENDANT, cut from sheet gold and inlaid with a central body in the shape of a fish, is similar to a number of others dating to the Middle Kingdom or slightly later.[261] Such ornaments are depicted being worn in the hair and were called *nekhaw* amulets. An Egyptian tale recounts that one of the pharaoh's concubines dropped her amulet in a lake and was inconsolable until a magician parted the water and retrieved the jewel for her.[262] It has been suggested that these amulets were intended to prevent drowning as well as to promote fertility; this tale would have been appropriate to both purposes. The abstracted fish represented here is probably a tilapia, which keeps its young in its mouth when a threat arises, giving the appearance of spontaneous regeneration.   PL

261 Carol Andrews, *Egyptian Antiquities in the British Museum IV: Jewellery I* (London, 1981) 62–3, 91.
262 The so-called "Three Tales of Wonder," from Papyrus Westcar, in Miriam Lichtheim, *Ancient Egyptian Literature*, vol. 1 (Berkeley, 1975) 216–7.

WRITING

114. Figure of a scribe
Dynasty 18, 1550–1292 BC
Steatite
H. 6.0 cm; w. 3.5 cm; d. 3.2 cm
UC 14820

As EARLY AS the Fourth Dynasty (2613–2494 BC), statues of men in the position of a scribe were symbols of prestige among the Egyptians. Literacy was the province of the elite, and the highest officials, even princes, chose the scribal statue as an expression of status, ability, and administrative experience.

This diminutive figure is seated in the characteristic pose, cross-legged, with his kilt pulled taut across his lap. The scribe wears a long, striated wig and broad collar, with his head bowed in concentration above the papyrus scroll spread over his lap.

The figure displays folds of fat on the torso that are also distinguishing features of the scribal statue, further emphasizing the prosperity and experience of the individual. A hole in the base of the statuette suggests that it was part of a composite group, perhaps facing an image of Thoth, the god of writing.[263]   BTT

263 From the New Kingdom on, such compositions were common votive offerings, depicting the dedicant kneeling or prone before their patron deity. In the case of a scribe, the individual usually appeared seated, in the act of writing, before Thoth in his incarnation as a baboon.

115. Scribal palette
Gurob[264]
Dynasty 19, 1292–1186 BC
Wood, pigment
L. 36.0 cm; w. 5.7 cm; d. 1.3 cm
UC 16055

THE PALETTE was the most important piece of equipment used by the ancient Egyptian scribe, with a compartment for storing reed pens, and two ink-wells containing red and black pigments. This example has a sliding lid covering the pen slot, with one reed brush preserved within. The square inkwells retain traces of both red and black ink.

A scribe's palette was a very personal item, which would have been carried and used daily, and in many cases, as here, buried with the individual. As such, many were inscribed with the name and title of the owner, as well as prayers to Thoth and Seshat, patron deities of writing. An inscription on the front of this palette reads "Hershef king of south and north," while the back is decorated with drawings of a lion and a figure of Hershef wearing the *atef* crown. A hieroglyphic inscription above the figure reads: "giving praise to your *ka*, Heryshef Lord of the Two Horns, Binder of the Brow." Another inscription in front of the figure reads: "I have given you prosperity and alertness (?) (at?) the *sed*-festival of the Lord of the Two Lands."[265]   BTT

264 Found "in a tomb." W. M. F. Petrie, *Kahun, Gurob, Hawara* (London, 1890) 36, pl. 24.
265 Stephen Quirke points out that this statement is perhaps more appropriate in a temple relief, as an address from a god to a king. Personal communication.

116. Ostraka

As PAPYRUS was quite expensive, Egyptian artisans used potsherds or flat flakes of the fine white limestone found in the desert for trial sketches and layouts of tomb decoration. Known as ostraka (sing. ostrakon), these stone fragments contained a wide variety of subjects, including satirical drawings, personal letters, legal documents, and literary texts.

A. Figure of Isis
New Kingdom, 1550–1069 BC
Limestone, pigment
L. 11.4 cm; w. 7.3 cm; d. 1.6 cm
UC 33194

A PRELIMINARY OUTLINE and partial grid are visible in this sketch of the goddess Isis, in red paint beneath the final black drawing. The goddess kneels, with her arms outstretched and wings spread, a posture characteristic of her role as a kite hovering protectively over the deceased. She wears the throne-shaped hieroglyphic sign for her name atop her head, and holds in each hand a lotus bouquet, a customary funerary offering symbolizing regeneration. Such a sketch was most likely executed in preparation for decorating a tomb wall or another item of burial equipment.

B. Figure of Bes
New Kingdom, 1550–1069 BC
Limestone, pigment
L. 11.7 cm; w. 11.3 cm; d. 3.2 cm
UC 33198

IN CONTRAST to the preceding example, this ostrakon decorated with an image of the god Bes, is almost certainly a finished piece. Only the final black outline is visible, and the details have been fully rendered in color. The god is depicted in his customary frontal pose, squatting, with arms outstretched. In each hand, he holds a shallow bowl; the left-hand dish contains a *was*-scepter. The image is atypical in that Bes usually appears naked; here, he wears four plumes atop his head, a short kilt with dangling sash, and a spotted garment around his shoulders, possibly simulating a lion pelt. An even less common feature is the pair of wings reaching from the god's shoulders to the ground-line.[266]

The completed state of the piece, in conjunction with the role of Bes as a guardian of pregnant women and children, suggests that this ostrakon was part of a personal or household shrine, securing the protection of the god.

C. Figure of Hathor
New Kingdom, 1550–1069 BC
Chert, pigment
L. 11.7 cm; w. 7.8 cm; d. 1.6 cm
UC 33193

THIS OSTRAKON highlights the creativity and inventiveness of the artist, who has cleverly united the subject- the goddess Hathor in her bovine form—with the medium—a piece of stone following the general shape of a cow.[267] The drawing, which retains traces of the initial red underline, depicts Hathor as a cow with piebald markings and hieroglyphic *wedjat* eye, wearing a *menat* necklace with a large counterpoise. She sniffs a large lotus blossom, curving up from the front of the sledge upon which she stands, with five papyrus stalks below her belly.

An inscription on the verso calls upon "Hathor, Lady of Heaven, Mistress of all gods. Made by the scribe Twr, justified of voice; the valiant scribe Ptnw." This bovine manifestation of Hathor was particularly revered in the area around the Theban necropolis and Deir el-Bahri. The ostrakon, replete with regenerative symbols such as the lotus and *wedjat*, was most likely a dedication invoking the funerary aspect of the goddess.

D. Head of a Bearded Man
New Kingdom, 1550–1069 BC
Limestone, pigment
H. 10.8 cm; w. 7.3 cm; d. 1.7 cm
UC 33211

OSTRAKA FREQUENTLY bear images of a more casual, less standardized nature than is normally associated with Egyptian art. In this instance, the artist has sketched the head of a man with long, wavy hair rather than the stylized wig typically worn during the New Kingdom. The man's face is stubbled, another feature rarely seen in formal settings, yet he wears a fillet securing a lotus blossom to his brow and an incense cone sits atop his head, both accoutrements worn for special occasions. The combination of formal and mundane elements suggests that the picture might be a caricature, particularly since it was drawn over a figure-eight. The secondary application of the sketch further emphasizes the "scratch paper" function of the ostrakon for artists in ancient Egypt.

E. Girl with a monkey
Thebes, Ramesseum
Ramesside Period, 1292–1069 BC
Ceramic, pigment
H. 9.4 cm; w. 8.4 cm; d. 0.8 cm
UC 15946

THIS POTSHERD is decorated with a whimsical, beautifully executed drawing of a girl and a monkey. The girl, depicted from the shoulder up, wears a graduated wig, incense cone, and two lotuses. The monkey faces her, holding its paw to her nose. The style of the wig and rendering of the girl's facial features suggest a date in the Ramesside Period. The monkey, rendered with less skill than the figure of the girl, was perhaps added later, as a caricature.

Stephen Quirke has hypothesized that this is, in fact, a caricature of the Opening of the Mouth ceremony, by which a mummy or cult statue was ritually animated.[268] Typically, Opening of the Mouth scenes show a priest or officiant holding an implement such as an adze to the mouth of the recipient. The posture of the girl, with her shoulders in profile, parallels the conventional representation of a statue, while the monkey performs the ritual action.   BTT

266 These elements are probably of Levantine origin. Anthea Page, *Ancient Egyptian Figured Ostraca in the Petrie Collection* (Warminster, 1985) 7.
267 The stone was in this shape before the drawing was executed, as evidenced by the horn of the cow that extends onto the rough edge.
268 Personal communication.

117. Pyramid texts

Saqqara, Pyramid of Pepy I
Dynasty 6, reign of Pepy I,
2321–2287 BC
Limestone, pigment
H. 24.5 cm; w. 25.0 cm; d. 5.0 cm
UC 14540

THE BURIAL EQUIPMENT and the chamber walls within the pyramid of Pepy I were destroyed in antiquity, and numerous fragments were left lying on the ground.[269] This fragment is one of the larger pieces outside Egypt; the adjacent parts of the walls have not been traced, and may have been reduced to dust centuries ago.

The inner chambers were inscribed in hieroglyphs with religious compositions relating to the funeral of the king, and designed to secure for him eternal life and power. These are the earliest extensive religious compositions from Egypt, first found in the pyramid of Unas, last king of the Fifth Dynasty (ca. 2350 BC), and have been named "Pyramid Texts" by Egyptologists. In subsequent periods, many Pyramid Texts continued in use, alongside later formulae used in funerals, such as the Coffin Texts and *Book of the Dead*.

On this fragment the hieroglyphs face left; in their original position on the wall this would be towards the burial chamber where the body of King Pepy I lay. These five columns contain formulae to be recited to ensure the ascension of the spirit of the king, and to equip him with food and drink to sustain his eternal life.

SQ

269 J. Allen in *Egyptian Art in the Age of the Pyramids* (New York, 1999) 445. The monument has been restored recently by the French Institute in Cairo.

118. *A Book of the Dead* with a sketch of a shrine[270]

Late Ptolemaic Period, 116–30 BC
Papyrus, pigment
H. 22.5 cm; l. 55.0 cm
UC 32374

A GROUP of funerary texts, consisting of nearly two hundred spells, many originating in the Pyramid and Coffin Texts, were gathered by the start of the New Kingdom into the work referred to by modern scholars as the *Book of the Dead*. Texts such as the *Book of the Dead* were designed to aid the deceased, providing the knowledge required during the challenging transition to the next world.

Known in Egyptian as "Spells for going forth by day," the *Book of the Dead* was illustrated with vignettes accompanying most of the chapters. Until the Late Period, there was no fixed order to the spells, which were most often recorded on papyrus. The deceased usually included a selection of chapters, rather than the entire collection.

This *Book of the Dead*, belonging to Padiwesir, son of Tefnakhtenwaset and Semes, contains corrupt versions of chapters 163 and 164, written in cursive hieroglyphics, below a register of vignettes.[271] The spells are intended to protect the body of the deceased from decay. A diagram of a typical *naos*-style shrine with accompanying captions in demotic appears on the verso. The notations are primarily numerals with no expressed units of measurement, apparently dimensions to be employed in the construction of a shrine.   BTT

170 I am grateful to John Tait for his comments on the papyrus prior to his publication of it: "A Papyrus bearing a Shrine Plan and a Book of the Dead," in F. Hoffmann and H. J. Thissen, eds., *Res Severa Verum Gaudium: Festschrift für Karl-Theodor Zauzich zum 65. Geburtstag am 8. Juni 2004* (Leuven, 2004) 573–582, pls. LII–LIV.
271 A grid and horizontal guidelines, executed in red ink, are visible on the side with the *Book of the Dead*. Neither the guidelines nor grid cover the entire surface of the papyrus and do not correspond to the arrangement of the text. The papyrus in its present form seems to have been assembled from two previously used sections.

ARTS AND CRAFTS

119. Craftsmen at work

Saqqara, tomb of Tepemankh
(*mastaba 76*)
Dynasty 5, 2494–2345 BC
Limestone, pigment
H. 30.2 cm; w. 70.5 cm; d. 4.4 cm
UC 14309

THE EAST WALL of the Fifth Dynasty chapel of Tepemankh at Saqqara was carved in raised relief with scenes of sailing boats, craftsmen working, a market, and rendering accounts. This block and seven other fragments, including another in the Petrie collec-tion (UC 14310), came from that wall.[272] Two partial scenes are depict-ed on this relief. On the left, a man and boy stand in the prow of a boat, with the caption "the *ka*-priest Nefer-khu." On the right, the block is divid-ed into two registers. The top depicts metal workers and the bottom regis-ter shows carpenters. The captions identify the craftsmen except for the inscription at the right end of the top register that indicates that "sloth is unbearable to Sokar."[273] Sokar was a patron god of craftsmen, especially metalworkers. These two registers continue to the right onto an adjoin-ing block, now in Moscow, that also depicts part of a market scene.[274] The other block in the Petrie collec-tion joins to the right of the Moscow block and continues the market scene.   SG-D

272 For a reconstruction of all the currently preserved fragments of the wall, see Metropolitan Museum of Art, *Egyptian Art in the Age of the Pyramids* (New York, 1999) 405, fig. 126.
273 Ibid., 407.
274 I.1.a.5566. Svetlana Hodjash and Oleg Berlev, *The Egyptian Reliefs and Stelae in the Pushkin Museum of Fine Arts, Moscow* (Leningrad, 1982) 33, 36

120. Vase in the shape of a trussed fowl
Middle Kingdom, 2055–1650 BC
Limestone
H. 13.2 cm; w. 8.3 cm; d. 7.6 cm
UC 69857

THIS DELICATE VASE takes the form of a plucked, trussed fowl, a motif found throughout the Dynastic Period, but particularly popular during the Middle Kingdom. Examples are known in calcite and anhydrite, as well as limestone.[275] These vessels may have been made to hold some precious unguent or medicinal potion, or as stand-ins for offerings of fowl in the tomb. The neck of the duck arching over its back acted as a clever handle and clearly provided an inducement to use the vessel. PL

275 Biri Fay. "Egyptian Duck Flasks of Blue Anhydrite," *Metropolitan Museum Journal* 33 (1998): 23–48.

121. Footed dish
Gurob
New Kingdom, 1550–1069 BC
Calcite ("Egyptian alabaster")
H. 12.1 cm; rim diam. 14.9 cm
UC 30085a, b

THIS SHAPELY FORM of vessel is commonly referred to as a tazza cup,[276] and is often shown in depictions of feasts, holding ointment with which to anoint the guests. It is possible that the separate foot was attached with an adhesive or it may have stood alone so that the dish could be removed and carried. Since parties of women are often shown using these vessels it is not surprising that a number were found in the *harim* palace at Gurob. PL

276 Janine Bourriau, "Dish on stand," in Edward Brovarski, Susan K. Doll, and Rita E. Freed, eds. *Egypt's Golden Age: the Art of Living in the New Kingdom* (Boston, 1982) 129, cat. no. 120.

122. Flasks

A. Piriform flask
New Kingdom, 1550–1069 BC
Bronze
H. 22.9 cm; diam. 7.6 cm
UC 16428

B. Miniature piriform flask
New Kingdom, 1550–1069 BC
Calcite ("Egyptian alabaster")
H. 11.5 cm; diam. 2.3 cm
UC 16429

THE EGYPTIANS delighted in repeating the same form in a variety of media. The tall, graceful flask that appears in the Eighteenth Dynasty is found in precious metal as well as glass and pottery. The bronze example, raised from a single sheet of metal and hammered into its final shape, is a masterpiece of craftsmanship. The body had to be beaten out against an anvil introduced through the narrow neck of the vase, reducing the metal to a mere 1/40th of an inch in thickness.[277] The vessel, inscribed for "the sandal-bearer of Amun, Djehutyhotep," may have been used in rituals at Karnak for the cleaning and dressing of the cult image in the temple. Such flasks also appear in tomb scenes being used to pour wine or perfume at parties.   PL

277 W. M. F. Petrie, *Arts and Crafts of Ancient Egypt* (London, 1909) 101.

159

123. **Lion gargoyle**
Koptos
Middle Kingdom, 2055–1650 BC
Limestone
H. 8.0 cm; w. 25.5 cm; d. 39.5 cm
UC 14319

LION-HEADED SPOUTS for rainwater are often found atop the outer walls of Egyptian temples. Examples have been dated from the Old Kingdom[278] to the Graeco-Roman Period.[279] This lion, with its broad muzzle and enigmatic face, is most like a complete limestone waterspout recently excavated at a Middle Kingdom pyramid temple at Lisht.[280]

Lions, associated with many deities, were worshipped and even kept in Egyptian temples.[281] Perhaps the use of lions as rain spouts can be linked with the leonine goddess Tefnut, who was born of the saliva of the sun-god.[282] Although the climate of Egypt is extremely dry, rainstorms do occur and can have a devastating effect on a land not prepared for them. As a result, many Egyptian temples have elaborate drainage systems.   PL

278 Ursula Schweitzer, *Löwe und Sphinnx im alten Ägypten* (Gluckstadt and Hamburg, 1948) 26–7.
279 Cf. an example in the Old Aswan Museum, #1087.
280 Now in the Cairo Museum, JE 63941. Dieter Arnold, *The Pyramid of Senwosret I* (New York, 1988) 81; pls. 57, 101.
281 P. Houlihan, *The Animal World of the Pharaohs* (London, 1996) 91–5.
282 Ursula Verhoeven, "Tefnut," *LÄ* 6: 296–304.

124. Model tower

Probably from the Ptah Temple at Memphis[283]
Late Dynasty 18, ca. 1300 BC
Limestone
H. 17.8 cm; w. 9.7 cm; d. 11.1 cm
UC 14543

THIS LIMESTONE MODEL of a tall building with crenellated wall bears across two of its four faces a depiction of worship in sunk relief. On the left, the Memphite god of craftlike creation, Ptah, stands on a plinth shaped as the hieroglyph for *maa'*, "smooth, straight, true," facing right to an offering stand beneath a vertical line of hieroglyphs reading "offering given by the king to Ptah the great, lord of heaven, lord of the Two Lands." On the adjacent face to the right, a woman is shown standing with arms raised, inclining slightly forward, facing left towards two large ears, carved in some detail, one above the other. She is shown wearing a long garment, flaring out above ankle height, the contours of her body beneath incised as if it were transparent. The plinth and the skin areas of the woman and the ears are painted in light red ochre.

Depictions of ears, often in conjunction with the funerary formula and/or a scene of worship as here, more usually occur on small votive stelae.[284] The ears seem to denote or encourage the hearing by the god, to ensure that prayers are answered; accompanying inscriptions do not record a specific wish, as if these votive offerings aimed more generally at a favorable reception for the donor.

The model building represents a three-dimensional variant within the same category. Relatively few models of buildings survive, complicating their interpretation. Rather than literally an image of a tower, the crenellated walls perhaps convey the impression of a temple enclosure viewed from the outside, as a sacred and so, separated, terrain. These votives may have been placed as near as many worshippers could come to the sanctuary of the deity.   SQ

283 Its find-spot is not recorded, but the reference to Ptah as "lord of heaven" makes it likely that it comes from a center of his cult, and it seems likely that Petrie acquired the piece at Memphis, probably during his excavations there 1908–1913.
284 A large group of the stelae were excavated by Petrie at Memphis, beneath the foundation sand-trench under the temple for the cult of Ramesses II in the domain of Ptah, the main religious structure now visible at the site. From the context, the stelae must date earlier, as confirmed by the style and the names of donors and kings found on them, all pointing to mid- to late Eighteenth Dynasty date.

125. Model column capital

Ptolemaic Period, 305–30 BC
Limestone
H. 17.0 cm; w. 15.5 cm; d. 9.8 cm
UC 28720

MODEL BUILDINGS and architectural elements appear to have been offered by the king during temple ceremonies.[285] The type of complex column capital represented on this piece was a development of the Ptolemaic Period. With elaborate, articulated parts, such as the scroll volutes and the pendant orbs, it is a type found on the west colonnade of the temple of Philae.[286]

PL

285 Alexander Badawy, *A Monumental Gateway of Seti I* (Brooklyn, 1975).
286 W. S. Smith, edited and revised by W. K. Simpson. *The Art and Architecture of Ancient Egypt* (New Haven, 1998) 241.

CERAMICS

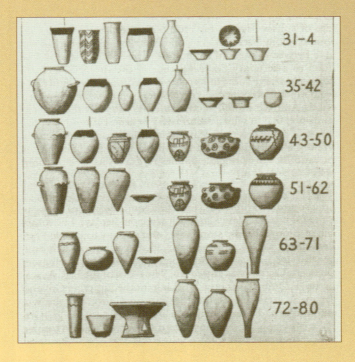

126. Black-topped jar

Naqada, tomb 1471
Naqada I (Amratian) Period,
ca. 4200–3700 BC
Nile clay ceramic
H. 19.1 cm; rim diam. 10.2 cm
UC 5688

THIS SLENDER, trumpet-shaped jar is typical of the black-topped pottery of the Naqada I Period. The pleasing color combination came about when vessels made of Nile mud with an iron-rich slip were fired upside-down, with their upper portion buried in ash at the bottom of the kiln. During the firing, the exposed part of the pot would oxidize and turn red while the lower portion would fire a dark black. Originally, this patterning was probably accidental, though it soon became an intentional and sought-after technique.

Vessels of this type are found in both Upper Egypt and Lower Nubia, indicating the close connection between the two culture areas. They also occur in both settlement sites and in graves as offerings to the dead. Such finely crafted and well-preserved specimens are usually part of tomb equipment, as was this example.[287] Much of our knowledge of the prehistoric period in Egypt comes from Petrie's pioneering study of the ceramic assemblages of the Neolithic or Predynastic cultures of the Nile Valley.[288] Of particular importance is the material from his excavations in Upper Egypt. Petrie's original sequences have been further refined and classified into several sub-periods based on the study of the remains from the "type site" of Naqada.[289]

PL

287 E. Baumgartel, *Petrie's Naqada Excavation. A Supplement* (London, 1970) 44. Cf. W. M. F. Petrie, *Naqada and Ballas* (London, 1896) 12, 30.
288 Petrie, *Prehistoric Egypt* (London, 1920).
289 Cf: W. Kaiser, "Zur inneren Chronologie der Naqadakultur," *Archaeologica Geographica* 6 (1957): 69–77; W. Needler, *Predynastic and Archaic Egypt in the Brooklyn Museum* (1984).

127. Bowl

Qau, tomb 991[290]

Dynasty 4, 2613–2494 BC

Marl clay ceramic

H. 8.9 cm; rim diam. 19.5 cm

UC 17658

MANY TYPES of Old Kingdom pottery vessels follow metal prototypes, as evidenced by the sharp, angular carination at the rim of this vessel. In addition, its deep red color, described by nineteenth century archaeologists as "sealing wax" red, was in imitation of polished copper. Such bowls are also known as Meidum-ware, from the site where Petrie first discovered them.

This bowl comes from the extensive provincial cemetery excavated by Petrie at Qau, dating to the Old Kingdom.[291] Despite their fine finish and beautiful shape, these vessels seem to have been used for almost everything, from eating and drinking to mixing plaster and feeding cattle. The contour of the rim also had a practical function, making it a no-drip cup for sipping soups and beverages. The shapes of these bowls change throughout the Old Kingdom, serving as an important dating tool.[292]   PL

290 According to a mark on the bowl.
291 Guy Brunton, *Qau and Badari* II (London, 1928) 4, pl. L.
292 P. Ballet, "Essai de classification des coups type Maidum-Bowl," *Cahiers de la ceramique egyptienne* I (Cairo, 1987) 1–16.

128. Vase with practice hieroglyphs

Dendera, tomb 480
Dynasty 11, 2125–1985 BC
Marl clay ceramic
H. 12.0 cm; rim diam. 6.0 cm
UC 18289

DURING THE Intermediate Periods, pottery, like sculpture and relief, sees great changes and regional variations with the breakdown of centralized production workshops.[293] This vessel, with a tall, corrugated neck and quatrefoil, folded-over rim is a departure from the finely finished wares of simple elegance that characterized the Old Kingdom. The surface is wet-smoothed and the base has been roughly trimmed with a knife.

This vase is distinguished by the hieroglyphic images of animals running around the body, perhaps comparable to the Letters to the Dead found on some vessels of this time (see cat. no. 145). There are examples of objects inscribed with "pseudo-hieroglyphs," presumably made by illiterate people. However, this particular vase seems more akin to the ostraka of the New Kingdom, as the artist seems to be playing with different versions of similar renderings of animals, including cats and dogs.   PL

293 Janine Bourriau, *Umm el-Ga'ab: Pottery from the Nile Valley before the Arab Conquest* (Cambridge, 1981) 51.

129. Pot

El-Kab
Dynasty 12, 1985–1773 BC
Marl clay ceramic
H. 11.7 cm; rim diam. 7.0 cm
UC 18371

DURING THE Middle Kingdom, a fine
marl clay that fired a white to pink-
ish-buff color became popular for
ceramic vessels.[294] This clay could be
highly burnished on the surface, giving it the sheen and appearance of a
stone vessel. The form of this vase imitates one commonly produced in stone
in the Middle Kingdom. A recurrent
theme in Egyptian material culture is
the use of faux finishes and the imitation of similar forms in varied media.

PL

294 Janine Bourriau, *Umm el-Ga'ab, Pottery
from the Nile Valley before the Arab
Conquest*, (Cambridge, 1981) 55.

130. Tell el-Yahudiya ware fish flask
Second Intermediate Period,
1650–1550 BC
Ceramic
H. 9.5 cm; l. 14.6 cm
UC 13477

THE CREATOR of this comical vessel skillfully employed the flask shape to evoke the form of a fish, incorporating dotted scales zig-zagging along the body to the bulging eye. The mouth would have extended into a spout joined to a ring handle, now broken away. During the Second Intermediate Period, small black juglets with patterns of pricked white dots appear, particularly in Lower Egypt, and become diagnostic of Hyksos rule over the divided land. The juglets themselves combine a typical Near Eastern ceramic shape with a design and ware native to Egypt.

In addition to the standard piriform juglet (see cat. no. 122), there are other decorative classes of vessels, including theriomorphic, or those taking the form of an animal. This unusual vessel is fashioned in the shape of a fish. The details of the eyes, tail, and fins, though partially missing, were carefully modeled and the surface decorated with lines and dots. A number of these fish vessels, representing the tilapia fish, were found at Tell el-Yahudiya.[295] The tilapia holds its young in its mouth at any sign of danger; seeing the fry swim out from the parent's mouth inspired the Egyptians to equate this animal with spontaneous regeneration. Consequently, it became a potent symbol of rebirth and is often found as a decorative motif on funerary offerings.   PL

295 W. M. F. Petrie, *Hyksos and Israelite Cities* (London, 1906) pl. VIIIa.

131. Lidded vase imitating a basket
Sedment, burial 1715
Second Intermediate Period,
1650–1550 BC
Marl clay, pigment
H. (overall) 8.9 cm; diam. 12.0 cm
UC 17886

THIS VESSEL represents a wickerwork basket with a conical lid. A number of examples have survived, showing a range of treatment, from very naturalistic with a carefully ribbed outer surface, to more abstract renderings of the overall shape, as in this case.[296] Though found far north in Egypt, it is similar in size and style to a number of vessels found at Kerma, in Sudan, dating to the Second Intermediate Period.[297]

Like the Kerma vessels, this one has been low-fired and the paint applied afterward in geometric patterns along the sides and lid, imitating an elaborately woven basket. Tick marks along the top simulate stitching, in order to represent the finished edge. The lid is pierced, so that it might hang from a string, as would a real basket. There was a significant amount of contact between Nubia, and even the north of Egypt, during the Second Intermediate Period, as this vessel illustrates.   PL

296 John K. McDonald, "Basket with lid, Rounded basket with conical lid," in Edward Brovarski, Susan K. Doll, and Rita E. Freed, eds. *Egypt's Golden Age: the Art of Living in the New Kingdom* (Boston, 1982) 151, cat. nos. 157, 159; George A. Reisner, *Excavations at Kerma, Parts IV–V* (Cambridge, 1923) 154–5, 159–61.
297 Reisner, ibid., 162.

132. Blue-painted amphora

Late Dynasty 18, 1352–1292 BC
Nile clay ceramic, pigment
H. 34.7 cm; diam. 12.7 cm
UC 8695

THIS ELABORATELY decorated amphora is one of a small number of similar vessels. The shape is probably derived from fancy presentation vases made from precious metals, depicted in Theban tomb paintings being delivered to court by Syrian envoys. The designs on the vessels vary somewhat, but all include the lotus petal garlands used to adorn plain pottery amphorae at feasts. The lotus pattern was not only attractive, but also signified rebirth, as the lotus opens anew each morning with the sunrise. The pendant petal ornamentation could be combined with other floral motifs, such as buds, as shown on the vessels.

In addition, plastic decoration is used on the amphora, in the strap handles and the applied ibex head. The ibex was another symbol of rebirth, perhaps because of the mother's extended period of care for her offspring. On some vases, the three-dimensional head is further embellished with a painted body, which often looks quite awkward. Here, the artist has instead cleverly painted a thicket of vegetation, through which the creature pokes its head.   PL

133. Pilgrim flask

Coptic Period,
Fourth-sixth centuries AD
Ceramic
H. 11.7 cm; diam. 11.1 cm
UC 19516

AS IN OTHER AREAS, the early Christians living in Egypt were subject to persecution. One such individual, St. Menas, was martyred in the late third century AD.[298] He was buried in the desert south of Alexandria, at a location chosen, according to legend, when the camel bearing his body lay down and refused to continue. In the fourth century, a complex known as Karm Abu Mena, "the house of Mena," was constructed for the throngs of pilgrims who visited the site from near and far.

Pilgrims would have received a terracotta flask such as this one, filled with oil from the lamps in the sanctuary or water from the sacred spring, as souvenirs. Referred to as "eulogy ampullae," the flasks bear a standard motif, depicting the saint in prayer, standing with uplifted hands between two recumbent camels. In this case, Menas is identified by an inscription. These flasks are found across the Mediterranean world, an enduring testament to the popularity of the shrine and its saint.   BTT

298 In AD 296, Menas was supposedly tortured and mutilated. Despite his injuries, he still rose and addressed the assembled crowd before he was finally slain.

134. Fragments painted with scenes of a warrior saint and musicians

Abbassid or Tulunid Dynasty,
about AD 900
Pottery, pigment
H. (large piece) 25.0 cm; w. 23.5 cm;
d. 13.5 cm
H. (small piece) 23.0 cm; w. 20.0
cm; d. 10.0 cm
UC 19481

THREE SEPARATE SECTIONS (two now joined) survive from this remarkable painted cylindrical vessel, with narrower foot and outward flaring rim. On one side, a central scene depicted a warrior saint on horseback, wielding a sword in his right hand. Among the several saints depicted in this guise, the St. Theodore known from the ninth century AD onwards as "the General," is perhaps the most popular in the Egyptian Church, rather than the St. George more familiar in Western Christianity. St. Theodore

Stratelates is probably also the figure on a closely similar vessel, also unprovenanced, now in the Louvre (AF 6940).[299] The saint is said to have been martyred in the reign of the Roman emperor Maximianus (ca. AD 285–310).

The focal area of the vessel has been repaired from two joining fragments; the rear legs of the horse are preserved on a third part, to the right of the lower area of a right-facing seated figure and, behind, the triangular earring and neck area of a large head. The remaining fragments preserved what would be the opposite side of the vessel, with, from right to left, the left side of the head wearing the triangular earrings, then three haloed figures forming an orchestral choir, and then a better preserved head wearing ball earrings, the nose modeled in clay, now abraded. The musical saint to the left is seated, and has hands to waist as if clapping the

rhythm, as ancient Egyptian singers or accompanying performers would. The figure at center stands, holding at the waist an object depicted as a rectangle with circle at each end, presumably a barrel drum. The haloed figure to the right is again seated and facing left, playing a long reed instrument. Below the saints on both sides runs a frieze of fish and birds.

On the comparable vessel in the Louvre, the group of saints at the opposite side to the warrior saint are shown holding papyrus scrolls, in a grouping reminiscent of late Roman Period sculpted sarcophagi. The musical group on the Petrie Museum jar is harder to parallel, and provides a lively image of religious art and life in the early centuries after the Arab Conquest.

SQ

299 C. Neyret, in J. Vercoutter, ed., *Hommages à la mémoire de Serge Sauneron, 1927–1976* (Cairo, 1979) pl. 21.

FUNERARY

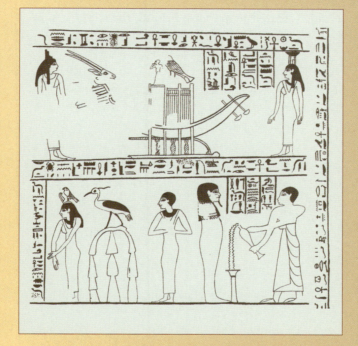

135. Relief depicting a tomb court
Memphis
Dynasty 18, 1550–1292 BC
Limestone
H. 29.5 cm; w. 60.0 cm; d. 4.0 cm
UC 408

As THE TRADITIONAL capital of Egypt for most of its history, Memphis and its cemeteries were home to some of the greatest Egyptian monuments. During the New Kingdom, high-ranking government officials built many lavishly decorated and elaborately conceived tombs in the area.[300] Sadly, many of these structures were destroyed and their carved reliefs spread far and wide.

Petrie found this block from an unknown tomb at Memphis.[301] It depicts exactly how such a tomb would have appeared, with a colonnaded central court bounded by papyrus-bud columns and a large offering table in the center. A libation is flowing off of the table through a spout into a basin flanked by kneeling images of the tomb owner and his wife. Two large statues wearing carefully pleated robes stand to either side of the basin. Inside the halls alongside the court, are two pyramidal stands piled with loaves of bread whose shape echoes that of the pyramid in front of which this funerary monument was located.   PL

300 G. T. Martin, *The Hidden Tombs of Memphis* (London, 1993).
301 Ibid., 205.

136. Pyramidion

Thebes
Dynasty 19, 1292–1185 BC
Limestone
H. 19.4 cm; w. 10.1 cm; d. 13.6 cm
UC 14574

WHEN THE VALLEY of the Kings became the site for royal burials during the Eighteenth Dynasty, the pyramid tomb ceased to be a kingly prerogative, and the form was adopted by private individuals, in a much-reduced form, for their own monuments. Although these small pyramid tombs are found from the area around Memphis down into Nubia, the best-known examples are from Thebes. The steeply-sloped, mud-brick pyramids were not very tall and were crowned with a capstone, known as a pyramidion. These tops were often inscribed with the names and titles of the tomb owner and prayers for his spirit.

This pyramidion came from the tomb of a man named Nebamun. All four sides are inscribed and decorated with relief. The front contains the remains of a niche that probably held a small stelophorous statue of the deceased (see cat. no. 21). On the front side, the tomb owner is shown wearing a long cloak before a table of offerings; above him an inscription names him as "the excellent spirit...." On the right side, the sun god is shown in a divine boat resting on the hieroglyph for "heaven." The inscription on this side, written above a depiction of the owner and his wife, reads: "O my lord Nebamun, justified (ie., deceased), we cry out for food and provisions for every spirit and abundance for Ren-nutet, we cry out...." The rear side of the pyramidion portrays Nebamun, his hands raised in prayer, with an accompanying inscription that reads: "Nebamun, true of voice (ie., deceased)" above him, and "[Neb]amuntet, justified (ie., deceased)." There are remains of a female figure, wearing an elaborate wig and long, flowing gown on the left side.[302]   PL

302 H. M. Stewart, *Egyptian Stelae, Reliefs and Paintings: Part 1* (Warminster, 1976) 61.

137. Funerary figurines

FUNERARY FIGURINES were known as *shabtis*, *shawabtis*, or *ushebtis* in ancient Egyptian, terms that are used interchangeably today, though inaccurately, since each has chronological, and even geographical, boundaries. The first shabtis, appearing during the Middle Kingdom, were simple, mummiform figures. By the Second Intermediate Period, the figures were often inscribed with Chapter 6 of the *Book of the Dead*. The spell magically animated the figures, which were depicted with tools in hand and a basket slung over the shoulder, ready to perform any labor required of the deceased in the afterlife. In a basic form, the spell reads:

> The Osiris [x]: if one counts off the Osiris [x] to do all the works which are to be done therein the necropolis, to make arable the fields, to irrigate the riparian lands, to transport by boat the sand of the East to the West, indeed, obstacles are implanted for you there, as a man at his duties; if one calls you at any time, "here I am," you shall say.

A. Shabti of Iwnty
Sudan
Dynasty 18, 1550–1292 BC
Granite
H. 40.8 cm; W. 12.4 cm; D. 7.5 cm
UC 40330

THIS MASSIVE stone figure, belonging to the Overseer of Works of Amun, assumes the traditional mummiform posture, wearing a striated tripartite wig and plaited beard. He carries the usual complement of tools, including a pick, hoe, and two baskets that are held in front, instead of slung over the shoulders, in the customary manner.

B. Shabti of Khaemwas
Dynasty 19, reign of Ramesses II, 1279–1213 BC
Steatite
H. 16.5 cm; W. 8.1 cm; D. 5.1 cm
UC 2311

KHAEMWAS, son of Ramesses II and Queen Isetnofret, served as High Priest of Ptah at Memphis, oversaw construction of royal monuments, and administered the cult of the Apis bull. Succeeding generations revered him as a magician, historian, and man of wisdom.[303]

Shabtis of the Ramesside Period often appear in the dress of daily life, rather than as mummiform figures bearing agricultural implements. Although the head is missing, the characteristic sidelock worn by princes curls onto the right shoulder. The figure wears an elaborately pleated garment with flared kilt. One line of inscription runs down the front panel of the skirt, while the remainder encircles the back of the body.

A

c. Shabti of Harwa

Dynasty 25, ca. 716–690 BC
Altered peridotite (serpentinite)
H. 18.1 cm; w. 5.8 cm; d. 5.1 cm
UC 10681

HARWA WAS ONE of the highest officials of the Twenty-fifth Dynasty, holding the title "Director of all Divine Functions." He served as the steward of the Divine Adoratrice of Amun, the chief religious office in Thebes, during the tenure of Amenirdis I.[304]

Serpentine and other hard stones were particularly popular materials for funerary figurines of the Twenty-fifth Dynasty. This figure is typical of the shabtis of Harwa and his peers, wearing a tripartite wig without striations, the arms completely enveloped in the mummy wrappings, and features clearly reminiscent of contemporary Nubian sculpture.   BTT

303 Khaemwas, who also held the title "Senior King's Son, His Beloved," indicating his status as heir apparent, predeceased his father, and was most likely buried at Saqqara.
304 Although his massive tomb in the Asasif (TT 37) is poorly preserved, Harwa is represented in seven statues. Three other shabtis belonging to Harwa are in the Cairo Museum (CG 47715, 47828, 48517). Battiscombe Gunn and Reginald Engelbach, "The Statues of Harwa," *BIFAO* 30 (1931): 791–815.

B

C

138. Stela of Thutmose
Deir el-Medina
Dynasty 20, 1186–1069 BC
Limestone, pigment
H. 22.4 cm; w. 13.3 cm; d. 5.1 cm
UC 14228

THIS FUNERARY STELA belonging to a man named Thutmose is of a type found at Deir el-Medina, primarily during the Nineteenth and Twentieth Dynasties, in which the individual was typically depicted seated, holding a lotus to the nose. In the lunette at the top of this example, *wedjat* eyes, one now missing, flank an image of the sun emerging from the horizon above six columns of incised hieroglyphs. Thutmose is pictured on the lower left facing his brother, who pours a libation with his right hand, while extending a censer toward the deceased with his left hand (see cat. no. 67). The brother is identified as "the scribe Pa-iry of the Place of Truth," the ancient designation for the Valley of the Kings. Pa-iry, and in all likelihood Thutmose as well, was one of the workers responsible for constructing and decorating the royal tombs, who resided in the village of Deir el-Medina.

The inscription designates Thutmose as the *3h ikr n R'*, "the effective spirit of Re," an epithet found on this type of stela, which R. J. Demarée has suggested were used in the celebration of a private ancestor cult.[305] The stelae likely served as ritual foci, before which relatives could make offerings or plead for intercession on their behalf, one of several methods employed by the ancient Egyptians to communicate with the deceased (see cat. nos. 144–5). In the *Book of the Dead,* the *3h ikr* is an individual who knows and

is united with the sun god, Re', and the lord of the dead, Osiris, who enters the afterlife "as an ignorant one," emerging as the *3h ikr*. The knowledge of Re' and Osiris gained by the deceased allows them to act effectively on behalf of their living relatives, providing aid or protection from evil spirits.[306]   BTT

305 R. J. Demarée, *The 3h ikr n R'-Stelae: On Ancestor Worship in Ancient Egypt* (Leiden, 1983) 283–4.
306 See T. G. Allen, *The Book of the Dead; or coming forth by day* SAOC 37 (Chicago, 1974) Spell 64. Also, Florence Friedman, "Aspects of Domestic Life and Religion," in Leonard Lesko, ed., *Pharaoh's Workers: the Villagers of Deir el Medina* (Ithaca, 1994) 113–4.

139. Stela of Nesykhonsu

Thebes, Deir el-Bahri (DB 320)
Dynasty 21, reign of Pinedjem II,
990–969 BC
Wood, pigment
H. 39.9 cm; w. 22.3 cm; d. 2.5 cm
UC 14226[307]

FUNERARY STELAE of this sort are characteristic of the burials of the Theban priesthood during the Third Intermediate Period. Made for Queen Nesykhonsu, wife of Pinedjem II, this stela was fabricated from a single piece of wood, with a vignette and seven columns of text painted on a white ground. The scene shows Nesykhonsu on the right, dressed in a sheer garment and tripartite wig, topped with a fillet and incense cone. She faces an offering stand with a large lotus blossom, presenting burning incense to Osiris, on the left, in his customary mummiform manifestation, wearing the *atef* crown and divine beard, holding the crook and flail.

The inscription invokes Osiris on behalf of the deceased and lists her very impressive titulary, including Great Chief of the Musicians of Amun, Prophet of Khnum, Lord of the Cataract, and Amun of Khenemwaset, Overseer of Southern Lands, and most extraordinarily, King's Daughter of Kush. The latter title, a feminine equivalent of the King's Son, or Viceroy, of Kush, was one of the highest positions of the New Kingdom bureaucracy. That Nesykhonsu held this title, is indicative of the shifting balance of power at Thebes during Dynasty 21, and foreshadows the authority held by royal women of the succeeding dynasties.

Nesykhonsu and her family were buried in a tomb at Deir el-Bahri (DB 320) in which more than fifty kings, queens, and nobles of the New Kingdom and Third Intermediate Period were also interred.[308] The cache of royal mummies at Deir el-Bahri came about as part of a state policy that sanctioned the exploitation of the royal tombs in the Valley of the Kings.[309] Inaugurated at the start of the Third Intermediate Period, the despoliation of the tombs was intended to finance the "reigns" of the High Priests who had gained control over Thebes. Although the tombs were stripped of valuables, including metals, precious stones, and wood, their occupants were carefully identified, reconsecrated, and moved to another location, such as the tomb of Nesykhonsu's family.   BTT

307 From the collection of Amelia Edwards.
308 The tomb was officially excavated in 1881 by Émile Brugsch, though it had been known to local tomb robbers for several years. The royal occupants of the tomb included Amenhotep I, Thutmose II, Thutmose III, Ramesses I, Ramesses II, and Seti I.
309 See Nicholas Reeves and Richard Wilkinson, *The Complete Valley of the Kings* (London, 1996) 204–207; K. Jansen-Winkeln, "Die Plünderung der Königsgräber des Neuen Reiches," *ZÄS* 122 (1995) 62–78.

140. Tombstone
Rifeh, Balyzeh Monastery
Coptic Period,
late second century AD–AD 642
Limestone
H. 32.1 cm; w. 31.8 cm; d. 6.8 cm
UC 14771

THE ADVENT of Christianity in Egypt dates to the early years of the first century AD when St. Mark established churches in Alexandria. When the Arabs conquered Egypt in AD 641, they referred to its Christian inhabitants as "Copts," derived from the Greek *Aigyptos*, "Egypt."

The art of the Copts shows many influences, including ancient Egyptian, Graeco-Roman, Near Eastern, and Byzantine. Unlike their Egyptian and Hellenistic predecessors, Coptic sculptors worked almost exclusively in relief, primarily for use in architectural contexts. This limestone slab, used as a funerary stela, depicts the head of a man flanked by crosses, seen frontally in contrast to ancient Egyptian convention. The highly stylized, almost geometric features, lack of individualized appearance, and schematic rendering of the uplifted hands are all characteristic of figural representations in Coptic art.[310]   BTT

310 The appearance of the body may be deduced from a similar tombstone, also found at Balyzeh and in the Petrie collection (UC 14772), depicting the body as shapeless and without natural modeling. W. M. F. Petrie, *Gizeh and Rifeh* (London, 1907) 30, pl. xxxvii.

141. *Hes* vase inscribed for Nesytanebetisheru

Thebes, Deir el-Bahri (DB 320)
Late Dynasty 21, ca. 969–945 BC
Bronze
H. 28.1 cm; diam. 3.7 cm
UC 14239

POURING LIBATIONS of wine, milk, water, or other liquids was an essential part of ancient Egyptian religious ritual. Tall, graceful vessels such as this, known as a *hes* vase, were often used in funerary rituals or included with the burial equipment, containing beverages for the deceased. The vases, fashioned of faience, ceramic, or metal, were frequently labeled with the name of the deceased and their contents.

The inscription indicates that this bronze vessel belonged to "the Osiris, the great chief of the musicians of Amun-Re, king of the gods, Nesytanebetisheru." The vase consists of an upper portion and a base, connected rather carelessly by five small rivets. As the daughter of King Pinedjem II and Queen Nesykhonsu (see cat. no. 140), Nesytanebetisheru was a lady of great status in Thebes, and was among the nobles interred in a cache of royal mummies at Deir el-Bahri.

BTT

142. Canopic Jar of Iunefer

Hawara, Tomb 57[311]
Dynasty 12, 1985–1773 BC
Limestone, pigment
H. (total) 31.7 cm; diam. 18.1 cm
UC 16027

THE PROCESS of mummification involved removing the internal organs from the body in order to prevent decomposition. The organs were preserved, wrapped, and placed in four ritual vessels, called canopic jars, which were stored inside the burial chamber. During the First Intermediate Period (ca. 2160–2055 BC), the lids of the jars began to be carved in the form of human heads, representing the deceased, a style that would continue through the Middle Kingdom.

In this example, belonging to a man named Iunefer, the lid, which does not fit the jar, represents a human head, wearing a striated wig, with no beard. During the Middle Kingdom, the full complement of four jars often consisted of three bearded heads and a single beardless one. It is during the Middle Kingdom that the jars are first associated with the Four Sons of Horus, each safeguarding a specific organ, and in turn, associated with a protective goddess.[312] This jar would have held the intestines, based on the inscription invoking the protection of Selkis and Qebehsenuef.[313]   BTT

311 One of two jars found in this tomb, located in the cemetery to the north of the Hawara pyramid. W. M. F. Petrie, *The Labyrinth, Gerzeh, and Mazghuneh* (London, 1912) pl. XXXI, 2.
312 Falcon-headed Qebehsenuef protected the intestines, human-headed Imsety the liver, baboon-headed Hapy the lungs, and jackal-headed Duamutef the stomach. They were linked with Selkis, Isis, Nephthys, and Neith, respectively.
313 In the New Kingdom, the jar lids customarily took the form of the particular deity, with a jackal, baboon, human, or falcon head.

143. Mummy tag

Dendera
Early Roman Period, 30 BC–AD 149
Limestone, pigment
L. 8.1 cm; w. 5.3 cm
UC 34471

DURING THE Roman Period in Egypt, mummies were often identified with labels supplying basic biographical information about the deceased, with the occasional addition of a brief prayer. These labels were typically inscribed on small wood or limestone tags and attached to the mummy with cord. Despite their humble appearance, mummy tags offer a tremendous resource to modern scholars, providing details such as the filiation, age, and date of death of the individual.

This label, carefully rendered in black pigment on limestone, identifies the deceased as "the Osiris Nesmin, the elder son of Padii."[314] The inscription is written in demotic, although many tags bear texts in Greek; in some cases, the text occurs in both Greek and Egyptian. Instead of the customary prayer, this example contains a depiction of a recumbent jackal above the inscription.   BTT

314 The name might also be read as Nakhtmin. Cf. Günter Vittman, "Die Mumienschilder in Petries Denderah," *ZÄS* 112 (1985): 155, pl. 4, no. 10.

144. Ancestor bust

Dynasty 18, 1550–1292 BC
Limestone, pigment
H. 20.0 cm; w. 10.0 cm; d. 4.8 cm
UC 16551

THE EGYPTIANS believed the living could call upon the dead to intercede with the gods or overcome evil spirits. Busts of the dead, along with offering tables and stelae, were set in niches in the houses of their relations. Many of these busts come from the village of artisans at Deir el-Medina; while they are generally thought to be a stand-in for all of the family's departed ancestors, some are inscribed for specific individuals.[315] They are also mentioned in the *Book of the Dead* under spell 151, "the spell of the head of mysteries," which reads: "hail to you whose face is kindly…your head will never be taken away."[316] Ancestor bust-shaped amulets also occur as jewelry in the New Kingdom.

Only traces of paint remain on this bust, though originally it would have had a brightly painted floral collar on the chest, symbolizing rebirth and the collars offered by the living at the "Beautiful Feast of the Valley," when they visited the tombs of their ancestors.   PL

315 Lynn H. Holden, "Ancestral bust," in Edward Brovarski, Susan K. Doll, and Rita E. Freed, eds. *Egypt's Golden Age: the Art of Living in the New Kingdom* (Boston, 1982) 300, cat. no. 409.
316 R. O. Faulkner. *Book of the Dead* (Austin, 1977) 145.

145. Bowl bearing a letter to Nefersefkhi from his widow

Hu, cemetery Y, burial 84
First Intermediate Period,
ca. 2100 BC
Pottery, carbon black
H. 9.5 cm; rim diam. 21.7 cm
UC 16244

FROM THE LATE Old Kingdom to the late New Kingdom (ca. 2200–1100 BC), there survive about fifteen letters written to relatives who had recently died.[317] Despite the small number, the range in time and place suggests a broader custom of communication between living and dead. They provide the most compelling evidence for the strength of belief in a life after death. These letters never have just the simple purpose of keeping in touch with the deceased. Instead, all contain practical and urgent appeals for help with insoluble problems of the living, from ill health to disputes over property. Evidently a negative spirit of a dead man or woman could be responsible for whatever might be going wrong in life. In the Letters to the Dead, the writer insists that she or he has treated the dead person well in life and, by maintaining the cult of the dead, after death, and that there can be no reason for allowing ill fortune to strike the writer. All refer to recently deceased members of the family—husbands, wives, parents—and not to ancestor figures.

Arthur Mace, Petrie's co-excavator at Hu in 1899, found this bowl broken into four pieces, since mended. The six columns of writing on the interior of the bowl were already then much faded, but successfully deciphered by Alan Gardiner and Kurt Sethe.[318] Without the bowl, we would not know whether people at a provincial town like Hu, men or women, had access to writing so early in Egyptian history. Such a chance survival in the cemetery may force us to rethink a dominant assumption that few people could read or write in the third millennium BC. In the letter, a widow appeals to her dead husband for help in protecting their daughter, apparently against an abusive guardian or spouse. This is one of the excessively rare moments at which the vulnerable widow can express herself in the ancient historical record.

A sister speaks to her brother, the sole companion Nefersefkhi.

A great cry of grief! To whom is a cry of grief useful? You are given it for the crimes committed against my daughter evilly, evilly, though I have done nothing against him, nor have I consumed his property. He has not given anything to my daughter. Voice offerings are made to the spirit in return for watching over the earthly survivor. Make you your reckoning with whomsoever is doing what is painful to me: my voice is true against any dead spirit male or female doing these things against my daughter.

SQ

317 Four of these fifteen surviving Letters to the Dead are written on simple pottery bowls of Nile silt, dating to the First Intermediate Period or just before, and were found at the place of burial. Small bowls were presumably common tableware, used for presenting food to the living or, here, the lately departed. The messages written upon them are thus in the ideal place for contacting the dead. In the setting of the immediate family, and with no one between living writer and dead reader, the letters are among the most personal expressions in ancient Egyptian writings. They also include the first recorded messages of women from Egypt, and the earliest examples of writing in the provinces.
318 In their publication of eight Letters to the Dead: *Egyptian Letters to the Dead: Mainly from the Old and Middle Kingdoms* (London, 1928).

TOOLS AND WEAPONS

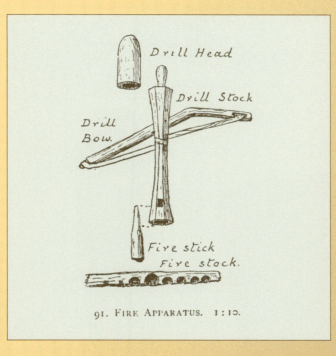

Drill Head

Drill Stock

Drill Bow.

Fire stick
Fire stock.

91. FIRE APPARATUS. 1:10.

146. Group of blades

Riqqeh, from surface deposit 611
Dynasty 19, 1292–1185 BC
Bronze

A. Hoe blade
L. 24.5 cm; w. 9.8 cm
UC 16338

B. Knife
L. 29.0 cm; w. 4.4 cm
UC 16337

C. Spearhead
L. 20.9 cm; w. 3.1 cm
UC 16334

D. Spearhead
L. 17.6 cm; w. 3.1 cm
UC 16339

THESE FOUR BLADES are part of "a set of weapons from a deposit near the surface in cemetery D. There was no trace of a burial," according to the Petrie excavation report on the 1912–1913 winter season at the cemeteries at Riqqeh.[319] The longer of the two spear heads bears a lightly incised hieroglyphic inscription reading "lord of risings, Ramesses beloved of Amun" (King Ramesses II), providing a date for the production, if not the deposition of the group. The shorter is incised with a depiction of a standing lion facing right, followed by the epithet "lord of strength." With these are a rounded knife blade, for cosmetic or other domestic, rather than military use, and a massive hoe-blade. Since tools and weapons are both represented in the find, it seems unlikely that they come from the equipment of, for example, a single soldier. Possibly they represent a smith's horde of material, or a tomb-robber's deposit, never retrieved.   SQ

319 W. M. F. Petrie, *Riqqeh and Memphis* VI (London, 1915) 15, pls. 9–10.

147. Bow and arrowheads

A. **Arrowheads**
Sedment, tomb 1586
Dynasties 9–10, ca. 2160–2125 BC
Wood
L. 20.0 cm; w. 0.9 cm
UC 63169a, b

B. **Bow**
Probably from Sedment
Dynasties 9–10, ca. 2160–2125 BC
Wood
L. 136.3 cm; w. 2.3 cm
UC 43508

IT SHOULD NOT be surprising that Petrie discovered numerous bows and arrows in the tombs dating to the First Intermediate Period at Sedment,[320] given the turbulent nature of that time.

This is an example of the simple, or "self," bow made from a curved piece of wood, a type used in Egypt before the New Kingdom, when the larger, more elaborate compound bow made of layers of wood veneer was introduced from the Near East.[321] The arrows had hardwood tips, which were slotted into reed shafts, made from the bulrushes that grow wild along the banks of the Nile.[322] The slight weight of the reed would have allowed the arrow to fly a longer distance. The separate tip would have dislodged on impact, making it far more difficult to remove from the target.   PL

320 W. M. F. Petrie, *Sedment* I (London, 1924) 7.
321 Cf. W. McLeod, *Composite Bows from the Tomb of Tutankhamun* (Oxford, 1970) 35–7.
322 V. Täckholm, *Student's Flora of Egypt* (Beirut, 1974) 696–7.

148. Scales from a suit of armor[323]

Memphis, from the guardroom at
the Palace of Apries
Dynasty 31 (Second Persian Period),
343–332 BC
Iron
H. (max.) 3.1 cm; w. (max.) 1.5 cm
UC 74787

DURING HIS SPRING 1909 excavation
at Memphis, Petrie made a find unique
in the history of Egyptology—the discovery of a mass of iron and some
bronze scales from perhaps a single
great suit of armor.[324] The scales were
found in a room on the ground floor
of the entrance to the very nerve center of ancient government, a column-
ed hall in the building that he named
"the Palace of Apries" (reigned 589–
570 BC) because the name of the king
is inscribed on the columns. From this
palace-fortress, Egypt seems also to
have been controlled in the following
century, after the Persian Conquest,
by the governors serving the Achaemenid Empire of Iran (rulers of Egypt
525–404 BC and 334–332 BC). Here,
the Achaemenid forces successfully
held out against the decade-long
rebellion from 463 to 454 BC.

The suit of armor seems closest
to Iranian parallels, but the ethnicity
of its wearer and his ruler cannot be
determined from the style of the armor
alone: indeed, in the famous Pom-
peian mosaic depicting Alexander the
Great in battle, the Macedonian hero
is depicted wearing just such Near
Eastern body armor, and so it is possible that the Memphis find dates to
the period after Alexander defeated
the Achaemenid Empire.   SQ

323 Iron scales of varying sizes, with perfo-
rations for stringing, some with medial ridge
to prevent slippage.
324 The find was distributed among several
museums sponsoring the Petrie excavations,
with about one and a half thousand scales
remaining in the Petrie Museum: in 2001
Fleur Shearman, conserved these and
prepared the set seen here for display.

FAIENCE AND GLASS

149. Bead-net dress

Qau, tomb 978[325]
Dynasty 5, 2494–2345 BC
Faience, modern string
H. 95.0 cm; w. 24.0 cm
UC 17743

ONLY TWO EXAMPLES of this type of Old Kingdom beaded net dress have survived. One is in Boston[326] and the other is this Fifth Dynasty example in the Petrie collection. The dress was found in the 1920s by Guy Brunton, a student of Petrie's, in tomb 978 at Qau. The tomb had been robbed but still contained some funerary goods, such as the box that held the thousands of faience beads and shells that constitute the dress.

An attempt to reconstruct the garment in the 1960s resulted in a rectangular network of beads bearing little resemblance to the present dress. In 1994, the beads were fully analyzed in order to be restrung.[327] The final form of the dress has a fitted body with a fringed hem of shells, each containing a small stone, to increase the rattling sound as the wearer moved. On the shoulder straps, two faience caps would have covered the breasts. The form and lozenge pattern of the dress have parallels in Old Kingdom statuary and painted reliefs. From such examples, it would seem that the beaded net dress was worn as embellishment over another garment.[328]

SG-D

325 From a box in a niche at the foot of the grave. Guy Brunton, *Qau and Badari,* Vol. 1 (London, 1927) 23, 64.
326 Museum of Fine Arts 27.1548. From Giza Tomb G 7440 Z. Sue D'Auria, Peter Lacovara, and Catharine Roehrig, eds. *Mummies and Magic: the Funerary Arts of Ancient Egypt* (Boston, 1988) 78–9, cat. no, 9.
327 Alexandra Seth-Smith and Alison Lister. "The Research and Reconstruction of a 5th Dynasty Egyptian Bead-net Dress," in Carol E. Brown, Fiona Macalister, and Margot Wright, eds., *Conservation in Ancient Egyptian Collections* (London, 1995) 165–72.
328 Rosalind Janssen. "An Ancient Egyptian Erotic Fashion: Fishnet Dresses." *KMT* 6, 4 (Winter 1995–6): 41–7.

150. Hippopotamus figurine

Dynasties 13–17, ca. 1773–1550 BC
Glass frit ("Egyptian blue")
H. 4.0 cm; w. 2.8 cm; d. 3.1 cm
UC 45075

SMALL FAIENCE FIGURES of animals became part of the burial equipment of non-royal people in the later Middle Kingdom. They frequently represent creatures that were thought to have some protective or magical significance. The hippo was both revered as a symbol of the household goddess Taweret and feared as a dangerous wild animal. These figures were often broken to render them harmless when placed in the tomb.[329] The front feet were broken off this little creature, which is made of the less common glass frit, also known as "Egyptian blue." The surface of this material would not accept painted designs as faience did, and so this example remains unadorned.   PL

329 Peter Lacovara. "A New Date for an Old Hippopotamus," *Journal of the Museum of Fine Arts, Boston* 4 (1992): 17–26.

151. Hedgehog rattle

Dynasties 5–6, 2494–2181 BC
Faience
L. 6.6 cm; w. 3.3 cm; d. 1.9 cm
UC 45081

THE TRADITION of placing faience votive animals in temples and sacred sites continued after the Archaic Period (see cat. no. 42) into the Old Kingdom and Later. This appealing hedgehog is very similar to a group recently excavated in the Old Kingdom Satet Temple at Elephantine.[330] Why some animals were chosen remains unclear. When shaken, this object works as a rattle; the shape of the hedgehog, which curls up on itself for protection, may have lent itself to this shape which fits easily in the palm of the hand. Perhaps these were used as sistra in temple ceremonies. Later, in the Middle Kingdom, small faience animal figurines begin to appear in the graves of private individuals, perhaps related in some way to their function as temple votives in previous eras. PL

330 G. Dreyer, *Elephantine* VIII, *Der Tempel der Satet. Die Funde*, AV 39.

152. Grapes and mold

Tell el-Amarna
Late Dynasty 18, 1352–1292 BC
Faience, Nile clay ceramic
L. 5.5 cm (grapes), 14.4 cm (mold);
w. 5.9 cm, 9.2 cm; d. 2.4 cm, 5.2 cm
UC 795 (grapes), 1700 (mold)

BUNCHES OF GRAPES are depicted in Egyptian art hanging from kiosks shading the royal throne and decorating palaces in friezes along ceilings. Rather than actual fruit, imitations in faience and glass likely served as more permanent architectural adornments. Examples have been found with a variety of means of attachment, probably for specific uses.

   This fragmentary example has a flat back with a groove at the broken edge and was fitted onto some sort of tang. The individual grapes appear to have been hand modeled, placed on a faience core, and then glazed. Other means of manufacturing such grapes would have involved casting in molds such as the open-face example shown here.   PL

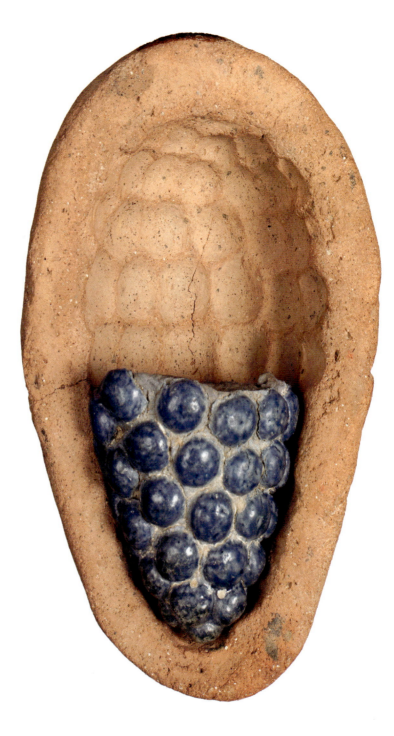

153. Inlays
Tell el-Amarna
Dynasty 18, reign of Akhenaten,
1352–1336 BC
Faience

A. **Lotus**
L. 6.3 cm; w. 6.6 cm; d. 0.4 cm
UC 909

B. **Fingers**
L. 5.0 cm; w. 4.0 cm
UC 23205

C. **Fish**
L. 4.7 cm; w. 5.1 cm; d. 0.6 cm
UC 476

D. **Duck**
H. 4.2 cm; w. 4.4 cm; d. 0.5 cm
UC 509

FAIENCE, the most common of the vitreous materials produced in pharaonic Egypt, is a glazed, non-clay ceramic composed of silica, which occurs in nature in the form of quartz, flint, or quartz sand, with small amounts of lime (CaO) and alkalis (soda and/or potash), which served the dual function of binding the quartz particles and reducing the temperature needed to melt the silica.

The next step in the process entailed the addition of water to the silica-lime-soda mixture. The result is a thick, malleable paste, which could be modeled by hand or pressed into a mold. Upon firing in a kiln (800– 1000°), the mixture hardens, creating a porous core surrounded by a dense outer layer containing fused interstitial glass.

The use of multiple colors, a characteristic of New Kingdom faience, was achieved by filling incised depressions within a faience body with faience paste of varied colors, as seen in the lotus inlay and the inlay with fingers. Later, at Amarna, the technique of painting with metallic oxide paints or adding a faience slurry incorporating the appropriate colorant was perfected. Both methods, carried out on pre-fired, moderately dry faience, were used extensively at Amarna, with a skill unsurpassed before or since. Most dramatic are the polychrome decorative tiles in which the slurry was applied in a painterly fashion to create naturalistic impressions of plants and animals, as seen in the fish and duck tiles.

To achieve the vibrant colors so fashionable at Amarna, the mineral oxides of copper (blue-green), cobalt (blue, violet), lead antimonite (yellow, light green), iron (red, black, green), manganese (black, purple), and titanium (white) were all employed. Many of these pigments were rare and had to be imported; some were never used after this period.

While colors had traditionally been employed in a discreet manner, faience artisans at Amarna experimented with subtle color shading and blending—a technique also seen in wall and floor paintings of the period. In addition, they were successful in producing a sparkling white body by adding ground quartz pebbles (rock crystal) to the basic formula. This white was often used as a background, offsetting the lively forms and brightly colored foreground.

The inlays were often used in architectural contexts, in stone doorjambs and wall reliefs, adding to the sumptuous appearance of the glittering, ephemeral capital.   PL

154. Chalice
Naqada, Temple[331]
New Kingdom, 1550–1292 BC
Faience
H. 13.4 cm; rim diam. 9.2 cm
UC 15891

THIS DEEP-BLUE CHALICE takes the shape of a blue lotus flower, with the petals forming the exterior of the cup. The lotus, which closes at night and opens during the day, was a powerful symbol of rebirth and resurrection. Such symbolism, combined with the fragility of the faience, indicates that this vessel, and others like it, were produced as votive and funerary gifts and did not serve a function in daily life.[332] These chalices were mold-made, usually with the foot made separately and attached to the cup.   PL

331 Found "on the first stage of footing of the wall, 50 inches E, 10 inches S of the S. W. corner." W. M. F. Petrie and J. Quibell, *Naqada and Ballas* (London, 1896) 70.
332 Porter in Sue D'Auria, Peter Lacovara, and Catharine Roehrig, eds. *Mummies and Magic: the Funerary Arts of Ancient Egypt* (Boston, 1988).

Tell el-Amarna
Dynasty 18, reign of Akhenaten,
1352–1336 BC
Glass
L. (max) 4.0 cm; d. (max) 0.3 cm
UC 22909, 22915–6, 22918–9

DURING PETRIE'S 1891–2 excavations at Amarna, he discovered what he believed to be a number of "glass and glazing" workshops, rich in the waste materials common to the faience and glass industries. The abundance of finely crafted, vibrantly colored, vitreous objects found at Amarna attests to the tremendous output, as well as the high level of craftsmanship, to be found at the royal court.

While glass making/working is closely related to faience manufacture, its basic composition—silica-lime-soda-alumina-magnesia—is more complex,[333] and the temperatures required for melting higher, somewhere between 1000° and 1150°.[334] Unlike faience, which appears in the Nile Valley during the fourth millennium BC, glass was a relative new-comer—a result, perhaps, of extended contact with western Asia during the early Eighteenth Dynasty, a period when foreign goods, new ideas, and craftsmen from abroad exerted a lasting influence on the decorative arts.[335]

Glass production in the ancient world was typically a two-step heating process. During the first phase (sintering), the raw materials were crushed, mixed, and heated in clay crucibles that were set in a furnace at temperatures around 800–850°. After a period of time, the materials were transformed into a viscous mass that solidified into frit upon cooling. Precipitated impurities were then chipped away, leaving a refined, vitreous core that could be ground into powder.[336] The second phase entailed heating the pulverized material at around 1000° until molten. At this point, the glass could be colored through the addition of opacifiers and pigments similar to those employed in faience manufacture (see cat. no. 153). For clear glass, substances such as manganese were added, although the exact decolorizing agent used at Amarna is unknown.[337] The viscous glass was then ready for working; the thick liquid could be poured into molds, rolled into thin rods, or wrapped around a removable clay or dung core to form small ornamental vessels.

While glass could be used for small, personal ornaments and as inlays in sculpture, relief, and architectural elements, the most notable products are core-formed, polychrome vessels. Hundreds of fragments and several near-complete vessels have been found at the site of Amarna. The vessels come in a wide variety of shapes and colors, the most common having a cobalt blue body with trails of yellow, white, and turquoise glass applied in bands or as trim. The technique required repeated heating of the body to shape it by rolling the pliable glass on a flat, hard surface and, if desired, decorating it by adding softened, colored glass threads. Once wrapped around the body, the threads were pressed into the soft glass. On many vessels, lively festoon, chevron, and swirl patterns were created by combing these filaments with a metal tool,

much like icing on a napoleon. Finally, the friable core was scooped out after gradual cooling of the vessel.

PL

333 W. E. S. Turner, "Studies in Ancient Glasses and Glassmaking Processes. Part IV. The Chemical Composition of Ancient Glasses." *Journal for the Society of Glass Technology* 40 (1956): 171.
334 Idem., "Studies in Ancient Glasses and Glassmaking Processes. Part I. Crucibles and Melting Temperatures Employed in Ancient Egypt at about 1370 B. C." *Journal for the Society of Glass Technology* 38 (1954): 443.
335 Christine Lilyquist and R. H. Brill, *Studies in Early Egyptian Glass* (New York, 1993) 43.
336 The continued importation of raw glass in the form of ingots from Asia is supported by the archaeological evidence as well as the Amarna letters. See Paul T. Nicholson, *Egyptian Faience and Glass* (Buckinghamshire, 1993) 49–51; William Moran, *The Amarna Letters* (Baltimore and London, 1992) 347, 351–2, 354–5.
337 Paul T. Nicholson, *Egyptian Faience and Glass* (Buckinghamshire, 1993) 42–4.

158. Inlay of two princesses

Tell el-Amarna
Dynasty 18, reign of Akhenaten,
1352–1336 BC
Glass
H. 9.5 cm; w. 4.9 cm; d. 0.9 cm
UC 2235

THIS INLAY is one of the most interesting pieces of glass to have survived from the ancient world. It is an opaque, dark red glass, colored by copper, which first appears in Egypt in the late Eighteenth Dynasty.[340] The subject matter is pure Amarna, showing a pair of nude royal princesses embracing. Though it remains unfinished, it is clear that an incredible amount of effort went into producing this beautiful composition.

It appears that the glass was first introduced into an open mold then the curves of the faces, bodies, and arms were modeled with a tool while the glass was still slightly molten. The ears and hand were then added using additional strips of red glass. Finally, details were etched onto the surface of the bellies and legs.[341]   PL

340 M. Bimson, "Opaque red glass: a review of previous studies," in M. Bimson and I. C. Freestone, eds., *Early Vitreous Materials* (London, 1987) 165–72.
341 Julia Samson, *Amarna: City of Akhenaten and Nefertiti* (London, 1972) 74.

159. Pilgrim flasks

A. New Kingdom, 1550–1069 BC
Glass
H. 11.2 cm; w. 8.0 cm; rim diam.
4.3 cm
UC 22081

B. Saft el-Hinna, burial 725[342]
Roman Period, 30 BC–AD 395
Glass
H. 9.7 cm; w. 5.9 cm; d. 3.8 cm
UC 22057

THE SO-CALLED "pilgrim vessel" first becomes popular in Egypt during the New Kingdom, inspired by Cypro-Mycenaean prototypes.[343] Though similar in form, these two vessels illustrate the evolution of glassmaking over time. Like all early Egyptian glass vessels, the small dark blue flask was formed over a core, coated by the viscous glass, which was then manipulated with tools to form the strap-handles and neck. Canes of yellow, black, and white glass were adhered to the rim at the mouth of the vase. Once the glass cooled, the core was carefully picked out, leaving a hollow interior.

A great innovation of the first century AD was the discovery of free-blown glass.[344] More efficient kiln designs melted the raw glass more thoroughly than before, so that when the mixture was affixed to the end of a hollow tube and air was introduced, it expanded into a clear, thin-walled bubble. This bubble could be introduced into a mold or modeled free-hand, frequently with ribbons of melted glass applied for decorative effect.   PL

342 W. M. F. Petrie, *Hyksos and Israelite Cities* (London, 1906) 41, pl. 38.
343 Janine Bourriau, *Umm el-Ga'ab: Pottery from the Nile Valley before the Arab Conquest* (Cambridge, 1981) 75–6.
344 K. D. White, *Greek and Roman Technology* (London, 1984) 41.

160. Medallion depicting Serapis
Roman Period, 30 BC–AD 395
Glass
H. 5.0 cm; w. 5.2 cm
UC 22063

THE HEAD AND TORSO of the god Serapis appear in the center of this emerald green glass medallion. The deity is depicted in his customary Hellenistic manner, with flowing hair and beard, wearing a tall modius crown. Introduced in the reign of Ptolemy I Soter (305–285 BC), Serapis was a hybrid of Egyptian and Greek divinities, originating with the Egyptian combination of Osiris and Apis.

Elements of various Hellenistic cults, including those of Dionysus, Zeus, and Asklepios, were eventually melded to create a universally revered deity, a patron of healing, fertility, and the afterlife. Although the cult center of Serapis was the Alexandrian Serapeum established by Ptolemy I, temples were dedicated to the god throughout the Hellenistic world, even as distantly as Britain.   BTT

ABBREVIATIONS

PERIODICALS

AJA
American Journal of Archaeology

ASAE
*Annales du Service des Antiquités
de l'Égypte*

BIFAO
*Bulletin de l'Institut Français
d'Archéologie Orientale*

BMFA
Bulletin of the Museum of Fine Arts

CRIPEL
*Cahiers de Recherches de l'Institut
de Papyrologie et d'Égyptologie
de Lille*

JARCE
*Journal of the American Research
Center in Egypt*

JEA
Journal of Egyptian Archaeology

JNES
Journal of Near Eastern Studies

LÄ
Lexikon der Ägyptologie

ZÄS
Zeitschrift für ägyptische Sprache

AUTHORS

SG-D
Sabrina Gomez-Deluchi
Independent scholar

TH
Tom Hardwick
Worcester College
University of Oxford

PL
Peter Lacovara
Senior Curator of Ancient Art
Michael C. Carlos Museum

SQ
Stephen Quirke
Curator of the Petrie Museum
of Egyptian Archaeology

BTT
Betsy Teasley Trope
Associate Curator of Ancient Art
Michael C. Carlos Museum

For additional information,
please see:
www.petrie.ucl.ac.uk
www.digitalegypt.ucl.ac.uk
http://carlos.emory.edu